CYBER SELF-DEFENSE

CYBER SELF-DEFENSE

EXPERT ADVICE TO AVOID ONLINE PREDATORS, IDENTITY THEFT, AND CYBERBULLYING

ALEXIS MOORE AND LAURIE J. EDWARDS

LYONS PRESS
Guilford, Connecticut
Helena, Montana
An imprint of Rowman & Littlefield

Lyons Press is an imprint of Rowman & Littlefield

Distributed by NATIONAL BOOK NETWORK

Copyright © 2014 by Alexis Moore and Laurie J. Edwards
Survivor's Guide in Appendix B © Survivors In Action

British Library Cataloguing-in-Publication Information available

Library of Congress Cataloging-in-Publication Data available

ISBN 978-1-4930-0569-7 (paperback)

♾™ The paper used in this publication meets the minimum requirements of American National Standard for Information Sciences—Permanence of Paper for Printed Library Materials, ANSI/NISO Z39.48-1992.

To cyberabuse victims everywhere who were once left behind:
May this book take you from victim to victorious

Contents

Acknowledgments

They say it takes a village to write a book, but we've found it takes much more than that; our help and support come from around the globe. Thank you to everyone who shared experiences, suggestions, and editing skills with us. We're deeply indebted to each of you, and we're grateful that you're a part of our lives.

Introduction

If you picked up this book, you're likely dealing with a cyberattacker or are hoping to protect yourself from online predators. If so, you're not alone. According to the US Department of Justice, more than six million people are stalked each year in the United States alone. With the advent of the Internet, many of these stalkers have taken advantage of the faceless, hard-to-trace crimes of cyberbullying and cyberstalking. Spurned lovers, angry neighbors, jealous coworkers, and bullying teens all find the Internet the perfect way to exact revenge—often with tragic results. Recent high-profile suicides, particularly of teens, are only a small sampling of the widespread and devastating consequences.

The Internet has added a whole new dimension to bullying, terrorizing, and stalking. It's also raised many moral issues: If you destroy someone's life or reputation in the news media, you can be sued for defamation of character. If you do it online, you might get away with it. If you murder someone, you'll go to jail. But if you bully someone enough that they commit suicide, are you guilty of murder?

Sadly, many victims find little or no help from law enforcement or domestic services. Cybercrime laws are on the books in many states, but penalties are rarely severe. With the exception of cases that involve online sexual predators, it can be difficult to persuade law enforcement to take cyberabuse seriously and prosecute offenders.

This book was written so you can protect yourself from online danger. Cyberabuse can cause lasting damage to your reputation, your self-esteem, your security, and your sanity. This manual will prepare you to fight back and regain control of your life.

Alexis Moore's Story

I was thrilled when I met my "dream" man. He was charming, affluent, and attentive—definitely the catch of the office. When we moved in together, I felt like I had it all. But that dream quickly died as I discovered my dream man was rotten inside.

When the physical abuse increased, I tried to obtain outside help but failed. One night, after I was beaten so badly it seemed I might not get up again, I fled, leaving behind my home, dogs, treasured photographs, and possessions—everything I owned—to keep from being killed. All I had, literally, were the clothes on my back. But I was free.

My freedom was only the beginning of a new nightmare. My ex was an abusive, controlling, vengeful person who, as a high-tech investigator, knew how to work the system. He wanted revenge and to show me he could control my life whether I lived with him or not. How did he do it? By becoming a particularly devastating cyberstalker.

I was cyberstalked until the last of my money was electronically drained from my bank accounts, my credit cards were canceled, and my email was tampered with. He destroyed my credit rating, making it almost impossible for me to buy a car, rent an apartment, or get a new credit card. My phone records were tapped into daily so that he could track the people I spoke with and monitor my whereabouts. It was painful financially, physically (the stress was killing me and I suffered latent effects from the beatings), and emotionally. He constantly found new ways to let me know that he was tracking my life from his computer and that he could make me miserable. It worked. My entire life was torn apart.

Extricating myself from his cyber-reach took four long, scary, and frustrating years. My experience is proof that even practiced investigators can fall prey to a determined stalker. As a result, I became a passionate advocate and educator for men, women, and teens in similar situations who discover that leaving does not necessarily mean the nightmare is over.

Survivors In Action

In 2007 I founded Survivors In Action (SIA) to help other abuse and stalking victims. Since I began my nonprofit, I have expanded my focus to help victims and potential victims of cybercrime. Through Survivors In Action, I work with victims who are experiencing or have experienced cybercrime as well as other victims whose stalkers find them through electronic means. I also lobby for greater legislation and stronger criminal penalties against cybercrime.

Every day the SIA inbox and voice mail are filled to capacity with messages from victims, advocates, and law enforcement agencies seeking advice and support. With backing from our volunteers (many of them former victims), we help as many people as we can. But with thousands of emails arriving every month (and sometimes every week), it is impossible to assist everyone; there are millions of abuse and cyberabuse victims in the United States alone. This book is our way of trying to reach out to more people who need help; we hope it will give you solutions to your own cyber-problems. The goal of this book is threefold—prevention, protection, and recovery from cyberabuse of all kinds. Our mission is to ensure that no victim is left behind.

Using This Book

Part I introduces ten different personality profiles and their dangerous online behaviors. A quiz in each chapter helps you identify that personality type.[1] An explanation of the personality type gives information about the cyberattacker's motivation and behavior, characteristics of potential victims, and typical relationship problems. Case studies detail how that particular cybercriminal operates.[2] Then Alexis Moore reveals how SIA helped the victims. She also offers tips so you can prevent and/or recover from each type of cybercrime. All chapters end with an action checklist, detailing simple steps you can take to protect yourself from that personality.

Part II offers strategies to protect yourself, reestablish your reputation, and rebuild your life if you've been cyberattacked. The techniques range from recovering data and regaining self-esteem to changing identities and going underground. We also outline self-help techniques to enable you to handle the trauma and live without fear.

The *appendices* provide checklists for action, additional self-help resources, and contact information for emergency services and support organizations.

---

1 These quizzes are only to identify potential cyberabusers and give insight into possible dangers; they are not psychological profiles or to be used for the diagnosis of mental or emotional illness. They are intended as general indicators, but each person is different. You are your own best judge of how the behavior affects you. Your partner may have a low score, but if the behaviors cause you more distress than the quiz answers indicate, read the information in the next levels up. And no matter what the score, if someone makes you feel uncomfortable, always trust your instincts and extricate yourself from the relationship.

2 Throughout the book you'll read a lot about SIA. Most of the case studies in the book are ones that SIA helped solve. Others are stories that were shared with the authors. In all cases, names and identifying details have been changed to protect the victims' identities.

Part I
Cyberattacker Profiles

CHAPTER 1

Attention-Getting: Hey, look at me!

Attention seekers are always on stage. They want all eyes on them and will go to great lengths to be the focus of any situation. The desire to be the center of a crowd isn't necessarily a problem; it may be a sign of a gregarious, extroverted personality. Only when that need becomes excessive does it become a concern.

Although most attention getters crave an audience and are happiest in a crowd, another type is less transparent. These quieter personalities act in secret, creating havoc behind the scenes. These individuals get more satisfaction by stirring things up and watching others squirm.

Recognizing an Attention Getter

Most attention getters are easy to spot: They're the ones who show off at parties, try to top everyone else's stories, and talk loudly or make outrageous remarks to attract notice. They're happiest with all eyes on them. They like to be the stars, gain adulation, and stand out from the crowd. They frequently dress in outlandish or stylish, fashion-forward clothes, drive flashy cars, and crack jokes or use sarcastic humor, hoping for a laugh. They become restless when others are talking and use tactics to divert everyone's interest back to them.

Not all attention getters put themselves in the limelight. Introverted attention getters have the same need for attention as their extroverted friends, but they don't feel comfortable showing off on stage. Quieter people may attract attention through pity. "Poor me" is their byline. Their lives are filled with drama and tragedy—health challenges, family problems, nasty bosses, unfair breaks, accidents, or betrayals. Whiners and complainers, some even cause their own problems or exaggerate them to gain more notice. Their cries for attention are more subtle, but no less intense than the extroverts'.

Other introverts get their attention more sneakily by jabbing other people. They often have a quick, sly wit and are masters of dry humor. They may not speak often, but when they do, people notice. Their remarks often make people gasp in surprise or horror, or make others laugh. Their cruelty is at another's expense. The spotlight is on the victim rather than the attention getter, but the attention getter basks in the glow.

Attention getters of either type can be annoying and persistent. Their behavior is often more bothersome than harmful, but when it gets out of hand, it can cause a lot of damage. They also may be dangerous if thwarted.

Signs of an Attention Getter

Does the person you're with have any of the following characteristics? Using a scale of 0–2, rate each behavior on either the Extroverted or Introverted scale as follows:

0-Never
1-Sometimes
2-Often

Most Extroverted Attention Getters:

____ are lively and talkative
____ get bored when others are talking
____ have short attention spans unless the activity revolves around them
____ try to stand out in a crowd
____ dress in outlandish or stylish, fashion-forward clothes
____ drive flashy cars
____ crack jokes, particularly at others' expense
____ are the first to take a dare
____ like to show off
____ usually talk loudly and quickly
____ always have to top others' stories
____ like to have the latest and best of everything
____ frequently interrupt others who are speaking
____ are filled with high energy and enthusiasm when people are looking
____ often check their appearance in the mirror
____ are quick with gibes and sarcastic remarks
____ make jokes at others' expense and then say "Just kidding"
____ are fake or shallow

Most Introverted Attention Getters:

____ feel sorry for themselves

____ appear self-absorbed and self-centered

____ always have to top others' tragic stories

____ open conversations with how they are doing

____ quickly turn conversations to their life or problems

____ always have more problems and tragedies than others

____ are often sick, hurt, or in crisis mode

____ have a "poor me" attitude

____ think the world is out to get them

____ dwell on the negative events in their lives

____ sulk if others get the limelight for too long

____ exaggerate their problems for additional attention

____ get bored when others are talking

____ may resort to hurting themselves or putting themselves in harm's way

____ may threaten suicide

Scale

0–8

Everyone likes attention at times, and people have different ways of attracting it. Although the behavior of attention seekers may be annoying, unless they are harming themselves or threatening suicide—both signs of deeper, underlying problems—there is little to worry about.

9–18

People in this range crave attention. How they go about it and how they treat you should be the determining factors in whether to continue the relationship. Extroverts often exhibit flamboyant personalities, making them rate high on the scale, but do not pose any danger.

If the attention getters are under age twenty-five, a score at the higher end of the scale could indicate a lack of maturity and the inability to see themselves as others see them. They may be emotionally needy or insecure, so they're trying to reassure themselves of others' interest in them. By their late twenties, most people have moved outside their own heads and have a clearer picture of how they appear to the rest of the world. They find more subtle ways to get the attention they need—by winning awards, competing in sports, vying for promotions, taking high-profile jobs, or choosing careers that place them in the spotlight. Introverted attention getters may opt for jobs as writers, illustrators, or other professions that give them credits or bylines but don't necessarily put them in the public eye.

18–36

The higher the score, the more wary you need to be. People with scores in this range most likely can and will cause trouble. They often have little or no capacity to put themselves into someone else's place, so they may do hurtful things without remorse.

If introverted attention getters don't receive the notice they were aiming for, they may hurt themselves or threaten suicide. Not all threats are done for attention or to manipulate (see chapter 5), which is why it's important not to dismiss or ignore them; treat them instead as cries for help. But don't be drawn into the drama. Let professionals deal with the situation.

Who Gets Hooked by an Attention Getter

Extroverted attention getters usually seek out quieter, more reserved friends and partners who give them the attention they crave and don't upstage them. The perfect partner is someone who is as enamored of the attention seeker as the attention getter is of him- or herself.

Sometimes attention getters choose partners who are needy or insecure, people who will look up to them. Someone who is repressed or fearful may be drawn to the attention getter's more uninhibited personality. The extrovert will do or say things the shyer person would never attempt. Inhibited partners watch in awe as attention seekers do things they only dream of doing. That admiration feeds the attention getter's need for appreciation.

Both introverted and extroverted attention getters are attracted to people with natural tendencies to help or encourage. A calm person who accepts the temper tantrums and acting out often provides a good match for the more flamboyant personality. The "poor me" syndrome works well with overly sympathetic types who like to nurse and care for others.

As long as the relationship remains in this balance, it usually works well. But once partners tire of stroking the attention getter's ego or realize their own needs are being ignored, the relationship can turn rocky.

Some attention getters hang out with wild friends who do crazy or outlandish things. When this happens the friends may attempt to top each other's behavior. This can lead to potentially dangerous situations for those around them and for the attention getters themselves. The friends may spur each other on to cruel or violent acts. This is sometimes the dynamic when a group of popular kids at school picks on loners or outcasts. They may choose a student they think will be easy to annoy. Emos or other emotionally vulnerable or volatile teens are favorite choices. Quiet students with few friends to protect them are frequent targets.

For negative attention getters, the most satisfying victims are people who react emotionally and "wear their hearts on their sleeves." These attention getters target people they can quickly and easily provoke to anger or tears. For this reason many negative attention getters are bullies. The need for center stage, along with a lack of empathy, allows them to hurt another's feelings with little or no remorse.

Stephanie's Story

The ringtone on Stephanie's phone startled her out of sleep. Caller ID showed it was her best friend, Aiko. Something terrible must have happened. Heart pounding and fingers shaking, Stephanie returned the call.

A sleepy-sounding voice answered. After Stephanie demanded to know what was wrong, Aiko responded with annoyance. Why had Stephanie woken her up in the middle of the night? "But you called me," Stephanie insisted.

Aiko was adamant that she hadn't made any calls. "You had a nightmare, Steph," she said. "Go back to sleep. And don't call me at two in the morning again unless it's an emergency."

After Aiko hung up, Stephanie stared at her phone. It showed her friend's number as an incoming call at 2:43 a.m. She hadn't been dreaming.

The next morning Aiko was regaling a small group of coworkers with the tale of the late-night call. Stephanie pulled out her phone and showed them the number. They all shrugged it off as faulty technology.

Later that day Stephanie's phone rang. With a quick glance at the number, she shut it off. Her mom knew she wasn't allowed to take personal calls at work. Why was she calling in the middle of the day? It must be an emergency. Sliding her phone into her pocket, she rushed into the restroom to return the call. As Aiko had the night before, Stephanie's mom claimed she hadn't called.

Still shaken, Stephanie stepped into the hall and almost ran into Ewan, one of the tech guys. He asked if anything was wrong. Stephanie mentioned the two calls, and Ewan expressed his sympathy. He made a joke about wires getting crossed and continued down the hall.

The strange calls persisted. Friends and relatives called and texted, yet when Stephanie responded, they acted puzzled and insisted they hadn't called or left messages. The hardest ones were the calls in the middle of the night. She couldn't ignore them because they might be emergencies. Yet after returning a few of the late-night calls and waking her friends from sleep, Stephanie stopped calling back. She'd toss and turn the rest of the night but wait until morning to text or call. Each time she did, she got the same response. None of them had called her.

She was starting to wonder if she was going crazy, and others wondered the same thing. Only a few people at work listened to her stories; most of her colleagues just rolled their eyes and walked away. Her friend Barb even asked if Stephanie was making up stories to get attention. After that Stephanie clammed up.

Then Stephanie began receiving calls in the middle of the night from the guardhouse of her gated community. Guards checked on single women who requested it, or they responded to alarm calls. Although she hadn't asked to be checked on, she answered in case they were issuing a security warning. No one was on the line when she picked up the phone.

The other calls had been more frustrating or embarrassing, but these scared her. This time, though, when she mentioned the calls to colleagues at work, most ignored her or told her to get a new phone. Only Aiko and Ewan still listened and sent sympathetic Instagrams or texts.

The fear and late-night calls were taking a toll on Stephanie. Her work was slipping, and she had trouble concentrating during the day. She was afraid to answer the phone, and she'd lost the sympathy of her family and friends. Even her own mother thought she was crazy.

Then came the most terrifying night of all. Stephanie woke to her house phone and cell phone ringing at the same time. Caller IDs on both phones indicated they were from the same number. She didn't answer either one. Then her answering machine clicked on. On the other end a deep, horror-movie voice said, "I know where you live, bitch." The message ended with an eerie laugh that echoed in Stephanie's head the rest of the night as she lay in bed, paralyzed with fear.

Stephanie's Answer: Spoof Calls

Desperate and terrified, Stephanie contacted Survivors In Action for help. She was relieved to learn that she wasn't going crazy. She'd been experiencing spoof calls. Using a simple spoof card, all the perpetrator had to know was Stephanie's phone number and those of her family and friends. The card allows spoofers to change their phone number to any number they desire. It's easy for spoofers to call or send text messages as someone else—the phone company, the gate guard, a friend, a neighbor, or a relative.

Some of the companies that sell these cards offer buyers a limited-time free trial; then they charge a subscription. In this case, because Stephanie had received multiple calls, her harasser must have signed up for the service.

As with every cybercrime case, SIA encouraged Stephanie to report it to law enforcement. Stephanie's small-town police force was not familiar with spoofing. Moore contacted them and provided documentation that such technology existed to help them realize Stephanie was telling the truth and her case needed to be recorded.

Understanding what was happening was a great relief to Stephanie. Her world had been spiraling out of control, but now she knew someone really had been messing with her mind. With the proof Moore provided, Stephanie convinced her family and friends that what had happened to her was real and could happen to them.

Protecting Herself

In addition to reporting the incident, Stephanie changed her phone number. She kept it unlisted and gave the number only to family members and a few trusted friends. In the past she'd shared her number with colleagues and social acquaintances. Now she kept that information private. She had no idea who the spoofer was, so she took no chances of the caller getting her information.

Action Steps

- Don't dismiss spoof calls as pranks; treat them seriously.
- Try not to react or give the caller any satisfaction.
- If you receive more than one or two random calls in the middle of the night, don't answer the phone.
- If you suspect it's the caller, allow calls to go to voice mail and save them.
- Save all texts and document dates and times of answered and unanswered calls.
- Ask friends and family to use a special code if they need to call late at night (for example, let it ring twice, then hang up and call again); then you won't need to worry that you're missing an emergency call.
- Get written statements from family and friends indicating they didn't make the calls; keep a paper trail.
- Contact your phone carrier and discuss the issue with the security department.
- Contact law enforcement and report the incidents immediately; having a record can help if the incidents escalate.
- When reporting incidents, stay calm and matter of fact. If you act overly emotional or hysterical, law enforcement may be less likely to take your case seriously.
- If you are distraught, ask a friend, advocate, counselor, teacher, or coworker to accompany you to a law enforcement appointment. They can not only back up your story but also provide some emotional support.
- Depending upon the severity of the situation, law enforcement may or may not react; many officers are not aware of the latest technology, so you may need an expert to explain it to them.
- If you are told that nothing can be done, continue to report the incidents. Persistence often pays off. And it's helpful to have an official record in case the laws change or the calls become more threatening.

Identifying the Harasser

When she realized that law enforcement would not be going after her harasser, Stephanie decided to see if she could figure out who was using the spoof card. Although it could have been a stranger, she believed it was most likely someone she knew. She looked for a person who:

- had a grudge against her or who enjoyed seeing her or others get upset;

- appeared happy to see her distressed or, conversely, spent time offering comfort;

- seemed extremely interested in hearing about the calls and her reaction to them;

- had a techy mind and was up to date on the latest gadgets and gizmos.

Most people don't know how to use spoof cards, which meant the perpetrator was tech-savvy. The spoofer most likely was someone who'd get a payback by making her upset. An angry ex or jealous coworker is often the culprit, but in this case, Stephanie had neither.

The only two people who'd showed any interest in Stephanie's ongoing saga were Aiko and Ewan. Because of his tech knowledge, Stephanie added Ewan to the list of possible suspects. Before the spoof calls, she had never spoken to him unless she needed tech help. Lately, though, he seemed to be around a lot, especially when she was lamenting the phone calls. And he'd sent her some supportive emails.

Confronting the Spoofer

This is not a step Survivors In Action recommends, because it could lead to danger if the spoofer is emotionally unstable. Even if the harassment is out of character and done in the heat of anger, while it's occurring that person is not making rational judgments, so you are at risk.

The more she thought about it, the more certain Stephanie became that Ewan was behind the calls. After arranging for Aiko and a few other friends to dine at a nearby cafe, she asked Ewan to join her there. She prefaced her request by mentioning how supportive Ewan had been recently. He looked startled and wary when she suggested meeting, but he stammered out a *yes*. When he arrived Stephanie confronted him. At first Ewan denied it, but finally he admitted he'd been trying to get her attention.

Hearing Stephanie gasp over the phone had been enough to fuel this attention getter. She may not have paid attention to him at work, but she sure did at three in the morning. Even better, he overheard her at work telling colleagues about the strange calls and smiled to himself, knowing he was causing chaos in her life. Meanwhile, he sent calming Instagrams that she answered, fulfilling his need for attention in several different ways.

Tracing Spoof Calls

Until recently, no legislation was in place to protect victims against such calls. The federal Truth in Caller ID Act of 2009 was passed to prevent people from falsifying their phone identities, but this law won't stop cyber-criminals from using technology illegally. And as long as the tool remains profitable for the companies who sell spoof cards, they'll continue to supply them until they're forced to stop. Many of these companies moved their businesses overseas so they wouldn't be affected by the act.

Although an experienced tech may be able to trace the calls, many spoofers are tech-savvy enough to prevent antispoofing technology from ferreting them out. Spoofers create fake accounts, use public computers, or take over an innocent person's computer to set up their scams.

Getting a conviction is also difficult. Tech evidence is not always fool-proof, meaning additional proof is needed to support the claims. Prosecutors can subpoena spoof company records, provided the company is in the United States. The difficulty with this is that law enforcement must have a strong reason and enough evidence to request a search warrant for a computer IP-address verification. The process can be long and involved, and victims may have to turn over their tech equipment for analysis. One final hurdle is that law enforcement must believe the case is important enough to prosecute.

Despite the fact that Stephanie's spoofer left a scary message saying he knew where she lived, the police did not feel she was in any imminent physical danger and never pursued her case. In fact, they discouraged her from reporting the incidents. Stephanie, though, at SIA's assistance, continued to do so.

What Motivates an Attention Getter

A major flaw of attention getters is the inability to get outside their own minds and view themselves as others see them. Every activity or action is evaluated by how it personally affects them, and they have difficulty putting themselves in someone else's place. Thus they have little understanding or empathy for others. Generally they are not deliberately cruel, just self-absorbed or thoughtless.

First and foremost, attention getters are motivated by attention and adulation. Most want fame or notice, but they go about attracting it in different ways. Whether quiet or extroverted, their goal is to create a stir. But underneath that external need lies a deeper, unfulfilled desire to matter to others.

Some attention getters grew up in a home with parents who doted on them, and they came to believe they were number one and that their needs should take priority. Taken to an extreme, this idea may result in them becoming narcissistic (see chapter 7).

But many children had the opposite experience. Their growing-up years were filled with inattention or neglect. They learned to compensate by seeking attention from others. Many still struggle with insecurity and low self-esteem. Although they don't appear to, they often have little self-confidence. They try to bolster themselves by making others pay attention to them. Lacking self-worth and self-love, they attempt to get it from their audiences. For example, younger children who feel overshadowed by older siblings may become show-offs to compensate for feelings of inadequacy.

Because of their insecurities, attention seekers can't tolerate criticism, which makes them angry. In this state they're liable to act out and hurt others around them. Some become drama kings or queens, throwing hissy fits or temper tantrums because they can't tolerate frustration.

Usually the greater the need for attention, the more emotionally immature the person is. In adults emotional development may have been arrested at an early age. Middle school and high school bullies also typically fall into this category. Many are less mature than their peers. They've also learned to use negative attention-seeking behaviors. Doing or saying inappropriate things will make people turn to look. If they can't get positive attention, they settle for disapproval.

At times attention getters have motives other than being noticed. If their behavior stems from jealousy (chapter 2) or revenge (chapter 9), they may be more dangerous and persistent. And some attention getters have psychological problems, such as histrionic personality disorder or narcissism, and need professional help.

How an Attention Getter Uses the Internet

Extroverted show-offs prefer a crowd. Unless they have friends who are watching and commenting on their activities either in person or online, their interest in cyberharassment is minimal. With their limited attention spans and need for an audience, they are more likely to engage in one-time cyberattacks unless goaded by a group. They may enjoy stirring up controversy, but their interest is generally short-lived.

Conversely, introverted attention seekers rely on the Internet for underhanded or secretive methods of gaining attention. They can remain faceless and anonymous while still gaining the attention they crave. Sometimes they behave like starstruck fans (see chapter 3) or try to outdo others in the number of posts or friends they have. Some engage in ongoing debates or post about controversial subjects. From dramatic announcements or bomb threats to smear campaigns, they may use the Internet as a weapon.

Computer hackers and others who operate behind the scenes sometimes do it for notoriety. Depending on the severity of their attacks, they may end up in the worldwide news, or at the very least, wind up posted as threats on antispam or antivirus sites. Even if no one knows they're behind it, hackers get satisfaction in seeing reports of the damage they've wreaked.

As long as attention getters provoke a response—either positive or negative—they'll continue their attacks. If they don't receive feedback, their interest will taper off. Although it's not always easy, the best way to combat them is to ignore them.

Leaving an Attention Getter

Those looking to end a relationship with an attention getter often can do so by withdrawing their attention or by spending more time talking about themselves, meeting their own needs, and dramatizing their own problems. Most attention getters soon tire of other-centered conversations. Their need for an attention fix is too strong to keep them in a relationship where they aren't center stage.

This mindset also makes attention getters the easiest cyberattackers to foil. Nothing frustrates them more than being ignored. They thrive on the reactions they get from others, so if their victims don't respond, they're disappointed. Often they'll increase their harassment, trying for a rise. Eventually, if they get no response, they'll look elsewhere.

If they feel slighted or thwarted, though, some attention getters become nasty and cruel. With their inability to put themselves in someone else's place, they can become dangerous. Beware of attention getters who are upset because they aren't getting the attention they feel they deserve. They can turn vindictive.

Combating Bullying from Attention Getters

As noted above, many attention getters will go away if ignored. Unrewarded behavior tends to disappear; psychologists call this *extinction*. But in some cases the bullying may get much worse before it ends. When bullies see that their tactics aren't working, they intensify their efforts to get a reaction. Unfortunately, at this point they often succeed. The victim can't help getting angry or upset. Bullies learn that to be successful, they need to be more outrageous. The next time they attack, they increase their cruelty, and it becomes a vicious cycle.

It's easy to suggest that victims not react, but this is difficult to do when someone is beating you up, trashing your reputation, humiliating you, and/or exposing your secrets.

Another good strategy to stop bullying is to report it, but that, too, is not without risk. Speaking out often breaks the bully's hold, but it's considered wrong to rat on your peers. To do so may make you the target of more abuse—not only from the bully but also from others who see you as a snitch. That leaves most victims feeling that there's no way out.

A few victims retaliate, leading to disastrous results as the war escalates. Some victims act out and do the things the bully accused them of. Many, though, just live with the pain, embarrassment, or shame. They shrink into their shells and avoid everyone. In the worst-case scenarios, victims turn their rage outward and harm others, as evidenced in school shootings. Or they turn the blame inward and commit suicide.

Camryn's Story

Camryn and Juliana had been friends for years. They shared everything, including the passwords to their emails, phones, and social media accounts as well as the combinations to their lockers. They also told each other intimate details of their lives.

Then Juliana began hanging around with the more popular kids. Soon after that, the practical jokes began. One day Camryn opened her locker to find it filled with shaving cream. Peyton, one of the popular girls, snapped a picture and circulated it. More locker sabotages and pictures followed. A few days later, Peyton had someone trip Camryn in the cafeteria, causing her to fall and splatter tomato soup all over her brand-new outfit. This time, Peyton posted a video of the fall and of Camryn on the floor, tomato soup dripping down her face.

Next tweets, posts, and blogs appeared on Camryn's pages, revealing many of the secrets she'd confided to Juliana over the years, intimate details about her dates and other private information that humiliated Camryn. Even worse were the fake "confessions," where she recounted her fantasies about what she wanted to do with her crushes; many of the posts were sick and vulgar. All of them looked as if they'd come from Camryn herself. She was so ashamed, she couldn't read most of them. For the next few days, she pretended to be sick to avoid going to school.

But over the weekend she received emails and texts from many of the jocks, inviting her on dates. She was horrified to learn that emails had been sent from her account saying that if they asked her out, she'd do whatever they wanted. After reading her "fantasies" online, they all had suggestions for what they'd like her to do.

CONFRONTING JULIANA

Because they had once been friends, Camryn wanted to talk to Juliana in person and let her know how much her actions had hurt. She believed her former BFF still had the same caring heart. Rather than calling, she showed up at Juliana's house. At first Juliana was reluctant to let her in, but Camryn insisted.

As they talked Juliana admitted that Peyton had pressured her to reveal the passwords and secrets. Juliana, who desperately wanted to be accepted, had given Peyton everything she'd asked for. While Juliana was doling out the information, she'd been the center of attention in the popular clique, something she'd always dreamed of. She regretted leaking Camryn's secrets but acknowledged that, given the chance to be admired by Peyton's group, she'd probably betray a friend again. For her, attention was more important than ethics.

Camryn learned a painful lesson about telling anyone, even a BFF, her logins and passwords. And she still had to face everyone at school. She knew her mother wouldn't allow her to stay home the following week, so her only choices were to skip school or endure the humiliation of walking down the halls.

CAMRYN'S SOLUTION

That weekend Camryn's mother insisted on finding out why her daughter was reluctant to attend classes. When she discovered what was going on, she called Survivors In Action. Camryn followed SIA's action steps of first documenting and reporting the posts, then changing her passwords. (See chapter 12 for more tips on handling cyberbullying.)

Preventing new posts and deleting the messages were Camryn's next priorities. Because the posts were on her account, she could quickly and easily delete them. What she couldn't do was erase their impact or the damage to her reputation.

She wrote a generic message, saying: *My email and social media accounts were hacked from 1/24 to 1/31, so if you saw or received any messages from me during those dates, they were fake.* She posted it on all her accounts and also emailed and texted everyone.

SIA helped her get the locker and cafeteria photos and videos removed from the Internet. Because her school had a strong antibullying policy,

Moore encouraged Camryn to report the incidents. Camryn, though, didn't want to start trouble or turn other students against her, so she declined.

Several weeks later Peyton started a smear campaign against Juliana, who had refused to help with any more bullying. That made Camryn realize she needed to report the incidents. Using the documentation she had and Juliana's evidence, Camryn overcame her reluctance and went to the school office. Peyton faced disciplinary action, but more importantly, she was also sent for counseling.

Not all stories end as well Camryn's. Every day, in schools around the country, students experience much, much worse. If you're facing bullying or harassment that has depressed you enough to consider suicide or violence, seek help immediately. Chapter 14 discusses depression and suicide and suggests some preventive resources.

For the victim, one of the hardest things is not to react to the taunting or bullying. If you can remain calm and act as if you are not bothered, it's often the best way to stop the harassment. Yelling, crying, gasping, or showing any emotion gives attention getters the payoffs they desire. A poker face, revealing no emotion whatsoever, takes away the attention getter's reward.

Remain aware that attention getters may escalate attempts to get a reaction. They may do things that hurt you or destroy your favorite possessions, not always out of malice, but to gain the drug that gives them their high: attention.

Action Steps

If you're dealing with an attention getter, here are some important steps to help you protect yourself:

- Follow the suggestions in appendix A and chapters 11 and 12.
- Make sure that any message you send out about hacking is unemotional, to prevent the harasser from getting additional attention.
- Take away the reward by ignoring the bully.
- Keep a poker face; refuse to give the bully any satisfaction.
- Although no one likes to be a tattletale, inform authorities immediately. You not only will help prevent future attacks on yourself and others, you also may be instrumental in getting the bully help.

Final Quick Tips

- **Adopt a poker face:** If you don't react, harassers get no payoff.

- **Seek protection:** Report incidents immediately; block access to your accounts.

- **Maintain your privacy:** Safeguard all your information; change passwords and phone numbers.

The attention getter is seeking a reaction, so don't overreact. Instead, take action!

CHAPTER 2

Jealous: I want what you have.

Many people think jealous partners really care about them. People who are jealous often call to see where you are, interrogate you about events you attend without them, and claim they won't survive if the relationship ends. At first all this attention can seem flattering, but there's often a darker side to these personalities. Not only do they sometimes make false accusations and/or fly into rages when they think you're looking at or flirting with someone else, but they also will often go out of their way to sabotage your next relationship or pit your friends against you. Jealous partners may use social media to keep tabs on you both during and after the relationship.

Recognizing a Jealous Person

One thing to keep in mind with jealousy is that it is the other person's problem. Your actions—no matter what they are—did not and cannot cause someone else's jealousy. That's not to say that you shouldn't be considerate of others' feelings and try not to hurt them, but jealousy is a choice the other person makes. The same behavior can provoke admiration in one individual and jealousy in the next. The behavior didn't change, only the person's perception of it.

There might also be different levels of jealousy. Someone might wish to be as thin or wealthy as a friend. Another person might covet someone else's boyfriend. The strength of these wishes will determine how envious each one is, but sometimes jealousy includes an additional component: a desire to take away what others have or to wish them harm. That's when jealousy spills over into the realm of danger.

Jealousy as a motive for cyberattack can be one of the most insidious. Knowing that your partner has a jealous streak is one thing, but you can stir up jealousy in others without being aware of it. The resulting attacks take you by surprise because the person may be a random stranger, a passing acquaintance, or even someone you thought was a close friend.

As you go through life, you're bound to stir up envy in others. Many people use that jealousy as a springboard to better themselves; others use it to fuel their attempts to knock you down from the pedestal on which they've placed you. And in some cases jealousy builds up until the person seeks revenge, making the jealous person more dangerous (see chapter 9).

Signs of a Jealous Person

Does the person you're with have any of the following characteristics? Using a scale of 0–2, rate each behavior as follows:

0-Never
1-Sometimes
2-Often

A jealous person may:

____ criticize the way you dress

____ call you constantly when you're apart

____ question you about where you've been

____ follow you when you go places

____ look through your wallet or purse

____ accuse you of lying to them

____ act suspicious about what you do when you're apart

____ watch you closely when you're around others

____ try to limit the amount of time you spend with family or friends

____ tell you how to act when you're out in public

____ worry about losing you to someone else

____ accuse you of flirting when you weren't

____ get angry when you pay attention to other people

____ want you to spend all your time together

____ listen in on your phone calls

____ pick fights with people you're close to

____ wonder if he or she can trust you

____ avoid social situations, preferring to spend time alone with you

____ expect to be informed of where you are at all times

____ get upset when you aren't where you said you would be

____ dislike you going out without him or her

____ suspect you of cheating

_____ spy on you
_____ act needy and clingy

Scale

0–7

If you're in a new relationship, you may see some of these behaviors as signs that the other person cares deeply. In the throes of new love, you want to be together all the time, and you may worry about losing this wonderful person. But if you're feeling stifled and unable to be yourself, chances are you're with a jealous partner. Keep an eye out for other warning signs.

8–15

You may find yourself doing many things that are out of character to avoid your partner's fits of jealousy. Family and friends may remark on changes in your personality. In a healthy relationship you don't have to change your behavior to make someone else feel secure. If you find yourself sacrificing who you are, it's time to find a way out of this relationship.

16–24

Most of the time you feel as if you're walking on eggshells. You never know when you're going to be falsely accused of something you didn't do. It's hard to live like a suspect all the time. No matter what you do, you never allay your partner's fears. A jealous person's distrust of you has nothing to do with how trustworthy you are; it's based on his or her own insecurities. For your own peace of mind, ease out of the relationship as soon as you can.

25–48

Some of these characteristics also fit the controlling personality (see chapter 6). The difference between the two is in their motivation. A jealous person is afraid of losing you, whereas a controlling person wants to dominate. Their motives are different, but the result is the same—they circumscribe your life to meet their needs.

It's possible this relationship could escalate into cyberstalking or other dangers. The higher the number, the greater your concerns should be. Take precautions when you leave this person.

Kate's Story

Exuberant and excited after winning their championship game, the under-30 coed football team clomped into the nearest pub, sweaty and still wearing their cleats and shin guards. They chose a large table in the back and jostled each other for seats. Lars stuck close to Kate, and when she pulled out a chair, he grabbed the seat next to her. But before she sat down, Colin beckoned from the other side of the table, and Kate rushed around to join him.

Lars slumped in his seat. Of course she'd prefer Colin's company; he'd scored the winning goal. Lars tried to console himself that he had a better view of her this way, but it didn't ease the jealousy eating at him as the night wore on. Lars hadn't seen much play, so it was hard for him to watch all the adulation being heaped on Colin and Harry, who'd scored the tie-breaking goal on a corner kick. He sat morosely, staring down into his beer as everyone around him chattered excitedly. They went over and over each detail of the three goals, the best plays, and brilliant defensive moves—none of which were his.

"You were awesome," Kate declared, leaning over to kiss Colin's cheek.

Lars cringed. He'd had his eye on Kate for some time now but still hadn't worked up the courage to ask her out. The more she drank, the more boisterous Kate became. And the more amorous. She was doling out kisses like candy to the teammates around her.

And the more Lars drank, the more irritated he got. He sulked into his beer. It sickened him that Colin, a married man, slung his arm around Kate's shoulders and pulled her so close she was practically sitting in his lap.

Arianna, the American transplant who still insisted on calling the game *soccer*, tried to include Lars in the conversation, but he could tell she was only doing it to be nice. After getting a few grumpy, one-word answers from him, she shrugged and turned to chat with the player on her right.

Lars had a strict religious upbringing, and the drunker he became, the louder his minister father's voice boomed in his ear. What Kate and Colin were doing was sinful. After watching the two of them share an amorous kiss, Lars shoved back his chair and stormed from the pub.

By the time he reached his apartment, he was steaming. He texted Kate: *Fooling around with a married man will send you straight to hell.* Then he texted warning after warning, quoting Scripture verses about adultery and fornication and cautioning her about the dire consequences of her sinful behavior.

The next morning he awoke, head pounding, but his fury unabated. When he turned on his computer, a string of posts popped up on Facebook about the game, but what caught his eye was Kate's mocking post: *Shared a few victory kisses in a pub and now I'm the "Spawn of Satan." Look at these texts I've gotten since.* She posted Lars's messages, and people's comments ranged from outraged to scornful.

Lars's face burned when someone asked who'd sent them and Kate posted his name for all the world to see. From the comments flying back and forth, it was obvious everyone thought he was a religious crackpot or worse. People advised Kate to stay away from him, to block him.

Before she did he was going to set the record straight. And although the messages and Kate's tone were hurtful, she was paying more attention to him than she ever had before. Lars reveled in that. He defended himself and pointed out that the kisses went well past the bounds of propriety. A short while later, Kate wrote: *Blocked the creepy bastard and plan to keep my distance.*

Furious, Lars set up a new identity and sent Kate a friend request. When she accepted he claimed to be a married man who'd read her previous posts, and then he made lewd suggestions. Each time Kate blocked him, he assumed a different name and continued to harass her.

Kate's Solution

It's important to act immediately when someone says something offensive. Kate was advised to take screen shots or print out the messages and then mark them as spam. One random cruel message may be a fluke if the person is usually kind, but more than one, or a string of messages, such as the ones Lars sent, demands immediate action. If anyone sends more than one message that seems mean, demeaning, or threatening, block that person right away and report the messages to the administration of your social media.

Alexis warned Kate to watch out for new friend requests soon after she'd blocked someone. Attackers may assume a false identity the way Lars did, intending to attack her again. Kate also needed to check all her social media accounts and phone. If Lars is using one means to send or post nasty messages, chances are he may post to other accounts as well. Kate also switched all her privacy settings to allow only friends to see her posts and make comments.

Who Gets Hooked by a Jealous Person

Lars and Kate were just acquaintances, but jealousy also can mar committed relationships. At first many people are flattered by their partner's constant attention. They feel loved and cared for and enjoy spending most of their time with their friend or lover. Soon, though, the jealousy becomes evident. Your lover accuses you of flirting, of paying too much attention to someone else, or of lying about where you were. At this point people with good self-esteem assert themselves and either work out these problems, if it's possible, or walk away.

Those who choose to stay might be afraid of being alone or may feel they don't deserve any better. Some have guilt about other things in their lives, so their partner's accusations feel justified. People who are uncertain or insecure often believe their partner's criticisms and worry that their behavior has caused the jealousy or anger.

Isaiah's Story

Isaiah met Jasmine during college orientation. Both psychology majors, they hit it off right away and soon became an item. Isaiah found Jasmine's brilliant mind, sexy body, and quick wit compelling, and they had fun together; however, a darker side to her personality emerged soon after they became exclusive. It began when they were walking across campus and Isaiah smiled and greeted a girl from one of his classes.

Jasmine quizzed him about how well he knew the girl. She badgered him, even when he said he was being friendly only because he recognized her face from class. He greeted guys from the class, too. But Jasmine wasn't satisfied. Whenever they were out and Isaiah even glanced at any passing female, Jasmine accused him of being a perv. One day a sociology classmate who was ill texted to ask about their homework, and Jasmine went ballistic, insisting he was sleeping with the girl.

Early in the relationship, Isaiah believed Jasmine's jealous streak showed how much she loved him, but as time went on, the accusations increased. It reached the point where he couldn't even walk past another female without rousing Jasmine's suspicions. She even followed him to his job at a fast-food restaurant, positive he was cheating on her with coworkers. If he didn't exit the restaurant immediately after closing, she peered through the glass or banged on the door until he came out.

As graduation neared, Isaiah was offered a job as a live-in counselor at a drug rehab center. He decided to take the position in spite of Jasmine's temper tantrums. When she demanded that he instead marry her and find another job, Isaiah refused, leading to a tumultuous breakup.

Jasmine wasn't ready to let go, though. Several months later Isaiah began dating a coworker, Camila. Yet wherever he went—restaurants, sporting events, and even the grocery store—Jasmine showed up. She sat near him and Camila in the movies, at concerts, and in bars. At first Isaiah put it down to coincidence, but as the sightings became more frequent, Isaiah became frustrated. When he spotted Jasmine driving by Camila's parents' house, an hour away from their hometown, he knew he needed to take action.

He went to his hometown police and reported the problem. Unfortunately, Jasmine had been there before him. She'd told the police that he'd been stalking her, and they had records of several complaints against him.

After he and Camila announced their engagement, the situation grew worse. Jasmine hacked into Isaiah's cell phone account and sent messages to all of his contacts, claiming he was a cheating bastard. Then she did the same to Camila's phone. Shortly after that, Isaiah discovered that Jasmine had installed spyware on his computer to hack into his emails. In fact, she'd been tracking him online for years after sending him a birthday card with spyware attached. Isaiah kept all his appointments in his online calendar, which explained how she always knew his whereabouts. Sometimes Jasmine sent emails to his friends, changing his plans. Instead of Raul meeting him at the local bar for drinks, Jasmine would be sitting there waiting. She canceled his plans to meet Juan at a basketball game and showed up instead, expecting to use Juan's ticket.

Once again, complaints to the local police resulted in accusations that he was the stalker and cyberstalker. More reports had been filed against him. With nowhere else to turn, Isaiah looked for an advocacy group that could help him.

Isaiah's Solution

Survivors In Action had Isaiah follow all the action steps for both stalking and cyberstalking (chapters 11–13 and appendix A). They had him keep a timeline with the following headings: DATE, TIME, INCIDENT DESCRIPTION, AND WITNESSES (see appendix B). The final column was especially important because the police didn't believe Isaiah's reports. He asked friends, family members, and sometimes random strangers to report the incidents and include a phone number and email so the police could contact them. Not everyone was willing to verify the information, but some, such as a bartender at his favorite bar and a ticket seller at the local movie theater, had seen Jasmine standing around waiting for him numerous times. They were willing to vouch that she'd been stalking him. Isaiah compiled a long list for the authorities.

Moore advised him that stalking and cyberstalking require repeated documentations before the incidents are taken seriously. Some states require threats of violence, whereas others take these occurrences seriously and view them as identity theft or a part thereof. Luckily, in Isaiah's case, his state considered it a crime. Because the police had ignored his previous reports, he went directly to an attorney and to the prosecutor's office with his reports. He and Camila were relieved to discover they had a strong case against Jasmine.

To stop Jasmine's harassment, Isaiah filed a restraining order. Because he had long ago broken up with her, he filed a CHO, or civil harassment order. Jasmine was ordered not to contact Isaiah or Camila by phone or Internet, and she was not allowed to come within one hundred yards of them. Restraining orders will not stop all perpetrators, but in Jasmine's case, she did not want to risk getting caught, so she stopped her stalking and harassment. (For information on filing a restraining order, see appendix D.)

What Motivates a Jealous Person

The three motivations for jealousy are competition, protection, and projection. Losers in competitions—for awards, grades, promotions, love, or attention—envy the person who receives what they desire. Jealousy in this case stems from a sense of inferiority, of not measuring up. Failure often leads to low self-esteem and feelings of unworthiness or insecurity. These painful emotions may result in anger or revenge.

Protection is a strong motivation for those who fear loss and abandonment. Deeply rooted anxieties from childhood can cause an insecure person to cling tightly to people and relationships. These worriers constantly watch for signs that others will leave them, but they frequently misinterpret the signals. Sadly, their actions often cause their fears to come true.

In the case of projection, some jealous partners attribute their own guilt to their spouses. Thus, if they're having affairs, they check up on their spouses, but in fact, the only reason they distrust someone else is because they know they themselves can't be trusted.

How a Jealous Person Uses the Internet

During a relationship jealous people often use the Internet to spy on their partners. They read their emails, check their social media posts, watch for their latest Instagrams, check their search histories, and may even install spyware on their computers or cars. If the non-jealous partner resents the surveillance or changes passwords or hides information, the jealous person will immediately suspect something sinister is going on. It can lead to accusations and fights.

A simple e-card or email from your lover or a jealous friend could actually be spyware disguised as a friendly message. It can contain technology that remotely allows the sender to read and review everything you do online. The jealous person can keep track of all your online business and appointments, all your emails and contacts, all your plans and ideas. This information makes it easy for him or her to stalk you. By opening that one card or email, you're providing the jealous individual with complete access to your life.

Once your relationship ends, your jealous ex-lover may continue to spy on you and try to cause trouble. Your ex might stalk you, subject you to abuse and harassment, or threaten you—not only online, but also in person. Jealous friends or lovers may also try to destroy your reputation or interfere with your new relationship. It is important to protect yourself and all your personal information before and after you leave a relationship with a jealous person. And you need to remain vigilant long after a relationship ends, as Isaiah discovered.

Leaving a Jealous Person

Because jealousy is rooted in fear and insecurity, jealous people will do whatever they can to prevent their partners from leaving. They may react with angry outbursts or refuse to accept that a relationship is over. Because most spend time following or checking up on their significant others, they are used to sneaking around and can be dangerous. Some will install tracking devices or keep tabs on their former partners through contact with friends, following their exes, or via the Internet.

Action Steps

If you're dealing with a jealous person, here are some important steps to follow:

- Regularly check your car, phone, and computer for tracking devices and viruses. If you are still in a relationship with the jealous person, it might be wise not to remove them until just before you leave, so you don't tip off your partner. Perpetrators may install tracking devices even after a breakup, so remain vigilant.

- Stay alert when in public and vary your routine to prevent the jealous person from tracking you. Take different routes to school or work. Go to places you normally don't frequent. Make some new friends.

- Warn friends and family that you are breaking up and that your ex is jealous. This will prevent them from inadvertently giving out information about your activities and whereabouts.

Final Quick Tips

- **Be on guard:** Prepare for spying and sneak attacks.

- **Be vigilant:** Check regularly for tracking devices on cars, phones, and computers.

- **Don't overshare information:** Every keystroke, image, and message can be a weapon for a jealous cyberattacker.

CHAPTER 3

Starstruck: I know you love me.

Many people admire celebrities; they watch every show or game and spend time and money collecting memorabilia. They rave about star sightings or getting their picture taken with their favorite celebrity. Generally, this adoration is harmless unless it turns into an obsession. Starstruck fans fixate on a celebrity and fanaticize about a relationship with their idol. If they lose touch with reality, they can become harassers, stalkers, or cyberattackers.

Recognizing Starstruck Fans

Some starstruck fans are easy to spot. They fight for front row seats at every appearance, follow all the tours, beg for autographs and pictures, and post effusive compliments online. The adulation of these groupies can be flattering if it doesn't get out of hand. They sing your praises to others and spread the news of your latest releases. Most stars are grateful for these diehard fans and don't want to risk offending them. Problems occur when the fans overstep normal bounds of propriety. If they do or say anything that makes you feel uncomfortable, trust your instincts.

Starstruck fans generally feel unworthy of their crush's attention. They daydream scenarios of a relationship between the two of you. In their imaginations everything is perfect. These fantasies can be simple crushes, in which the fan collects a few photos or mementoes and dreams and writes about his or her idol. The "celebrity" category can also include popular students at school, athletes, politicians, TV or movie personalities, or other public figures. For example, a teen pining for the most popular person in school may doodle their names together in hearts and think about going out on a date or getting married someday. Teens aren't the only ones who get crushes; people crush on colleagues at work or acquaintances in a social group. Even fantasizing about movie stars or rock stars is normal and harmless as long as the person doesn't lose touch with reality.

Danger Signs

When fans start confusing their daydreams with actuality, they become dangerous. They move beyond keeping a few souvenirs to collecting hundreds of star-related items or even erecting shrines. Some fantasize that the star has similar feelings, and they may believe the star is sending special messages or signals only for them. They may email or call the star describing their imaginings, which can range from romantic to crude and dirty.

When real life intrudes and the star finds a lover, some fans become angry and vengeful. They lose touch with reality altogether. Their behavior can escalate to physically stalking their crushes. The news has many reports of fans who maim or kill stars or their significant others, so it's important to report any contact from fans who seem unbalanced or who make threats.

If someone is leaving gifts or following you, also notify the authorities. Gifts may seem like a thoughtful gesture, but they could be a sign that someone is interested in you but too shy or insecure to approach. That person is starstruck and could be dangerous.

Categories of Stalkers

Experts have identified five main categories of stalkers, and these profiles apply equally well to cyberattackers. The first two types rarely attack their victims; the latter three pose the greatest risks.

- **Socially Incompetent Stalkers** have difficulty forming relationships, so they worship their victims from afar rather than approach them.

- **Resentful Stalkers** feel sorry for themselves and issue threats but generally don't follow through with them.

- **Intimacy Seekers** believe they have a special relationship with someone; in more extreme cases they are delusional, and their personality disorders make them dangerous.

- **Rejected Stalkers** become angry and want to make the person who hurt them pay; the majority of the time, they know their victims and are determined to regain their partners and/or their damaged self-esteem.

- **Predators** may target strangers, and their motives are control, violence, and/or sexual gratification.

Signs of a Starstruck Fan

Does someone around you have any of the following characteristics?
Place a checkmark beside any statements that are true.

____ Someone follows me around and tries to start conversations as if
we're close when we're not.

____ This person frequently bothers me for autographs and small
favors.

____ This person makes suggestive remarks or offers sexual favors.

____ I feel uncomfortable when I meet this person face-to-face.

____ I get a sick feeling whenever I see online or text messages from
this person.

____ Being around this person makes me nervous and/or wary.

____ Some messages I receive indicate that this person knows my
plans or appointments.

____ Friends have received requests for information about me.

____ Someone I don't know keeps sending me email or text messages.

____ A random stranger posts effusive compliments about me online.

____ A random stranger posts nasty comments about me online.

____ Someone I don't know well (or at all) acts as if we're best friends
online.

____ I've received flowers, presents, or unsigned cards and don't know
who sent them.

____ I've received messages that make me feel uncomfortable or
uneasy.

____ Some of these messages have a threatening tone or contain
actual threats

____ I've noticed someone following me.

____ A certain person shows up at many of my events or activities.

____ Sometimes I see this person when I exit my house, school, or
office.

Scale

Unlike the other quizzes, if you've checked more than one or two
items on this list, you could be in danger. If any of your checkmarks

are in the last five lines, contact the authorities immediately. There's a good chance you're being stalked. Physical stalking is extremely dangerous. Even if you know this person, it's important to make law enforcement aware of the situation. Police may not be able to act unless you receive an actual threat, but let them know your concerns. If the situation gets worse, they'll have a record of your previous complaints.

If you are a celebrity you need to be particularly watchful. Sending messages and gifts is often a fan's first step in actively pursuing you. If the fan becomes overly complimentary, sends messages, or starts following you, be sure to watch that person closely. If he or she does anything that makes you even slightly uncomfortable, report it immediately. Having a trail of complaints will make it easier to get a conviction should that fan cross the line.

Many stars find that a fan becomes obsessed with them, follows them to appearances, and contacts them online or in person. Having people who love what you do can be gratifying, but these behaviors can be danger signals. The greater the number of checkmarks on the quiz, the more likely it is that this person is unbalanced.

Jennifer's Story

Jennifer, an attractive newspaper columnist and TV personality, was used to having fans gush over her in her hometown. When she went out shopping, people sometimes stopped her for autographs or asked if they could take their pictures with her. Inside she was secretly pleased at being recognized and always obliged to keep the public happy. She also enjoyed getting fan mail and complimentary comments whenever her columns were posted online.

One man, who went by the screen name Big Guns, responded to every post she wrote. He also commented on each show. At first the remarks were general: "good job," "well researched," or "excellent points." Over time his compliments grew more effusive, and Jennifer basked in his praise. It was nice to publish columns that drew such wonderful accolades, and she looked forward to seeing how her "super fan" would respond to each new column—until his remarks became personal. They progressed from "You are the greatest! I love what you do!" to "Jennifer, you are hot! I watch your TV show every morning!"

The posts that followed made it sound as if they shared a connection outside of work, and at times his comments almost seemed as if he had been following her. She felt a bit nervous and uncomfortable but shook off her bad feelings, rationalizing that it was a fairly small town and likely he'd seen her out and about.

Jennifer wrote her next column about a recent cyberstalking case. She contacted Alexis Moore from Survivors In Action for some information and quotes. As she and Moore talked, Jennifer's uneasiness increased. Many of the early warning signs of cyberstalking that Alexis listed matched Jennifer's situation, but Jennifer was too embarrassed to confess that she'd been ignoring them.

After she got off the phone, Jennifer started to worry. The more she looked at her notes, the more obvious it became she'd been dismissing a situation that might be a potential problem. One of the things Moore had stressed was paying attention to gut feelings. "If something feels off to you, it probably is," she had said.

Honestly, Jennifer's gut had been warning her for months now, but she'd pushed those doubts aside. Her fears increased when Big Guns called the studio to talk to her. The call was passed on because he claimed to be a close friend. The receptionist, who'd seen the personal comments he'd made on Jennifer's shows and columns, believed him.

Jennifer was busy when the call came in and let it go to voice mail. Her stomach clenched when Big Guns introduced himself as her favorite fan and told her he was looking forward to seeing her when she got off work. He said he loved watching the way her ass swung as she walked down the street to her red Miata. "And those legs when you get in . . . the way your skirt slides up to expose your thighs. . . ." He wolf-whistled.

Shaking, Jennifer snapped off the answering machine. Next, he texted her on her cell phone. The studio's number was public, but this guy had managed to obtain her personal number. The texts were even more explicit than the phone message and, even more terrifying, they revealed that he knew private details of her life, including where she lived. The text that frightened her the most said he had plans to meet her in person soon—real soon.

Jennifer picked up the phone and called Moore. Under the pretext of confirming some quotes for her column, she gradually brought the conversation around to her real reason for calling. The minute Moore heard the story, she confirmed that Jennifer needed to act immediately to protect herself from a cyberstalker who could well be dangerous.

Jennifer's Solution

Moore stressed that Jennifer should make some changes to her looks, her routine, and her technology to deter the cyberstalker. Anyone in the public eye can use these tips to avoid becoming a victim.

VARYING APPEARANCE

In addition to having Jennifer follow all the action steps for both stalking and cyberstalking (see appendix A, along with chapters 11–13), Moore suggested that stars should always create two separate personas by using a different hairstyle at work, going by a different name (even if it's as simple as being called Jennifer at work and Jenny at home, or adopting a pseudonym for TV), and dressing and acting differently in professional versus personal realms. If fans are used to seeing Jennifer on TV with hair expertly coiffed around her face, wearing tailored suits and heels, she'd look different as Jenny with little makeup, hair in a ponytail, dressed in jeans. Moore suggested making the transition before she left the studio. Hats, wigs, and sunglasses can also add to the disguise, as can a more casual posture, stride, and speech. Even adding cosmetic changes for the camera, such as a beauty mark or a temporary tattoo in public, can make people uncertain if it's really Jennifer when they pass her on the streets.

Maintaining a totally different persona on camera might mean that fewer fans would recognize her when she was out, but at this point Jennifer was more concerned with safety than stardom. And unless she started wearing wigs, it would be hard to disguise herself in her hometown. But she did have a job interview for a position in another state and planned to use these strategies if she got that job.

STAYING SAFE

The other thing Moore stressed, especially if someone was following Jennifer, was for Jennifer to vary her routes to and from work as well as her arrival and departure times. Being unpredictable throws off stalkers. Jennifer was also advised to spend as much time as possible in groups or with friends when she went places. Walking alone made her an easier target, should the cyberstalker become a physical stalker.

She learned that the most dangerous places to be alone are bathrooms and stairwells. Many times super fans and stalkers will use these spaces to wait for a victim. As tempting as it was to take the stairs to burn off those extra calories, Jennifer avoided them unless a colleague or friend accompanied her. Sarah, one of her friends who worked at another TV station, had been accosted in the office restroom by a naked fan who'd hidden in one of the stalls. This man managed to sneak into the bathroom several times before management installed a key code lock. Because her building had minimal security, Jennifer double checked the bathroom stalls and her surroundings to be sure she was alone. She did the same when she entered public restrooms, and she always had a friend accompany her. When she was out on dates with her boyfriend, he walked her to the door and waited for her outside.

Jennifer made a self-defense class part of her exercise routine. Knowing she could defend herself if she were cornered or attacked gave her greater confidence, a confidence that showed in her stride and posture. Stalkers want to instill fear, and a frightened, cowering victim is easier to assault. They get no payback if their target disregards them and their threats, and they're less likely to attack someone who is walking with self-assurance and purpose.

PROTECTING PERSONAL INFORMATION

Getting an unlisted phone number and a post office box gave Jennifer one more layer of protection against unwanted advances. So did letting her friends and family know about the problem. Her colleagues and relatives not only stayed alert for signs of a stalker, but also knew not to respond if someone contacted them for information about Jennifer.

Moore also recommended having a "bat phone." This secret prepaid cell phone is useful for making plans, contacting relatives and best friends, and reporting emergencies. It gave Jennifer peace of mind to know that if the phone rang, it would only be people she knew. She could silence her other phones or even leave her regular cell phone behind without compromising her security.

In addition to recording and reporting the phone calls from her cyberstalker, Jennifer followed Moore's advice to have the IT department check out the IP address of Big Gun's posts. They blocked his posts and phone calls. Unfortunately for Jennifer, law enforcement did not feel the messages were threatening enough to act on, and they refused to take a report. Moore supported Jennifer in insisting on having a record in case the super fan became more dangerous.

Dangerous Crushes

Celebrities aren't the only ones who need to be cautious. Crushes can occur at work or in social settings. At school popular students may find themselves the object of unwanted attention. Sometimes the starstruck person tries to attract the crush's notice, hoping to start a relationship. Other times that person may idolize another student, including someone of the same gender, and seek to imitate them or gather souvenirs.

Jackson's Story

After a semifinal game at a rival school, the team members left their sports bags and equipment in the hallway while they waited for the bus. A group of girls from the other school joined them at the concession stand and flirted with all the players, especially Jackson, who was not only a standout athlete but also extremely handsome. One girl in particular cozied up to him. So much so, he felt uncomfortable. He'd seen Scarlett in the stands at all his games, and she'd wait for him after every game to tell him how awesome he'd played.

Jackson had a girlfriend from his hometown, and he was shy, so he edged away whenever she invaded his personal space. He was too tongue-tied to discourage her advances, so this particular night, he was relieved when she excused herself to use the restroom. As soon as she was out of sight, he wedged his chair between two of his teammates' seats, leaving no room for her.

Scarlett's disappointment was obvious when she returned. Still, she kept flashing him smiles as if they shared a secret. Jackson was grateful when the bus pulled up. Scarlett sidled up to him and asked for his number, but he pretended not to hear and hurried up the bus steps. She wrangled numbers from several of his teammates and promised to keep in touch. As the bus pulled away, she blew him kisses, prompting several teammates to remark, "That girl's got the hots for you."

In the locker room back at school, Jackson couldn't find his jersey. He shrugged, assuming that someone else had picked it up and would toss it in the communal laundry pile and that he'd have it for the next game.

Two days later Scarlett texted: *Missing anything?* She attached a picture of herself in his jersey, lying on a rumpled bed, hair mussed, legs spread, no pants on.

Jackson's face burned when he saw she'd sent it to several teammates.

Remember this? We had fun, didn't we? she wrote next, accompanied by more lewd pictures. Each message made it sound as if they'd been together.

Sick to his stomach, Jackson blocked her number, but he couldn't erase the pictures from his mind. And the photos quickly made the rounds at school. A few classmates made ribald comments or congratulated him; most, especially the more pious ones in his religious school, treated him like a pariah. One student reported him to the dean.

No matter how much Jackson protested his innocence, his classmates didn't believe him. Neither did the school disciplinary committee. Again and again, they returned to his claim that the jersey was stolen and questioned why he hadn't reported it. They pressured him to confess to his sin and stop lying about it. When he clammed up and shook his head, they suspended him.

His coach and teammates were upset. His girlfriend called in tears, wanting to break up. Even his parents looked at him skeptically. Alone in his room the night of the championship game, Jackson questioned why God had let this happen. A few weeks ago, he'd been an honor student headed to a prestigious college on a rugby scholarship. Now he'd lost it all. Suicide seemed his only option. Although he struggled with doubt, in the end, his faith stopped him from pulling the trigger.

JACKSON'S SOLUTION

A female investigator from SIA took on the case pro bono and went to Scarlett's school to interview students, many of whom had heard Scarlett bragging about stealing the jersey. One of Jackson's teammates confessed he'd given Jackson's phone number to Scarlett when she'd begged for it.

After collecting statements from the students and other witnesses, such as the coaches and teammates who'd seen Scarlett stalking Jackson after games, the investigator contacted school officials with the information. She convinced them that Jackson had neither given Scarlett the jersey nor been seeing the girl romantically.

Chagrined that they had jumped to conclusions without investigating the situation, the administration contacted Scarlett's school to request a meeting. When confronted, Scarlett admitted that she'd had no contact with Jackson except in the presence of others. The headmaster at her school insisted she write a letter of apology to Jackson and that she stay away from his sporting events. Jackson's school extended an official apology, reinstated him with all his previous honors, and, to avoid a possible lawsuit, waived his tuition for the remainder of the school year.

Because of their religious beliefs, Jackson's parents refused to press charges against Scarlett or the school. If they had, Scarlett would have been charged with theft, and they could have sued for the distress and anguish they'd endured.

What Motivates a Starstruck Fan

Starstruck individuals range from fans to fanatics. Those who develop unhealthy and delusional attachments to stars tend to be loners who lack close relationships. Often they were subjected to harsh or unfair punishments as children or they lost a primary caregiver, so they never learned to develop loving bonds with others. They have low self-esteem and may fear intimacy. At the same time, they are self-absorbed, possibly even narcissistic, which leads them to believe they have a close connection with a celebrity.

Interestingly, many are well-educated but unemployed, leaving them with plenty of time to concentrate on learning more about the person they idolize. Most also suffer from depression and anxiety. They are prone to fantasies; some have had hallucinations or intense paranormal or religious experiences. In the more serious cases, they lack the ability to integrate feelings and thoughts, and may completely lose touch with reality. Those who cross the line into stalking or violence also may have anger and control issues, sadistic tendencies, or various personality disorders. Alcohol and/or drug abuse is also common. These characteristics make it important to be extremely cautious when dealing with this personality type.

How a Starstruck Fan Uses the Internet

Anyone from high school students to big-name celebrities can find themselves targets of starstruck fans. Whether these fans have an unrequited crush on you, admire your skills or prowess, or hope to gain some advantage by befriending you, they can learn a great deal about you via the Internet. Many follow you, friend your online contacts, and read all your posts. If they adore you from afar, this may not be a problem. At times, though, they may bother you by commenting on posts, acting as if you have a special connection, or even cause trouble between you and your friends or significant other. They may use your posts to figure out where you're going and follow you around.

If someone's online behavior makes you feel uncomfortable, unfriend them immediately. Also set your status to private. And be sure not to accept any new friend requests from people you don't know. Your starstruck fan may be posing as someone else. Also ask your friends to unfriend this person. Keep in mind that in some cases your information can be visible to people who access your friends' sites. And always be careful what you share online. Announcing that you're attending a concert or other social event may mean your fan will show up there.

Additional Internet Tips for Celebrities

In the past fans had fewer ways to communicate with stars. Contact was limited to reading about them in magazines and newspapers, watching them on TV or in movies, or attending live performances. They could send letters or packages, but unless they knew the star's home address, they were confined to sending correspondence or gifts to an agent or studio address.

With the advent of the Internet, many celebrities went online to connect with fans. This opened them up to greater contact with groupies and stalkers. Many TV networks, radio stations, and studios have an online presence, and they allow people to leave comments. Social media offers immediate access to stars, giving fans the opportunity to interact with their favorite idols. If you have social media accounts, limit your posts to publicly available information. If you suspect you have a stalker, it might be wise to throw in false clues to your whereabouts and plans. Be creative in what you share. It's better to share information about events after they've occurred rather than before. Satisfy your fans with post-event pictures rather than revealing your excitement leading up to the activity.

It has become much harder for celebrities to maintain their privacy. Internet sites offer personal information for a fee, including addresses, phone numbers, and names of significant others. Any stalker, with a little investment of money and time, can find out where his or her target lives.

Action Steps

The news is filled with stories of rabid fans turned stalkers. Famous celebrities and their studios pay millions of dollars for bodyguards and protection, and still many stars live in fear. They curtail their activities to keep themselves and their families safe. Not everyone can afford bodyguards, so here are some tips for protecting yourself if you're in the public eye.

Physical Safety Tips
In addition to following the same steps Jennifer did, such as varying your routine, walking with others, learning self-defense, and carrying a prepaid phone, here are some other tips to help you stay safe:

- Always park in well-lit areas and consider your safety first and foremost.

- Know your area and select safe zones in case you need to get away or fear you're being followed. Choose places with video cameras and twenty-four-hour security. If you believe you're under threat, head for a safe zone while you call the authorities.

- Create a safety plan that lists your action steps if you're followed or have a stalker confrontation at home, at the office, or while driving. These safety plans are not complicated; they are simply steps to take in an emergency situation. They need to be rehearsed and updated when you change jobs, travel out of town, attend classes, appear at an event, or visit a foreign country.

- For added protection, contact a risk management consultant, one who specializes in personal protection. Usually one or two consultations will provide enough information to create a safety plan and avoid violence. Some consultants discount their rates if the client goes to a class sponsored by a nonprofit agency, such as Survivors In Action. Risk management consultants are also wonderful advocates in court because they are familiar with the legal system and can provide evidence to garner law enforcement attention, restraining orders, and successful prosecution.

- Some stalking victims carry handheld alarms, pepper spray, or weapons. If you choose the latter two options, familiarize yourself with state laws and obtain the proper training and permits. Observe all cautions when using any weapon, and remember that it can be used against you, so learn to protect yourself in these situations.

Home Safety Tips

- Consider installing security cameras at home. These can be expensive, but it's possible to get them at a discount or even donated if you're working with an advocate or nonprofit group.

- As a temporary measure, find something that looks like a camera and place it in your window. Most stalkers won't risk getting close enough to tell it's fake. One man set his computer mouse on the window ledge. The flashing red light on the bottom even fooled the police officer who came out to investigate his report of a stalker. Tiny nightlights hung from the top corner of the window can also look like security devices. (See chapter 8 for additional strategies to make your property look protected.) Actual protection is better than trying to fool stalkers, but these tricks may help deter predators until the system is set up.

- Consult with security companies who specialize in risk management (see previous page); ask for their recommendations for protecting your home and property.

Phone and Online Safety Tips

- Use an answering service or booking agent for incoming phone calls. If you can't afford a service, perhaps a friend or relative would be willing to act as a buffer.

- Have someone else record the outgoing message on your answering machine. Stalkers like to hear the voice of their victims to feel close to them and maintain their illusion of a relationship or love affair. Although it's false, they thrive on the feeling of connection. Hearing your voice or seeing your response empowers them and feeds their fantasies. If they can't hear you or can't get directly to you, they may stop calling.

- Avoid publishing information online regarding your personal life or day-to-day activities without first considering the possible outcome.

- Never publicly mention the names of family members or friends, as they may wind up being stalked, too. Starstruck fans have shown up at schools that a celebrity's children attend. They frequent a celebrity's favorite restaurant or attend a club or event, hoping for a glimpse of a star.

- Before you advertise an appearance, a book signing, or a celebrity charity event, be sure you have adequate security in place, and never attend the event alone. The more people you have with you, the better.

- Be careful not to use logins, passwords, or security questions that relate to your interests. Fan sites and interviews reveal everything from your favorite colors and foods to the names of your significant other, children, and pets. Birth dates, graduations, anniversaries, and other data are readily available to avid fans. They can look up places where you've lived, parents' names, and other information typically chosen as answers to security questions. Rather than using information that may be public knowledge, try to find creative answers to the questions. But always choose answers you'll remember, or write them down and keep them in a safe place.

- Web counters on your site can record incoming IP addresses, city, state, time, and duration of visit. Monitor these for spikes in activity from a certain area or computer. Keep logs of the IP addresses of frequent commenters. Incoming calls to your work number also can be recorded.

- Try to find out as much as possible about rabid fans—their real names in addition to screen names, where they live and work, their daily schedules. You can furnish the police with this information later should the problems escalate.

- If you feel threatened and can afford it, hiring a private investigator may offer important clues to the fan's life, whereabouts, and mental health.

Final Quick Tips

- **Monitor super fans:** Identify overeager groupies; keep printouts of their comments and records of their calls, and have someone keep an eye on their activities, or hire a professional risk management consultant to do so.

- **Protect private information:** Direct all calls and correspondence to a third party; use an unlisted number and post office box for additional privacy; never share information about your home or family; get a "bat phone" to stay in touch with those closest to you.

- **Disguise yourself:** Change your looks and persona as you move between your personal and professional life.

CHAPTER 4

Entitled: I deserve it all.

People with a sense of entitlement believe the world owes them something simply because they exist. They don't feel they should have to work, strive, or struggle. They expect others to do things for them, but they rarely do much in return. Often they aren't grateful because they believe they deserve what they receive. If others don't meet their needs, they have no qualms about lying, cheating, stealing, or demanding what they see as rightfully theirs.

Recognizing People with a Sense of Entitlement

One way to spot entitled individuals is to watch them in social situations where work is involved. For example, in a recent Facebook post, Adia described moving day at her house. Four people were loading the truck, two were scrubbing the house, one was watching everyone's children, and she was—in her typical entitled fashion—busy looking through the phone book to find charities to pick up the outmoded furniture. And once she found a place, she'd make sure someone else made the call.

Most likely you know someone like this, someone who always ends up with the easy tasks while everyone else does the hard work. People like this frequently complain about how hard they've worked, while ignoring others' more significant contributions. And the truth is, they have worked extremely hard in their opinion because they don't think they should have to lift a finger.

People with a sense of entitlement feel that the world owes them, and they reach out to take what they believe they deserve. The sense of entitlement can be as simple as expecting others to drive them places, pay for a joint cab, let them go first in line, or wait for them when they're running late. Whether in small ways or large, their belief that they deserve certain benefits may lead them to harm others through lying, cheating, stealing, or demanding favors.

Signs of an Entitled Person

Does the person you're with have any of the following characteristics?
Using a scale of 0–2, rate each behavior as follows:

0-Never

1-Sometimes

2-Often

People who feel a sense of entitlement:

____ expect first-class service even if they haven't paid for it

____ don't care how you feel, but expect you to care how they feel

____ mooch other people's possessions, food, drinks, and equipment

____ push to be first in line

____ make their own rules

____ expect others to treat or pay

____ act like they're doing people a favor by being around

____ wear or use items they've bought, then return them

____ complain loudly about service and often send food back in restaurants

____ make you wait, but get annoyed if you keep them waiting

____ take credit for others' work

____ treat themselves to things outside the budget because they believe they deserve it

____ expect others to wait on them

____ complain they're not appreciated

____ say "That's not fair" or "I deserve more or better" or "I deserve it"

____ let others pay their bills

____ show up at events when they haven't been invited

____ ask people, even strangers, to do things for them that they're capable of doing

____ blame others for their mistakes or bad feelings

____ take items intended for others (e.g., help themselves to charity baskets, take numerous condiment packs in fast-food restaurants or large handfuls of candy in waiting rooms)

____ always have their hand out for more

____ never say "thank you"

_____ treat favors as their due

_____ expect people to move out of their way

_____ put their needs first

_____ think the world owes them a living

_____ get furious when criticized or corrected

_____ don't take responsibility for their actions

_____ never like to "get their hands dirty" or do menial jobs

_____ always have an excuse for why they aren't at fault

_____ often treat the people around them like servants

_____ expect others to do their bidding

_____ have no qualms about lying or cheating to get what they want

_____ say what they think without regard for others' feelings

_____ don't feel laws apply to them

_____ consider themselves special or privileged

_____ look down on others

_____ believe they deserve more or better than others

_____ expect people to fawn over them

Scale
0–10
Having a few of these characteristics may just be the sign of poor manners. Some children are raised to grab the best or the first before it's gone. These are not endearing character traits, and if this person is toward the upper range, you should ask yourself if you truly want to be in a relationship with someone who acts this way.

11–22
Chances are you're doing most of the giving in this relationship. It's time to evaluate whether what you're receiving compensates for what you're expending. If you truly care about this person, you need to take a stronger stance and expect him or her to take more responsibility. You're not really helping or being loving if you allow the entitled person to trample on your (or others') feelings or to use you.

23–42
Sometimes these individuals have special talents or status that adds to their feeling of entitlement. Everyone around them is in awe, which contributes to their inflated opinions of themselves. Others scurry to do their bidding, either because they're paid to do so or because they

hope to curry favor with the superstar. Maybe you've even fallen into this trap yourself, feeling that a superstar's elevated status accords this celebrity certain privileges.

If these individuals are not celebrities (or even if they are), you may be feeling angry and resentful that they treat you like a servant and ignore your feelings. If this is the case, it's time for a reality check. Ask yourself if they have the right to treat you and others this way. Chances are they won't acknowledge their boorish behavior, because, after all, the rules don't apply to them. They see themselves as different and special. But you need to take care of yourself.

43–78

Again, many celebrities fall into this category; they expect others to fawn over them. But for anyone, superstar or not, the higher the score, the more likely they are to be out of touch with reality. If these individuals can't see how their behavior affects those around them, they lack the basic empathy needed to have normal, healthy relationships. Continual lying, cheating, or stealing may be indicative of a deeper and more serious personality disorder.

Who Gets Hooked by an Entitled Person

Those with a sense of entitlement look for people who will indulge and wait on them. Their ideal partners look up to them and are people pleasers, hard workers who enjoy serving others and rarely complain about onerous duties. These helper types may be generous in spirit, or they may be insecure and eager to placate others. For example, partners who idolize their spouses and see them as better looking, smarter, or more worthy of love often spend a lot of time trying to please.

If insecure people gain a sense of their own self-worth, they may demand some attention and refuse to continue indulging another's whims. Unless the entitled person learns to accept responsibility, share duties, and become supportive, the relationship may become rocky or even dissolve.

Bill and Evelyn's Story

Marita was born to parents who had struggled to have children for fifteen years. Overjoyed to have this long-awaited baby, Bill and Evelyn showered her with attention, affection, and toys. Over the years Marita became increasingly spoiled and rebellious, testing limits and acting out, but her parents smoothed over any difficulties and bribed or negotiated to keep Marita from experiencing the consequences of her folly. They wrote falsified excuses when Marita skipped school, hired a high-powered lawyer to fight Marita's shoplifting offenses and drug charges, and paid to fly her to another state for an abortion.

When Marita flunked out of college, she moved home with her parents, who urged her to get a job. But she preferred to party at night, sleep late, and do what she pleased during the day. Against her parents' wishes, she had friends over for loud parties every weekend and often spent her days smoking pot with various boyfriends. If her parents complained or criticized her, Marita flew into rages and screamed that she hadn't asked to be born. That usually silenced them.

Bill was past retirement age, but he couldn't quit his job because Marita racked up huge bills for clothing, parties, and alcohol. From time to time Bill would insist that Marita apply for a job, and her mother filled out numerous applications, falsifying some of Marita's work experience with jobs and references that couldn't be verified. Marita was usually personable enough to get hired, but she soon lost the jobs.

Then Bill had a heart attack. The doctor warned him to reduce the stress in his life. He and Evelyn knew the major source of tension in their lives—Marita. Evelyn bribed Marita to move out by agreeing to pay the rent and utilities on an apartment. At last they were free of their daughter and all the stress she'd brought into their lives. Or so they thought. Marita had gained access to their credit cards, and the bills began to roll in. But they decided not to confront her. Their peace of mind was worth more than the hundreds of dollars added to their accounts each month.

An even greater shock occurred when Bill opened the statements for his retirement accounts six months later. A total of seventy thousand dollars had been drawn out in five-thousand-dollar increments. They drove to Marita's condo to find a brand-new Hummer parked outside.

Marita wasn't at all apologetic. "That money was coming to me when you die," she said with a casual wave of her hand.

Despite how worried and upset her actions made them, Bill and Evelyn agreed they could never prosecute their daughter. They changed their passwords, but Marita still managed to tap into their retirement accounts and use their IDs to open new lines of credit. Her parents continued to pay the bills. They felt they had no choice if they wanted to keep their credit rating intact. But their retirement accounts dwindled.

Bill and Evelyn's Solution
Following an SIA suggestion, Bill and Evelyn changed all their passwords again. Yet they were unable to stop the charges on their accounts. SIA discovered that Bill, who had memory problems, had stored a document on his computer with all his personal, bank account, and investment information as well as the online passwords to his accounts. Initially, Bret, Marita's boyfriend, had hacked into the document remotely to access the account information.

SIA suggested the following measures:

- Remove the document with account passwords from the computer.

- Open new accounts at different banks and transfer the money in person to new investment and retirement accounts.

- Explain to bank personnel that the online accounts were hacked and request all information on paper until the issue is resolved.

- Pay off and close out all credit card accounts. (Although they could have used the strategy SIA recommended for Simon in chapter 5 of requesting exoneration for charges they hadn't personally incurred, Bill and Evelyn did not want to implicate Marita in any way.)

- After returning to banking online, change passwords monthly.

- Be sure that the password retrieval email is your email rather than someone else's.

- Change all security questions to make sure the answers are very difficult and not ones the cyberattacker can easily to figure out. (Because Marita knew her parents' answers, SIA recommended choosing someone else's information rather than their own.)

- Write down new passwords on paper and keep them in a safe place; if you need to protect them from someone in your household, store them under lock and key or write them in code (see chapter 12 for additional ideas).

They also discovered that Bret had been using a keylogger to keep track of all Bill's online activity. Removing the device cut Bret's access to changed passwords and account information.

ABOUT KEYLOGGING

Keylogging, or keystroke logging, can be done in many different ways, and it is usually hard to detect, except that it will often make a computer run more slowly. While you're typing, a delay or pause may occur before the letters appear on the screen.

Sometimes it's installed directly into the computer hardware. Because Bret had access to Bill and Evelyn's computer, he took advantage of it to add a simple USB connector, knowing that Marita's parents knew little about computers. They never noticed the tiny plug connected to the back of their CPU. It kept track of all the keystrokes on Bill and Evelyn's computer, which Bret could access remotely. It didn't matter how often Bill changed the computer or bank passwords online. Bret had a record of every keystroke, so he knew the new passwords immediately.

A variety of hardware devices, some more noticeable than others, can be added to computers, including laptops. Many are obvious additions that can be seen by those who know what computer hookups look like. If you notice new wires or plug-ins on your computer, that can be a tip-off.

Keylogging also can be done by software-based programs. You may inadvertently download the software along with another program or by opening an attachment that has a virus. The program can run silently behind the scenes, either under the operating system or as part of it, making it difficult to detect. If it's a virus, most antispyware programs will detect it. It is also a good idea to have a computer pro check out the machine if there's any suspicion of keylogging.

Keylogging programs collect each keystroke and relay it to another party via email, a file transfer protocol (FTP), or directly to another computer. Keylogging bypasses the security of *Https* sites because it does not affect those sites in any way; it records only the information that's typed in, meaning it easily gains access to all passwords and login information.

Tough Love

Bill and Evelyn may believe they're protecting Marita, but in fact, they are enabling her criminal behavior. Practicing tough love, forcing Marita to face the consequences of her actions, would be better for all of them in the long run. By suffering in silence, they're sending the unintentional message that they agree with her actions, and they're letting her get away with crime. In addition, their daughter has learned no discipline and is lacking job skills, so she'll always need someone to support her. Once Marita empties their bank accounts, she will likely justify stealing from others.

If the person who gains access to your bank account or personal information is a stranger, an ex, or an enemy, it's relatively easy to follow these steps. When it's someone who is close to you, it can be much more difficult to follow through. Remind yourself that you are acting in the best interests of all concerned and that one of the most loving things you can do for this person is to force him or her to take responsibility for his or her actions.

What Motivates a Person with a Sense of Entitlement

In a society where parents indulge their children, youngsters learn to expect—and even demand—the same or more from everyone around them. Whether they're given material items, excessive attention, or both, these children eventually come to believe they are entitled to have their needs met by others. Especially in homes where they are shielded from the consequences of their actions, children never learn that privileges come with corresponding responsibilities. Like Marita, children who are spoiled and coddled often lack respect for their parents and everyone around them. If they never face the negative outcomes of their mistakes and wrongdoings, they don't learn to accept responsibility for their actions. In some cases they don't realize there are consequences.

Overindulged children develop a sense of entitlement, but so do those whose feelings are not acknowledged. They don't learn to trust and process their feelings, which means they never learn to understand themselves or to empathize with others.

Special Case of Superstars

Some people, because of their status or profession, develop a sense of entitlement. Enjoying a lifestyle in which they are idolized and catered to, many stars develop an attitude of superiority. Sometimes their rudeness is a result of shyness or a desire for privacy, but often they have come to expect others to tend to their needs and to do their bidding. They are used to having lackeys and groupies who are more than willing to serve their every need.

Additional groups with a strong sense of entitlement include the wealthy, heads of corporations, and politicians. They, too, have people who do their bidding. Some consider themselves and their needs more pressing than those of others. Because they receive so much deference in public and at their jobs, they often carry that attitude home and treat family members' needs as less important than their own.

In an interesting turn of events, people with a sense of entitlement sometimes hang around superstars because they believe they're as good, or better, than the celebrity and expect to gain recognition and/or hope to break into the field that way. They are so convinced of their worthiness for the position, honor, adulation, or material possession that they justify any means of getting it. They may even attack perfect strangers to obtain what they want.

How an Entitled Person Uses the Internet

Entitled people feel they deserve the best of everything, and they use the Internet to acquire it. To get what they want, they've learned to be crafty. Online, they're likely to make sudden sneak attacks, and they may even get underlings to do their dirty work. They may attempt smear campaigns or use their tech knowledge to crash your computer. The media frequently reports about politicians who have encouraged campaign workers to send out false and/or defamatory messages about their opponents.

In some ways entitled individuals are easier to thwart than most cyber-attackers because they don't like to exert effort to achieve their goals. If you can block them quickly, they'll be angry but are not likely to exact revenge unless they have minions who will do it for them. If you have something an entitled person wants—a job, a relationship, business contacts, or customers—be on guard against possible attacks. He or she will justify any means to take it from you and will usually do it in a stealthy and unexpected manner.

Leaving an Entitled Person

Perhaps early in the relationship, you gave freely without expecting anything in return. If you're a naturally giving person, you may have continued to give until disappointment or resentment set in. In long-term relationships, partners of entitled people usually feel put upon. Their spouses may order them around as if they're slaves. Many fear the entitled person's wrath.

It can be difficult to get out of such a relationship, especially if your partner believes he or she is entitled to you. Some people see themselves as "owning" their spouses. This attitude means they won't give up easily if someone leaves them. An entitled person will often use trickery, emotional blackmail, or other sneaky tactics to get you to return. They are skilled manipulators, so be wary of engaging in confrontations or conversations, because they will usually find a way to gain the upper hand. Do all your planning in secret, and when you're ready, go quickly before they realize your intent and try to thwart you.

Action Steps

Once you've secured your accounts with the strategies Bill and Evelyn used, it's important to prevent the fraud from happening again. Here are some additional safeguards for protecting your accounts:

- Watch for signs of keylogging on your computer. Have it checked by a technology professional if you notice any new hardware or experience operational delays.

- Phone the three national credit bureaus to place a credit freeze and fraud alert on your credit reports; request that all creditors contact you prior to issuing any new lines of credit or banking accounts or making changes to existing accounts.

- Verify that the information has been received and is being passed on to creditors by applying for a new line of credit; if you are granted one, you'll know the credit freeze/fraud alert was not applied and needs to be reinstated.

- Complete an affidavit of forgery and have it notarized for any account that has been opened without your consent or permission (see appendix B for form and instructions).
- Check your credit bureau information at least twice a year and pay close attention to online activity.

Final Quick Tips

- **Safeguard passwords:** Do not keep records of account passwords online or email them to others, because they can easily be intercepted.

- **Proceed with care:** Realize that *Https* sites are not safe if a keylogger is recording your transactions.

- **Use tough love:** Don't let sentiment or family ties blind you to criminal activity.

CHAPTER 5

Manipulative: Do what I say or else.

Manipulators are often charming and kind when you first meet them. They appear caring and totally interested in you. It's not until you get into a relationship with them that you realize they use the information you've confided to control you. Some manipulators use guilt, illness, tragedy, and even self-inflicted pain to keep people in a relationship. And when the relationship ends, they're good at twisting facts so others believe you're at fault.

Recognizing a Manipulator

Identifying manipulators can be tricky because this personality appears charming, loving, and generous early in a relationship. Manipulators are good listeners and rush to fulfill your every wish. An ideal partner may do the same, so it's easy to mistake a manipulator for a dream come true.

But once you've fallen in love, everything changes. At first a manipulator's requests are subtle or even unnoticeable, but these demands escalate over time. Manipulators play mind games and often use the personal information you've confided to control you and get you to comply with their wishes. Making sarcastic remarks, giving dirty looks, or rolling their eyes are other ways they try to keep you in line. If you still don't give in, they may move on to threats or bursts of rage.

But when you do what they say, they reward you with tenderness and kindness. Constant shifts between critical and loving behavior may make you feel unbalanced and unsure of your relationship. You never know where you stand and often blame yourself for the problems in the relationship. Manipulators increase that uncertainty by lying about what they did or said, making you wonder about your sanity.

They also control through guilt or by putting themselves in the role of victim. Some manipulators pretend to be sick or actually hurt themselves to get your attention. If you have a problem, they have an even greater one. If you criticize them or point out their faults, they counter with how you caused that problem or behavior, or they act so devastated that you feel guilty for hurting them.

Healthy relationships are built on trust and honesty, which means relationships with manipulators are shallow. Early in life manipulators learned not to trust others, and as a result, they avoid sharing their deepest thoughts and feelings. Some even construct a fake persona. Frequently, the secrets they confide turn out to be false. When you confront them about lies or mistruths, they claim that you misheard or misunderstood.

If these symptoms sound like those in your relationship, you'll need to extricate yourself carefully. Manipulators don't want to let go of their victims. They are also adept at twisting information to make themselves look good and you look bad. Expert manipulators are used to being sneaky, and they'll try to turn your friends against you or harm you in ways that won't reflect them in a bad light. The Internet provides the perfect tool for getting back at you anonymously, so be sure to take precautions against cybercrime before you break up (see chapters 11 and 12).

Signs of a Manipulator

Does the person you're with have any of the following characteristics? Using a scale of 0–2, rate each behavior as follows:

0-Never
1-Sometimes
2-Often

Part A: Early in the relationship, manipulators:
_____ are charming and thoughtful
_____ are sympathetic listeners
_____ shower you with attention, affection, and presents
_____ make you feel like you're the most wonderful person in the universe
_____ fulfill your every wish
_____ confide many personal secrets
_____ fall in love quickly
_____ say you are their "one and only"
_____ speak well and easily, and are never at a loss for words

Part B: Later in the relationship, they:

____ are hot and cold toward you

____ change their stories, depending who's listening

____ lie by omitting certain facts

____ refuse to admit to mistakes or wrongdoing

____ claim that hurting or embarrassing you was a joke

____ say "If you really cared about me . . ." or "I'm not like the rest of these people . . ." or "I don't want to hear it"

____ do not give straight answers

____ always want the final word in arguments/disagreements

____ often claim to have illnesses, emotional issues, or other traumas

____ issue veiled or overt threats

____ use putdowns and sneers

____ gain sympathy by playing victim

____ use the silent treatment when upset

____ make you feel guilty if you point out a problem

____ act innocent after hurting someone

____ put their needs first

____ forget their wallets so you have to pay

____ turn things around so it appears you are at fault

____ volunteer to help but then act like martyrs

____ claim everyone hates them

____ always have an excuse for why they aren't at fault

____ use secrets you've confided to hurt you

____ always have worse problems than you do

____ threaten to end the relationship

Scale

0–14

If you're in a new relationship that's going well and most of your total is from Part A, your partner may not be a manipulator. But if the relationship seems too good to be true, keep an eye out for signs that all is not as it appears.

If the majority of your score is from Part B, you need to be careful. Everyone likes to have their own way sometimes, and some people will even lie, exaggerate, or fake illnesses for attention. It's possible your partner is just immature or selfish, but it's likely that the manipulation is beginning. The higher the score, the greater the likeli-hood that you're with a manipulator.

Ask yourself what you're getting from the relationship. Are your needs being met? Are you truly happy? Do you feel like you can be yourself around your partner? If not, try to figure out why you feel tied to this person. If your score is in the higher range, it's time to look for a partner who supports you and cares about your needs.

15–26

If most of your score is from Part A, see **0–14** above. But do try the experiment below to see if there's a manipulator hiding behind that mask of kindness.

If the majority of your score is from Part B or comes equally from both parts, it's highly likely your partner is a manipulator. You may often find yourself giving in to your partner's demands or feel like the problems between you two are mainly your fault.

Experiment by standing firm in your opinion or by asking to go to a different movie or restaurant than your partner prefers. See how they react. It's okay for your partner to disagree, state an honest opinion, and try to come to a compromise. But if there's no compromising, or if your partner pressures you, puts you down, threatens, insists, or makes you feel guilty, you're with a manipulator. Get out of the relationship as soon as you can.

27–48

If your score is on the lower end of this range and most of your total comes from Part A, see **15–26** above.

If the majority of your score is from Part B or comes equally from both parts, you are most likely with a true manipulator who loves to control others and may engage in risky or hurtful behavior to get his or her way. The higher the number, the greater your concerns should be.

It is possible this relationship could escalate to cyberstalking or other dangers. Some manipulators move on if they find they can no longer control you. If you stop being compliant, but do it quietly and reasonably without getting upset or giving in to their demands, your partner may look for someone else to manipulate. If, however, the manipulator becomes violent or threatening, take safety precautions and enlist help from others, including school or work authorities, law enforcement, domestic violence organizations, and support organizations such as Survivors In Action.

Who Gets Hooked by a Manipulator

Some people are more easily conned by manipulators than others. People who are trusting and generous often become targets. They have a tendency to ignore slights and hurts, or to excuse them, so they may be deeply into a relationship before they realize the truth. Even then, they try to give the manipulator the benefit of the doubt.

Other victims who fall into manipulators' traps are people pleasers. They work hard to make others happy and have trouble saying no. Often they have low self-esteem and dislike conflict. As a result, they give in easily to the manipulator's demands to keep the peace. They usually accept the manipulator's view that they're at fault for problems in their relationship.

Others at risk for falling for a manipulator are those who are lonely, longing for love, or desperate for attention. Those who are anxious or depressed are also more likely to become victims. Being needy or naïve may make people more vulnerable to a manipulator's flattery and deception.

At first manipulators listen well and are attentive. They shower their victims with attention, gifts, and compliments. Usually by the time they show their real personalities, the other person has already been hooked into an intimate relationship. The victim has fallen in love and is emotionally tied to the manipulator, making it hard leave.

Simon's Story

Simon, a successful software designer, had worked his way up to a management position in a large computer company, and on the side he was beta testing a video game he'd developed. One Friday evening after work, he went to a trendy local eatery to mingle with area business people, winemakers, and wine enthusiasts. While enjoying wine flights and tapas, Simon met Oliver. Simon had a quiet, gentle personality, was interested in and genuinely concerned about others, and had a big heart. Oliver, by contrast, was bold, outgoing, and self-confident.

Oliver's muscles and tan skin were the bait, and his hook was always out as he trolled for his next prey. He was between boyfriends and down on his luck. His last relationship had ended, as they all did, because Oliver didn't like to work. Lounging by the pool was more his style. His life of leisure had left him without a car or a bank account, but Oliver was good at finding someone eager to give him what he needed and wanted. For the next two weeks, he'd be house-sitting for someone he'd met at a club, and he was driving the man's Lexus convertible. The clock was ticking for Oliver to find a new friend soon, or he'd be sleeping on the street.

Simon noticed Oliver right away. He was interested but shy about approaching the tall, toned stranger. He finally caught Oliver's eye. When Oliver responded with an enthusiastic smile, Simon sauntered over and started a casual conversation. Then he offered to buy Oliver a drink. Later, Oliver shared some of his wine. Simon was so mesmerized that it never occurred to him that Oliver had only reciprocated with a free drink. He was too amazed that this personable and good-looking man seemed interested in him.

Meanwhile, Oliver was sizing up Simon. His potential victim seemed gentle and kind, and he was easy on the eyes. Simon was also generous; he'd paid for Oliver's meal and several more drinks. Once Oliver discovered that Simon had a good job at a major computer company, he knew it was time to reel in his catch. After more small talk (mostly about himself), Oliver told Simon how much he enjoyed meeting him and that he hoped to get to know him better.

Flattered, Simon offered to meet at the bar again the next evening. Oliver had to work fast because he'd soon be without a car and house. The next night he asked Simon to spend Sunday afternoon with him.

He picked up Simon in the Lexus and planned a picnic with delicacies the homeowner had left in the house. Afterward he invited Simon back to the house for a romantic evening of music and drinks from the homeowner's store, giving the impression that he was wealthy and financially secure.

When Simon reciprocated and invited Oliver to his spacious rental home with a huge built-in pool, Oliver knew he had found "the one." This was the perfect setting for him to live the life of leisure he desired. Simon always paid the tab and saw to Oliver's comfort. In return, Oliver showered Simon with attention, sent him cards and loving emails, and brought him small but meaningful gifts. A few days before the homeowner returned, Oliver made up a sob story about losing his job and his house. As he'd expected, Simon offered to let him move in until he was back on his feet again. Oliver rewarded Simon with kindness, compliments, and romantic gestures.

Over the next few months, Oliver offered tearful excuses about why he couldn't find a job. He even lied about going on interviews, then claimed to be despondent over losing out on the nonexistent job. Simon would sympathize with him, make special meals to cheer him up, and not bother him about job hunting.

Oliver continued to woo Simon until he was certain that Simon couldn't live without him. Once their romance was secure, Oliver started sleeping in until noon and lounging by the pool all afternoon. If Simon criticized him, Oliver complained about his aching back, his allergies, or his migraines. By the time Oliver finished making excuses, Simon had tears of sympathy in his eyes and often apologized for being so hard on Oliver. He offered Oliver massages, baked him treats, and waited on him.

After a year together Simon grew tired of Oliver's failure to find a job. The utility bills were twice their normal amount with Oliver living there, and Oliver still didn't have a job or a car, so Simon chauffeured them to all events and picked up the tab. And after long hours at work, Simon came home and found Oliver asleep outside in a lounge chair with dishes piled in the sink, the bed unmade, and dirty clothes heaped in the laundry room.

Simon panicked when his salary couldn't cover the monthly expenses. He had to pay rent and utilities on his credit cards, which were nearly maxed out from all the nights on the town, clothes shopping for Oliver, and gas for the car.

His patience ran out when he arrived home to find Oliver asleep, surrounded by shopping bags. This wasn't the first time Oliver had used Simon's charge cards without permission. Usually Simon didn't complain, but this time he woke Oliver and launched into an angry tirade that ended with him telling Oliver to leave.

Furious, Oliver jumped off the sofa and grabbed Simon's arm. He twisted it and slammed Simon against the wall. When Simon struggled to break free, Oliver punched him in the side, and Simon crumpled to the ground. Oliver stood over Simon, fists clenched. Simon threatened to call the police, and Oliver fled.

The next morning Simon discovered that Oliver had texted all his friends and coworkers, saying Simon had kicked him out of the house. Ashamed, embarrassed, and a bit guilty, Simon refused to talk about it. He ignored all the text messages Oliver sent saying he couldn't live without Simon. Fearful for his safety, Simon went to stay at a friend's house.

Oliver cyberharassed Simon, bombarding him—and his friends—with messages. He posted up to fifty messages a day on Facebook declaring his love and begging for a reconciliation. Dozens of times a day, he texted Simon's friends and coworkers, telling them how much he loved Simon and that all he wanted to do was be there for Simon and be part of his life. Photos of the two of them together, romantic texts, and love poems appeared on all of Simon's social networking sites, including his business sites.

Simon had always enjoyed posting video game reviews and news about the latest computer products. He'd worked hard to establish his reputation as an expert in the field, so people would trust him when he launched his video game. Now he avoided his marketing and networking sites. He was embarrassed by how unprofessional Oliver's posts made him look. And with Oliver's calls and texts coming in continually, Simon stopped answering the phone.

He changed his Facebook status to single, hoping Oliver would get the message. Instead, a neighbor told him that after Oliver saw it, he'd gone on a rampage in the house and destroyed many of Simon's possessions. Simon was afraid to unfriend Oliver after hearing that.

Then the messages turned abusive. Oliver leaked information about the video game and criticized Simon's work. Oliver's cyberharassment also affected Simon's career. Clients couldn't get through to the office because Oliver tied up the phone lines with incessant calls, Simon's coworkers were annoyed by Oliver's frequent texts and emails, and Simon's boss became irritated because productivity had dropped significantly. After several warnings, Simon was fired. His credit cards were maxed out, and he couldn't go home because he feared for his physical safety with Oliver still living in the house. He moved to another state and took an entry-level job in a small computer company.

Simon's Solution

Many people panic when faced with bullying, abuse, shame, humiliation, and cyberstalking. Like Simon, they choose to run. In some cases, especially if their lives are in danger, this may be the only option. They may decide to take on a new name and/or persona. Some people even opt to cut all ties from the past, remove any traces of their personal history, alter their looks, and start over with a brand-new identity.

A technique called going black ops is used as a last resort when victims fear for their lives. They must erase all clues to their previous life and become someone totally different. It means a loss of identity and reestablishing a whole new life. They lose everything from their past—credit histories, diplomas and degrees, licenses, work histories, and other forms of identification, including medical records and insurance coverage. (Strategies for doing this are discussed in chapter 13.)

By moving out of state, Simon chose a less confining form of black ops. He kept his name and took his diploma with him. To maintain secrecy he did not share previous references when applying for jobs. Without previous credentials and proven work experience, he started in a lower-paying job and had to work his way up. His skills soon became obvious, but getting his reputation reestablished took a great deal of time and effort. Simon also cut off all contact with long-term friends and acquaintances to prevent Oliver from manipulating them to find out his whereabouts. Simon chose what he felt was the best solution at the time, but the move and job change resulted in a great deal of pain and loss.

By the time he contacted Survivors In Action, Simon had already established a professional reputation at the company where he was working. But after his experience with Oliver, he hesitated to get involved in his new community or in a relationship, so he kept to himself. Previously, he had acted in community theater productions, but now he refused to try out for plays or do anything that would make him visible. He dreaded getting his name in the media because Oliver might trace him.

Given that Simon had made the choice to start again in a new place, Survivors In Action worked on solutions to free him from debt and make him more secure in his new home. SIA representatives began by getting many of the charges on his credit card removed. They helped him report the identity theft and theft of his credit cards. Because Oliver did not have permission to use the cards, a police report and an affidavit signed under oath were sufficient to get the majority of unauthorized charges removed.

Simon got a domestic violence protective order against Oliver, which empowered Simon and gave him legal standing to have Oliver arrested if his ex tracked him down or bothered him in any way. SIA also recommended home security and called in tech experts from the sheriff's office to check Simon's car for GPS tracking devices. Because Simon still feared for his physical safety, he took self-defense classes and kept pepper spray in his car. SIA taught him self-defense moves specifically against stalking, which empowered him and helped him take control of his life rather than live in terror.

SIA also encouraged Simon to tell his present employer about his past. Moore provided information to the computer company owners so they understood Simon's situation. Citing her experience as a risk management consultant, she explained that she had seen thousands of cases like this and that the victim is not at fault but should be commended for ending the abusive relationship. She also pointed out that by refusing to accept the violence, stalking, and cyberstalking, Simon had revealed his strength of character. Simon's bosses agreed to do what they could to protect him and his identity.

Moore worked with Simon to reconnect him with his life. Eventually, he reached the point where he could function in business again and was no longer living in constant terror. By the time they finished working together, Simon had learned techniques to overcome his fear. He no longer felt intimidated and knew he could defend himself. Because he had been honest with his employer, he could talk about his true credentials, which led to a higher-level position. He still had not achieved his previous status at work but was on his way to greater career success.

OTHER STRATEGIES

If Simon had contacted SIA before he fled, he would have discovered other options for dealing with Oliver. Simon could have chosen to stay in his hometown. Using the technique called hiding in plain sight (see chapter 13), he could have set up protection strategies, taken control of the situation, and regained his reputation.

Sometimes leaving and going to a new, unknown place is more difficult than remaining in familiar surroundings and fighting back. Often staying where you are is the only choice. Some victims are still living at home, are in school, or lack the money to move. Others have established professional reputations and have clients they do not want to lose.

It is important to assess your threshold for fear, your ties to the community, and your willingness to face down the perpetrator. Sometimes it helps to take a week or more to get away from the situation. If possible, stay with trusted family members or friends in another city. After time away from your usual routine, you'll have a clearer head and can make better decisions about the future. Also discuss your options with a risk management service; they can often suggest innovative strategies to stop the cybercrime and stalking. They are trained to support and help you implement solutions. (In addition chapters 11–13 and appendix A contain lists of action steps for dealing with stalking and cyberstalking.)

What Motivates a Manipulator

Manipulators need to be in control and to prove that they're superior to others. They like power, but they don't feel comfortable getting it by being leaders. They learn to work behind the scenes to secure what they want. They may use others for money, status, attention, or ego-stroking.

Underneath, many have self-esteem problems, and they fear being vulnerable. Manipulating others makes them feel strong and powerful, and compensates for the deep inadequacies they feel. Early in life, they learned to meet their needs using underhanded tactics or to protect themselves by giving out false information. As children they found it wasn't safe to ask for what they wanted, and, as a result, they learned to cope by being sneaky. They lie, cheat, or steal to get what they want. They're afraid of letting people know their true needs or of exposing their feelings.

Some manipulators have problems with self-centeredness or narcissism, some crave attention, and others may be sociopaths. Manipulators with psychological disorders are the most dangerous. Be extra careful when leaving those relationships.

How a Manipulator Uses the Internet

Manipulators are as deceptive online as they are in person. They like to use the Internet as their control center, influencing you from afar, often without your awareness. Because they do it so subtly, they draw you in before you realize it. They may text to say hello and offer a compliment, then ask you to do something for them. If you refuse, they try to cajole or guilt you into it. If you continue to resist, they will act hurt or strike back with a stern text or criticism. Or they will invent a crisis that makes it hard to refuse their requests.

Manipulators are usually careful about the messages they send. When they put things in writing, they stick to verifiable facts but present them in a way that's misleading. It's hard to rebut the messages because everything they say is true, but the way they present the facts distorts the truth.

After a breakup manipulators often use the Internet to make you feel guilty. They claim to love you, remind you of promises, and play on your sympathy. If you already feel bad about the breakup, they may even convince you that the problems were all your fault and make you doubt your choice of leaving them. If that doesn't work, they sometimes resort to more drastic measures, the way Sergio's girlfriend Lilly did.

Sergio's Story

Every time Sergio went out with friends, his new girlfriend had a crisis. One night he went to a bachelor party even though Lilly pouted and begged him to stay with her. He'd been at the party only a short time when she called to say she had a blinding headache and . . . the phone clunked to the floor.

Sergio's favorite uncle had died suddenly the year before of a brain aneurysm. Terrified, he rushed from the party to find Lilly sprawled on the couch, acting unresponsive. He called 911 and stayed with her all night as she went through rounds of tests at the hospital. Sergio was so relieved when tests all came back fine that he never questioned Lilly's fake attack.

But Sergio soon noticed that Lilly texted him whenever he met friends, using a dramatic message to get him to return home. During Sergio's all-night basketball tournament, she texted about being in a motorcycle accident. When he arrived he discovered the motorcycle had tipped over on her in the garage, leaving Lilly with a few bruises and a sprained ankle. She hadn't wanted him to go to the tournament, and now that she'd gotten her way, she was loving and seductive. After many similar incidents, Sergio realized she was manipulating him and broke off the relationship.

Lilly flooded Sergio's email, phone, and social media sites with messages. She also tried more emergency phone calls. When she texted that she was home alone and someone was breaking in, Sergio called the police and one of Lilly's neighbors to help her. It turned out to be a false alarm. Lilly was furious that Sergio hadn't shown up, and she sent nasty messages about him to all his friends.

After a few more unsuccessful attempts to get Sergio's attention, Lilly called to say she had taken alcohol and pills. Sergio wondered if Lilly was lying, but he didn't ignore her. Instead of going to her house, he called 911, a suicide help line, Lilly's parents at work, two neighbors, and several of Lilly's friends. The neighbors rushed over to find Lilly unresponsive, and she was hospitalized. After undergoing psychological therapy Lilly no longer bothered Sergio.

Not everyone's story will end like Sergio's. Your manipulator may still cause trouble and try to involve you. You'll be torn about whether to respond. Remember, you don't need to go in person, which is often what manipulators want. If the manipulator is involved in dangerous or life-threatening behavior, contact the appropriate authorities. Send others, such as the manipulator's friends, neighbors, or parents. Usually they will arrive before you and will be better equipped to handle the emergency.

If the manipulators are faking, like Lilly did at first, they'll soon realize they can't draw you into their drama. At that point many manipulators look for new victims. Few go to the point Lilly did and attempt suicide. If they do, you need to realize that it's not your fault. Although it is normal to blame yourself, remember that the manipulator made the choice. If you are dealing with someone who's suicidal or if being stalked has made you upset and depressed enough to consider suicide, call 911 or (1-800) 273-TALK (8255). If you are outside the United States, contact www.suicide.org/international-suicide-hotlines.html. (See chapter 14 for more advice about dealing with depression and suicide.)

Leaving a Manipulator

The charm and social graces of manipulators can make it hard to break up with them. Friends and family who don't know the truth may encourage you to stay together. They may even question why you left such a wonderful person. Manipulators take advantage of this by involving others in the breakup. They tell everyone how much they love you, how hard they tried, how good they were to you, and that they don't understand why you're leaving. They may enlist your friends, coworkers, and family members to influence you to stay in the relationship.

If that doesn't work, they're likely to twist facts or subtly turn people against you, all while appearing kindhearted and caring. At times you may even wonder if you're wrong to leave, but trust your gut instincts. Many people say that something felt "off" when they first met the manipulator, but the manipulator's magnetism won them over.

Don't let down your guard if a manipulative person starts acting kind. This is a ploy to get you to return. Remind yourself that this behavior is part of a cycle and that, if you fall for it, the whole cycle will only begin again.

After leaving a manipulator, you may feel guilty and blame yourself for the relationship troubles. Some people even believe they deserved to be treated badly or that their partner's violence was justified, and the manipulator encourages or plays on those false beliefs. You should never be hurt physically or emotionally in any relationship.

If you were struggling with self-esteem issues before you met the manipulator, you may find it even harder to accept yourself after the relationship ends. Even if you went into the relationship feeling good about yourself, you may struggle with low self-esteem, especially if you mentally replay all the criticisms the manipulator used to keep you in line. It's hard to forget those messages, so counseling can help. (Chapter 15 describes additional techniques to regain or bolster your self-esteem and get rid of guilt.)

Finally, try to understand what drew you to this person. What needs did the manipulator meet? How did the manipulator con you into believing he or she was wonderful? Watch for these same characteristics in other dates to be sure you aren't taken in again.

Action Steps

If you're dealing with a manipulator, here are some important steps to follow:

- Work on asserting yourself in the relationship unless it will result in physical harm.

- Move slowly to extricate yourself from the relationship, unless the situation has progressed to physical violence. Take time to plan and consult with a risk management expert to learn the best ways to protect yourself.

- If you share a home or space, change the locks or move to a space of your own. If possible, install a security system.

- If you fear for your physical safety, get a restraining order and take self-defense classes.

- Let family, coworkers, and friends know that you want no contact with the manipulator.

- Change all social media accounts, passwords, and any links that give the manipulator access to you or information about you.
- If the manipulator flames (attacks) you or your business online, ask friends, family, and/or loyal customers to post positive comments or reviews. Be sure your supporters don't engage in online dueling with the critic, because that could cause additional harm to your reputation.
- Be cautious about getting involved in future relationships that seem too good to be true.

Final Quick Tips

If you need to have contact with a manipulator, always follow the **Three-Second Rule**—Pause, Assess, then take Action—especially if you are considering a manipulator's requests.

- **Stop and block:** Cease all contact with the manipulator. This not only slows him or her down but also keeps you from being manipulated again.

- **Delay:** Time is your friend when dealing with a manipulator. Most manipulators want their needs met immediately. If you aren't there for them, they'll look for someone else.

- **Stay safe:** If the manipulator becomes abusive, get away and immediately seek outside help and support.

CHAPTER 6

Controlling: I'm king of the world.

People with an excessive need to control are often referred to as control freaks. These perfectionists generally keep a tight rein on themselves and those around them. People who are controlling want to impose order on their environments and may become neat freaks or workaholics. They are not content to run their own lives, however, and they tell everyone else what to do and how to act. To lessen their own inner anxieties and insecurities, they fight to be top dog in business or at home, where they tend to bark out orders that they expect others to obey—or else.

Recognizing a Controller

Being outspoken doesn't necessarily indicate that someone is controlling. A person may have definite opinions and not appreciate having them challenged. The way to tell the difference between people with strong, determined personalities and those who are controlling is to look at their end goals. Trying to convince you that they are right about a particular topic is different from insisting that you change in some way to meet their expectations. If someone makes decisions for you or tells you how to act, what to wear, or whom you may see, they are controlling you. If you fear doing anything without your partner's permission, you're with a controller.

Controllers often have forceful personalities and may use rages or threats to get others to comply with their will. Some use more subtle means of control, such as guilt or manipulation. Often these quieter forms of domination are less noticeable, but they achieve similar results: They get others to alter their behavior. Whether overt or covert in their actions, controllers have one goal—to get what they want at any cost—and they have little regard for whom they hurt in the process. This personality type does not respect others' boundaries and is likely to engage in physical, verbal, emotional, and/or sexual abuse.

Signs of a Controller

Does the person you're with have any of the following characteristics?
Using a scale of 0–2, rate each behavior as follows:

0-Never

1-Sometimes

2-Often

It's easy to spot controllers because they:

____ are charming and thoughtful

____ are always right

____ get annoyed when people question them

____ sulk or get moody when things don't go their way

____ have temper tantrums when you don't do what they expect

____ make you feel you must ask their permission before you
     do things

____ prefer to be in charge of things

____ usually supervise others or tell them how to do things

____ threaten or bully to get their way

____ talk to people in a condescending manner

____ expect their needs to be met first

____ give backhanded compliments that are actually criticism

____ will not take *no* for an answer

____ claim you are the problem in relationship troubles

____ expect you to read their minds

____ insist you change plans that don't suit them

____ are critical of you and others

____ make you feel you have to do what you want in secret

____ threaten to leave you if you don't do what they say

____ become jealous or try to distance you from friends or family

____ make you feel as if nothing you do is good enough

____ insult you in front of people

____ infringe on your personal space

____ belittle your accomplishments

Scale

0–8

Some people enjoy being in charge. They may have knowledge or skills that enable them to take over and do a good job supervising. If this person got 2s on "prefer to be in charge of things" and "usually supervise others or tells them how to do things," chances are they are natural leaders.

9–14

People with a score in this range are self-centered and determined to get their own way. They may not be full-fledged controllers yet. If it's early in the relationship, these are definite signs of a person who will expect others to give in to their demands.

15–48

You are with a domineering partner who will try to control what you do and when you do it. You may have learned to give in to keep the peace and sacrificed your own needs and desires in the process. The higher the score, the more controlling this person is. Those at the high end are likely to be abusers. You need to seriously consider getting out of the relationship as soon as it is safely possible.

Who Gets Hooked by a Controller

It's easy to get caught up in a relationship with a controller who appears, at first, to be concerned and caring; he or she may even dote on you. Often it's hard to distinguish this from manipulation. After you've been in a relationship for a while, you may feel you don't have a right to make decisions on your own, or perhaps you've even been beaten down so much with physical and/or verbal abuse that you're afraid to make choices.

Many times people in abusive relationships came from families in which abuse was the norm, and they learn to accept or even expect it. Controllers look for people who are easy to boss around. This may include people pleasers, peacemakers, or gentle people who give in easily. People with low self-esteem or who are insecure often accept abuse, as do those who are guilt ridden and ashamed, or who consider themselves unworthy.

You need to respect yourself and set boundaries; otherwise you'll find your partner will continue to intimidate you and exploit your weaknesses. Learning to say *no* and standing your ground isn't easy, but it's necessary to prevent controllers from running roughshod over you.

Avery's Story

Avery had a crush on Max all during high school, but he never paid attention to her. Several years after they graduated, she went to a party on a friend's boat, and to her surprise Max was there. They enjoyed reconnecting and soon began dating. He was finishing a degree at a nearby university, and she was student teaching. It wasn't long before they moved in together. They had fun whenever they weren't busy with classes. Weekends were filled with boating and partying.

After Max graduated he and a classmate started their own computer tech company. To get it off the ground, he worked long hours, often until the wee hours of the morning and most weekends. Avery, who had been substitute teaching, was thrilled to be offered a full-time position when one of the teachers retired, and soon she too was spending long hours planning lessons, grading assignments, and developing activities for her students. She and Max rarely saw each other.

Neither of them had time to party, go boating, or just relax together. Both of them were so stressed out by their jobs that when they did have time together, they often wound up fighting. Many of their arguments began with Max accusing Avery of spending more time with her friends or on her work than with him. Whenever he was home he expected her to drop everything and pay attention to him. Yet he'd fly into rages if she disturbed him during his free time. His attitude was that he deserved downtime after working long hours, and her needs could wait.

The longer they were together, the more demanding Max became. He decided what they watched on TV, where they went, what they ate, and who they saw. Max gradually pushed more and more chores off on Avery, and she did them without complaint. At first she gave in to keep the peace. And she still had a crush on him and didn't want to lose him. She also rationalized that he was working much longer hours than she was, so it was only fair for things to go his way when he was home.

But when Max ordered her not to see her best friend, Darcy, because he considered her a bad influence and to discontinue the data plan on her cell phone because it cost too much, Avery balked. Defying him, she scheduled her visits and texted her friends and family when Max wasn't home. When he discovered she hadn't listened, he threw a fit. Usually Avery gave in, but this time she didn't. She stomped off and locked herself in the bedroom. A short while later Max banged on the door.

This pattern continued most weekends, with Max becoming more controlling and demanding. When he didn't get his way, he lost his temper and often made her pay for resisting his directives with cruel, cutting remarks or by doing things he knew would hurt her.

One Saturday after a bad fight, Avery, crying and shaking, called Darcy. Darcy, who had been encouraging her to leave Max, offered to let Avery stay at her apartment. Relieved, Avery packed her car. She didn't know how long she'd stay, so she took most of her things. Max arrived home as she was putting the last of her suitcases in the trunk and demanded to know what she was doing.

"I'm tired of fighting," Avery told him. "It's obvious things aren't working out between us. I thought—"

"Thought? You thought what?" Max yelled. "That you'd sneak away while I was gone? You planned to walk out without saying anything?" He cut off Avery's protests and stormed into the house. Before he slammed the door, he said in a low, menacing voice, "If you think you can leave me like that, you have another thing coming."

Tears streaming down her face, Avery drove to Darcy's apartment, where her friend greeted her with open arms. To cheer up Avery, Darcy suggested going to their favorite bar that evening. They unpacked the car and then primped for their night out. Avery was still feeling glum and uncertain about her relationship with Max, but she was determined to put him out of her mind for a while and enjoy herself.

As she and Darcy joked and laughed at the bar like old times, Avery relaxed. When she excused herself to go to the restroom, she was sure she'd made the right decision to leave Max. She was feeling happier than she had in a long time.

She had no sooner locked herself in a stall than a woman entered the restroom chattering on her cell phone. "Yes, I got the pictures. How disgusting. She's a teacher at Lakewood Elementary?" The woman practically screeched, "Who would want someone like that teaching our kids?"

Avery taught at Lakewood, so she'd know the teacher. She remained in the stall and eavesdropped, hoping to hear more.

The woman continued to rant. "You see it in the news all the time—teachers who are pedophiles. And we have this Avery Williams right in our community. Someone should report her to the police."

Avery gasped. She rushed from the stall and demanded to know what the woman was talking about.

The woman's eyes widened and her cheeks reddened, but her face screwed up into an expression of distaste. "Posting obscene pictures of yourself on the Internet. You're disgusting."

Avery stood there in shock. Then the restroom door banged open, and Darcy rushed in. She dragged Avery out the door as people stared and snickered. In the car Darcy handed Avery her phone, with her email account open.

There were pictures of Avery naked in suggestive and lewd poses. Some of them Max had taken during their intimate moments together; for others he'd photoshopped her head onto a body that was somewhat similar to hers. The most disgusting one was of her grinning head pasted on a woman sitting on a toilet. Avery's cheeks burned when she saw the pictures had been sent from her account to every person on her email list—fellow teachers, administrators, her mother, her minister, and parents of her students.

She checked her own phone and discovered shocked and disgusted messages, hate mail, lewd responses, and twenty-two texts from Max. Every one of them said the same thing: *No one leaves me.*

Even worse, the pictures had gone viral. People were forwarding her picture (with her private parts blocked out) under huge bold headings such as "Do you want Avery Williams teaching your children?" and "Suspected Pedophile, Avery Williams." For all she knew, Max had done that as well.

Avery buried her head in her hands. What was she going to do? She could never appear in public again, and she'd never be able to teach at Lakewood. Even if the administrators let her through the door, how could she face all the students, parents, and colleagues who'd seen her naked?

Avery's Solution

Avery was too distraught to think, but Darcy went online and found the contact information for Survivors In Action, an organization she hoped could help. SIA told her to get the evidence to the police right away. Because Avery was a teacher, the high-tech crimes unit took the case very seriously. The local police force had been flooded with calls from parents, demanding Avery's arrest because they feared she was a pedophile. At first the police detectives who questioned her treated her as if she were a potential sex offender. They demanded that she turn over her cell phone, iPad, and laptop for examination. School administrators put her on leave pending the outcome of the case, and Avery hired an attorney.

During their relationship Avery had recognized Max's need to control. He demanded to know her passwords and private information. She loved him and gave him whatever he asked for. Although he knew how to get into her accounts, he never gave her access to his.

Because Avery's decision to leave Max happened suddenly, she had little time to plan for her protection. In fact, she didn't even consider the possibility that he'd try to hurt her. If she'd paid more attention to how he reacted when she did things he forbid her to do, she might have been prepared for his cruelty after the breakup. But because she'd never dream of hurting someone who broke up with her, it didn't occur to her that she'd need to protect herself.

Darcy started the damage control by hitting "Reply All" and typing, "LOL. I can't believe your ex was stupid enough to think people would believe these pictures are of you. Anyone with any brains can see they've been photoshopped. What a loser!" Then Darcy attached a close-up of the neck of one of the altered pictures, and it was obvious that Avery's head had been attached to another body.

Darcy's mom also sent out an email that went to everyone on the list. "Honey, I told you that Max was trouble. I'm so sorry you had to find out this way."

Another girlfriend wrote, "You poor thing. I dated that bastard Max Livingston, and you wouldn't believe the nasty things he did to me when we broke up."

A high school friend wrote, "Max Livingston? The one who graduated from Lakewood High with us? Figures he'd be behind this. He was always a sneaky SOB."

They sent out these emails as if they'd accidentally hit "Reply All." They counted on people being curious or voyeuristic and reading Avery's "private" emails. The goal of the emails was to change people's attitudes from censuring Avery to sympathizing with her and to focus people's attention away from the pictures.

In addition to the four people Avery asked to send messages, several other people chimed in, mentioning things Max had done. It hadn't been Avery's intent to bash Max; she'd only wanted to let people know that she hadn't sent the emails and to focus attention away from the pictures. It seemed, though, as if Max had hurt quite a few other people, judging from the emails flying around.

At SIA's request, people sent emails to the school board and to the detectives handling the case, vouching for Avery's character and reputation. Friends, colleagues, and even several university professors made clear statements that Avery was not the kind of person those email images portrayed. The principal of Lakewood contacted Avery privately to tell her that she and several other administrators didn't believe the rumors that were circulating, but given the outcry from the community and the nature of the charges, the school board had no choice but to keep her on administrative leave until the case was settled.

While she waited for the case to be resolved, Avery rarely went out because people sneered and jeered as she passed them on the sidewalk. The first time she entered the grocery store, people stopped and stared. Some men undressed her with their eyes; parents yanked their children away as if afraid she'd snatch them. The cashier recoiled from touching Avery's money. While she was in the store, someone spray painted the word *slut* on her car door. She returned from the grocery store in tears.

After that Darcy ran errands for her and brought her groceries. Darcy was one of the few friends who stood by Avery. Work colleagues avoided her, and acquaintances who visited mainly came to ferret out gossip.

As time dragged on with no paychecks coming in, Avery couldn't pay her bills. Darcy offered to let her stay rent-free until things were settled, but Avery hated imposing on her friend. She had little choice, though, unless she returned to Max, the last thing she'd ever do.

She rued agreeing to deposit her paychecks into Max's account. While they were together he'd paid all the bills and given her weekly spending money. Anything they'd saved together was in his name. Now that they'd split, she had nothing. She had one credit card from her single days, but that was soon charged to the hilt with the lawyer's retainer, her food, and paying Darcy a small amount toward utilities.

Avery was an emotional wreck. She avoided all of her usual activities, and no one invited her to social events. She'd become a pariah in the community, and she had no idea if or when her name would be cleared. While she was virtually a prisoner, Max was roaming free, enjoying his victory.

The police continued to question Avery as they built their case. Most treated her as a soon-to-be-convicted criminal, but Detective Hudson had been working in the high-tech crimes unit for years, and his particular area of expertise was child and sexual exploitation. He realized on the first diagnostic of her computer that it was not Avery in the majority of the pictures. He took a special interest in the case and was impressed by the many testimonial letters he'd received on her behalf. His background check on her came back clean.

He made her case his top priority, working long hours on weekends and holidays to issue search warrants for information from the social media companies and Max's cell phone carrier. The tech experts turned in their reports after examining Max's and Avery's electronics, but it took the usual three months to obtain the results from the search warrants. Eventually Detective Hudson had all the proof he needed to solve the case.

Avery was thrilled to know that Detective Hudson had solid evidence proving Max was behind the photos. She and Darcy celebrated that night, excited that Avery was soon to have her day in court. They were both relieved, picturing Max behind bars. Avery met with her lawyer, who cautioned her not to get her hopes up about the outcome.

Although it was humiliating for Avery to sit in the courtroom while each picture was projected onto the screen and analyzed for alterations, she was determined not to let Max get away with destroying her reputation—or anyone else's. She kept her head high and her face neutral and took deep calming breaths. Although she was serene on the outside, her heart was racing and she was sweating.

It turned out her lawyer was right. Max accepted a plea bargain for misdemeanor stalking and harassment and served no jail time. He was ordered not to have contact with Avery and to do community service. His sentence was six months of home detention, which was later reduced to three months. Max could leave home for work, medical appointments, and approved outings.

Tears ran down Avery's cheeks. It didn't seem like punishment at all because Max could come and go as he pleased, whereas she, the innocent one, had already served a more stringent confinement for the past three months. On the other side of the courtroom, Max beamed.

Distraught, Avery rushed from the room following the proceedings. Detective Hudson caught up with her in the hallway. He, too, was noticeably upset, but he explained that this was a typical outcome in many cases involving cyberstalking. He admitted that quite a few detectives in his unit had become frustrated and burned out because the punishment rarely fit the crime.

But one thing he said stood out in Avery's mind: "You are an amazing young woman, and with time you will be stronger and wiser for this experience." Avery knew she had been through all this for a reason, and she determined to take action and do something to help others.

A few days later at a special school board meeting, Avery was reinstated. Shortly after that she visited VolunteerMatch.org (a website that connects volunteers with community needs) and noticed postings from Survivors In Action seeking volunteers. It clicked that victim advocacy was what she needed to do.

A local reporter who'd been following the case contacted Avery and offered her a chance to tell her story. Although it was embarrassing for Avery to reveal the truth about her failed relationship with Max and to remind people of the pictures, she was determined to help others if she could. The story hit the front page of the local newspaper and was one of the lead stories in the online edition.

That was Avery's start. In addition to working for SIA, Avery became a leader in her community by starting an antibullying campaign. She also volunteered to be a speaker and help others impacted by cyberstalking, abuse, and bullying.

As she counseled other cybercrime victims, Avery discovered that laws vary state by state, even county by county. Some law enforcement agencies took on cases and worked hard to help victims. Other victims had to sort out own their cases, even when laws against cybercrime were on the books. Avery came to appreciate how lucky she'd been to have a good lawyer, help from SIA, and a passionate detective who saw early in the case that she was not the villain and deserved to be protected. She also realized how important it was to make wise choices in relationships. Never again would she let physical attraction blind her to a controlling nature.

What Motivates a Controller

Childhood traumas or unstable home lives often lead to controlling natures. Children who grew up with an alcoholic or abusive parent, or in the midst of turmoil, try to create stability by ordering the world around them. Likewise, children who experienced a death of someone close to them or went through another similar tragedy may have a strong need to control all the circumstances in their lives. Often insecurity and fear of abandonment underlie their outward blustering. Although their behavior is an attempt to stabilize their lives, they do not have the right to destabilize yours.

How a Controller Uses the Internet

Controllers try to take over people's lives online as well as offline. They monitor their partners' incoming and outgoing calls and messages. If you live with a controller, assume that he or she has access to all of your accounts and knows your passwords, and proceed with caution. Remind yourself not to send private messages or reveal any secrets you don't want the controller to know. Make friends and family aware that any messages they send are being monitored, so they are careful about what they write.

If at all possible, get a new phone number and social media accounts, but do not close out the old ones. You may need to use someone else's computer and phone to establish these new accounts so the controller can't trace them. (Public libraries usually have free Internet access. Some require you to have a library card, but signing up is free and takes only a few minutes of your time.) After you open new accounts, continue to use your old accounts in the usual manner to prevent the controller from becoming suspicious.

If you leave them, controllers can be vicious in their attempts to get you back. Don't allow them to hurt you. Close out all social media accounts they have access to if you've set up new ones. If you had no way to change your accounts prior to leaving, immediately change all passwords. Send their texts to spam, block their calls, and unfriend them on social media. It's easy to get caught up in the control cycle if you keep in contact.

Leaving a Controller

Controllers must be in charge in their relationships. When they feel that control slipping, they grasp for power in any way they can, which means they can be cruel and punitive, deliberately hurting their partners. They've learned that if they punish their partners enough, their significant others give in.

Freeing yourself from a controller is extremely difficult. Controllers keep a tight rein on their partners' activities. If you're dependent on the controller for support, it may seem almost impossible to free yourself. Many controllers do not let their spouses work and limit their spending, leaving them with no means to take care of themselves if they do leave. Being dependent on the controller puts victims in a difficult situation.

Controllers who suspect their partners are moving out from under their control increase their vigilance and may become angry, vengeful, and more demanding. Living a double life for a while is sometimes the best option. Remain compliant on the outside and continue to accede to your partner's wishes. Secretly go about making your preparations to leave.

Plan to leave when your partner is absent. Be sure to allow enough time to pack and get away before he or she returns. Do not leave any notes or clues to your destination, particularly if you are fleeing a violent situation. Give your contact information only to those who are trustworthy and absolutely need it. The fewer people who know where you are, the better. Follow the additional steps in chapters 11–13 as well as appendix A to prevent stalking and cyberstalking, and to keep yourself safe.

People who are leaving a controller should prepare for retribution. They must be extremely careful to protect their property, their reputations, and their lives. Sometimes controllers threaten to harm their partners, children, or pets to get their way. They may hold your favorite things as collateral, agreeing to return them only if you do what they say. In this respect they are very similar to vengeful partners (see chapter 9), but their motives are different. Controllers use the threat of harm to elicit a desired behavior, whereas vengeful partners follow through to destroy and punish. Controllers want power; the vengeful want blood. To leave either type, it's important to proceed with caution.

Cautions for Teens

It's important to differentiate between overly concerned parents and controllers. Parents who care about their children may seem intrusive when they monitor phone and Internet time, question their children's comings and goings, or call to check up on them. Sometimes, though, they step over the bounds of concern and become intrusive and controlling. This can be annoying and frustrating, as Yael discovered (see the story below), but may not be a reason for leaving or for breaking off the relationship.

If, however, a parent is making you do anything unethical, illegal, or immoral, you need to leave. Parents who abuse you physically, emotionally, or sexually have no right to do so. In situations like these, often the only solution is to get away. This can be difficult when the controller is a parent or guardian. (See Ryker's story in chapter 10.)

In addition to having no way to support themselves and nowhere to live, teens have few options for victim support, unless they can prove they are being physically or sexually abused. Shelters and domestic violence assistance providers require minors to have parental permission to receive services. SIA is one of the only organizations that works directly with minors because they understand that teens may have absent or uncaring parents, lack parental support, or need protection from the parents themselves.

Yael's Story

Growing up in a home with a controlling mother, Yael had learned to circumvent most of her intrusive behaviors. Those he couldn't avoid, he endured, but he resented that she decided whom he could associate with, where he could go, and what activities he participated in. His mother called his friends and grilled them for more information about him, and several times his mother severed his friendships with people she felt were bad influences. Yael had no idea why certain people suddenly started avoiding him until a classmate taunted him about being so much of a mama's boy that he couldn't end his own friendships, but let his mommy do it for him. Yael was humiliated and glad that once he went off to college, he'd be out from under his mother's thumb.

The following fall he started at the Ivy League school his mother insisted he attend, and he reveled in his new freedom. He hadn't dated much in high school because his mother scared off most girls, claiming they were unsuitable. After Yael met Devi in his business management class, they soon started dating. Without his mother's usual interference, the relationship blossomed.

A few weeks later, Yael was totally unprepared for his mother's wrath during his weekly phone call home. His mother blasted him, demanding he break up with Devi. Yael had no idea how she'd found out. He'd been careful never to mention Devi's name. In an unusual show of defiance, he told his mother he loved Devi and had no intention of ending the relationship. Mom issued an ultimatum: If he didn't leave the girl, she'd stop paying his tuition and his cell phone bills.

Yael hung up, feeling defeated. Whatever he did, his mother would get her way. If he didn't leave Devi now, he wouldn't be back next semester. As he texted Devi, asking her to meet him, It dawned on him that his mother must have been reading his texts. The phone was in her name, so she'd have access to the records. No doubt she'd also found a way to read his emails. Yael realized he'd never be free of his mother's domination as long as she was paying the bills, unless he could find a way to circumvent her surveillance.

Although it bothered him to be duplicitous, he purchased an inexpensive phone with a plan that allowed him to text Devi privately. He used his other phone for making plans with groups he belonged to, sending messages to classmates about assignments, and writing texts he didn't care if his mother read. He went to the college library and used the computers there to set up a new email account for contacting Devi; he also used this account for other emails he didn't want his mother to see. To keep his mother from becoming suspicious, he still sent emails from his other account. Yael decided what aspects of his college life he was willing to share with his mother and kept the rest private.

Action Steps

If you want to leave a controller or at least establish some distance, here are some important steps to follow:

- Plan your escape in secret. If controllers find out, they'll cut off your options and may hurt you, physically or emotionally, to prevent you from going. Don't leave clues to your whereabouts.

- Change your passwords, phone number, bank accounts, and other personal information right before or after you walk out the door. Do it before the other person discovers you're gone.

- When setting up new accounts, do it from a safe computer. Consider that the controller may be monitoring friends' and family members' accounts, so set up accounts at a public library or request computer time from someone the controller doesn't know. Be sure to erase all traces of your sessions after you use another computer.
- Maintain your old account with the old password if the controller knows it. Send unimportant emails or texts from that account to keep the controller from becoming suspicious, but send private emails or texts from the new account with your secure password.

Final Quick Tips

- **Maintain the status quo:** Let controllers think they have the upper hand; as long as they believe they are in control, they're less likely to bother you. If they think they're not dominant, they will step up their attacks or cyberattacks.

- **Be cautious:** Remember that the controller likely has access to all of your accounts; filter the information you send and warn others that your messages are being monitored.

- **Protect your privacy:** Establish new accounts (including credit cards, bank accounts, and social media accounts) that the controller doesn't have access to; have the post office forward your mail beginning on the day you leave or even a few days before.

- **Avoid all contact:** Once you've left, don't respond to texts, calls, or messages; save and document them, but remain silent.

CHAPTER 7

Narcissistic: It's all about me.

The word *narcissist* originates from the Greek myth about Narcissus, who fell in love with his own reflection. That describes people with this personality type, who are so self-absorbed that they overlook the needs of others. They share many of the traits found in entitlement (chapter 4), believing they deserve things they haven't earned, but their outstanding characteristic is excessive self-love, or self-adoration. Like Narcissus, they see no faults in themselves, only beauty, and while busy gazing at that beauty, they fail to see how they are hurting others. (Psychiatrists have identified a disorder they call *narcissistic personality disorder*, or NPD; however, the term *narcissist* is used here to refer to a less extreme form of egotism.)

Recognizing a Narcissist

Often the easiest way to recognize a narcissist is by outward appearance. They are often the best-looking and best-dressed people in the room. Their hair is styled, their grooming is flawless, and they frequently check their appearances in a mirror. Many have had plastic surgery or cosmetic enhancements and like to show off their bodies in tight or revealing clothes. At parties they spend much of their time charming, flirting, or seducing.

Once you spend time with narcissists, you'll realize they are cocky, vain, and shallow. They turn every conversation to themselves, fish for compliments, and see situations from only their own point of view. When they don't get their way, they may pout, hold grudges, or use other forms of emotional blackmail. They need to win arguments and have no qualms about hurting others in the process. Believing they have the right to self-gratification at any cost, coupled with an inability to empathize, they have little or no remorse about injuring others. Taken to an extreme, this attitude can lead them to become tyrants, con artists, or sexual abusers. Some, especially those diagnosed with a personality disorder, can be scary and dangerous. All narcissists can be wily about having their needs met, and you often don't realize it until you've fallen into their traps.

Signs of a Narcissist

Does the person you're with have any of the following characteristics?
Using a scale of 0–2, rate each behavior as follows:

0-Never

1-Sometimes

2-Often

You can identify narcissists because often they:

____ are charming early in the relationship

____ are fun and likeable to be around, especially at first

____ are good at attracting sympathy

____ frequently use the words "always" and "never"

____ rarely consider long-term consequences

____ make impulsive decisions

____ prefer to be the center of attention

____ borrow things and don't return them

____ take credit for other people's work

____ believe they are special

____ blame others for problems they caused

____ cheat on a partner or juggle multiple relationships at the same time

____ spend joint money without consulting partners, believing they deserve what they're buying

____ use emotional blackmail to control others

____ interfere with their friends' or partners' relationships with others

____ manipulate others into conflicts

____ try to control others' thoughts or feelings

____ exaggerate talents or achievements to gain recognition

____ want to associate only with individuals of high status or the best in their fields

____ need constant admiration

____ spend excessive amounts of time and money on appearance

____ have plastic surgery and/or cosmetic procedures

____ expect to be recognized for any and all achievements

____ take advantage of others to gain what they want

____ have little or no empathy for others

_____ are haughty and arrogant

_____ believe others are envious of them

_____ continue to lie even when confronted with proof

_____ exaggerate, especially about their achievements

_____ use emotional blackmail to get others to comply

_____ cannot put themselves in someone else's place

_____ hate it when others outshine them

_____ can be generous, but usually have strings attached

_____ lie even when they can tell the truth

_____ become angry when people contradict them

_____ may be addicted to alcohol, drugs, gambling, sex, or food

_____ focus on their needs at the expense of others

_____ have a sense of entitlement

_____ refuse to grow up

_____ never admit they're wrong

_____ like to flirt

Scale

0–16

Some people may be self-absorbed but are not necessarily narcissists. If most of the score is from the first eight characteristics, you are probably not dealing with a narcissist. If it isn't, your partner is likely to be egotistical and more concerned with his or her own needs than yours. Perhaps it's time to look for a partner who supports you and cares about your needs.

17–39

If the score is in the low range and is mainly concentrated on the first seven characteristics, you may be dealing with an outgoing person who likes attention and/or may be impulsive. Scores in the mid to upper ranges are more problematic. As long as you're stroking narcissists' egos or giving in to their wishes, you'll get along well with them, but chances are that when you're around them, you feel demeaned, diminished, overpowered, or unheard. Frequently your needs are relegated to a lesser status, even to their frivolous or unimportant desires. It's time to ask yourself how this relationship is benefitting you. If it's not, plan to ease out of it in a way that won't leave you vulnerable to attack.

40–82

The higher the number, the greater your concerns should be. People with scores in this range are definitely ego-driven and will likely retaliate if you leave relationships with them. Their behavior could escalate into cyberstalking or other dangers. Narcissists will go to any lengths, even illegal ones, to destroy anyone who threatens their status or self-esteem. If the narcissist becomes cruel, violent, or threatening, take safety precautions and enlist help from others, including school or work authorities, law enforcement, domestic violence organizations, and support organizations such as Survivors In Action.

Who Gets Hooked by a Narcissist

People who grew up with a controlling, uncaring parent may be drawn to narcissists. They are used to sublimating their own needs to cater to another's whims. And deep down, they may be looking for the validation and love they missed as children. They won't find it with narcissists, but the relationship pattern feels familiar, so they stay and accept whatever tiny bits of affection they receive.

Narcissists gravitate toward partners who are self-effacing, caring, and sensitive to others' feelings—those who don't mind stroking their egos and are willing to let them take all the credit. Sometimes narcissists choose partners who are less attractive or less educated or who have insecurity or self-esteem issues, in the hopes that a less confident partner will idolize them.

Nico's Story

Nico completed his real estate training and landed a job with a large firm a few months before Brooklyn joined. On her first day Brooklyn made a whirlwind entrance that attracted a great deal of attention from everyone in the office. With a business suit molded tightly to her curves and a blouse that dipped low enough to reveal her impressive cleavage, Brooklyn breezed into the office, greeting each person with a friendly smile, letting her hand linger on an arm or coat sleeve after she shook hands. Her voice dropped to sultry and seductive when she spoke to the men in the office. Other women might have been jealous, but Brooklyn turned her sweet Southern accent and charming manner their way too, complimenting each of them.

Because office policy was to work in pairs, Nico and Brooklyn—as the two newest arrivals—were assigned to work together. Nico, shy and reserved, was glad Brooklyn was so outgoing. He preferred working up figures; he'd moved into real estate after helping with his father's mortgage business, so he was most comfortable with that part of the business. He also enjoyed showing clients around houses. He'd found that his quiet mannerism often made them forget he was there, and they'd start feeling at home in the house. He had a good sense of when to speak and when to remain silent. His clients liked that he wasn't high pressure, and they trusted him, so much so that they heartily recommended him to their friends. Although he hadn't been at the firm long, he'd already closed several deals and had quite a few showings lined up. The only part of the job he didn't like was making phone calls and drumming up new business. Brooklyn, with her friendly, outgoing manner, seemed a perfect match. She readily agreed to take on that part of the job.

The two of them got along well, except for Brooklyn's flirting. Nico had been raised rather conservatively and preferred to take relationships slowly. He also dated only women he'd consider marrying. In fact, his goal was to get established in the business, find a nice girl, settle down, and have a family. Brooklyn definitely wasn't the type he was looking for, but he didn't know how to discourage her advances. Most of the time, he used work as an excuse to evade her. Or the phone would ring, distracting her. Several times she cornered him in the empty meeting room, pressing her body up against his and issuing a silent invitation. The first time he'd been so flustered, he'd dropped the papers and pen he was holding. As he scrambled on the floor to retrieve them, Brooklyn dropped to her knees to help and angled her body to show off her cleavage. If he'd been a different type, he might have taken advantage of her offer. Instead, he hurriedly gathered his papers and jumped to his feet, ignoring her outthrust lip and disappointed look.

After that, if they were ever alone in the conference room, he always held his clipboard or laptop in front of him to avoid physical contact. In the office, though, she'd come up behind him and run her fingers through his hair or lean over his shoulder so her breasts brushed the side of his face. When they walked to meetings, she'd sidle close and tuck her hand in the crook of his elbow. Other men in the office gave him knowing looks, assuming he and Brooklyn were in a relationship. Yet Brooklyn enjoyed flirting with all the men, and Nico suspected her frequent and overly long lunch meetings and private conferences with their boss, and her time sequestered in the conference room with various male colleagues, weren't all real estate–related discussions. He figured it was none of his business as long as she did her job well.

And she did. She loved making calls, connecting at social events, doing open houses, and promoting their team. Although most of the time her spiel made it sound as if she worked alone, Nico shrugged it off. Brooklyn offered to redesign the sign and ad to include her picture, and Nico was happy to let her. When the signs arrived Nico was startled to see that Brooklyn's name and picture were prominent and that his had been relegated to a small space in the lower corner. He gritted his teeth and tamped down his irritation; after all, her pretty face would attract more clients. Plus, he'd never liked seeing his cheesy smile in the ads. He also tried not to resent that she made herself the focus of attention at every client meeting and open house. Most of the time, she swooped in when prospective buyers came through the door and rarely bothered to introduce him unless they had financing questions. Then she made it sound as if working up numbers were his only function. She'd flash him a killer smile and prettily beg him to help the buyers with their money questions, and then make sure she thrust her card in their hands before they walked out the door.

She let Nico do all the follow-up work but often cut him out during closings. Sometimes she told him the wrong time or place, or she'd "forget" to tell him when plans changed. Other times she recorded the details on the office sales sheet with only her name. He'd have to squeeze his name into the tiny space as an afterthought.

Because they quickly became one of the top-selling teams in the office, Nico kept quiet. And that year they made top sales team for the region. Onstage, Brooklyn practically elbowed him aside to grab the award, and in the photos she stood in front of him so that he was barely noticeable. A few days later, Nico was passing the boss's office and overheard Brooklyn saying that although Nico had closed a few deals, she'd asked those clients to work with him so his numbers didn't totally suck. Outraged, Nico stopped where they couldn't see him to listen to the rest of the conversation. Brooklyn went on to say she'd probably do better paired with a stronger seller, but she'd prefer to keep working with Nico because she enjoyed a challenge and she thought she could help him with his technique. She added that he was good with numbers, so he was an asset to the team. Then she bragged about all she'd done to close the sales, even claiming credit for many of Nico's accomplishments.

Fuming, Nico stormed down the hall to his desk. When Brooklyn returned he asked her to go with him to look at a new listing. He wasn't about to blast her in the office where others could hear. As soon as they got in the car, all his pent-up resentment spilled out. He emphasized that he was done letting her take charge of everything. He didn't mind doing all the math and letting her make all the calls, but in everything else, they'd be equal partners, sharing the sales, the leads, and the credit.

Brooklyn's wide-eyed innocence disappeared, and in a nasty voice she said, "This partnership is over."

Shaken by the encounter, Nico went home for the day, which turned out to be a mistake. The following morning he discovered she'd told everyone in the office that he had tried to force himself on her and had become furious when she rejected him. One of the female agents took Nico aside and told him she didn't believe Brooklyn's story, but Brooklyn had returned to the office, hair and suit slightly mussed, with tear-filled eyes, and declared she couldn't work with Nico ever again. Because of the situation and her stellar record, their boss had agreed to let her work alone. Many of Nico's colleagues gave him the cold shoulder because they believed Brooklyn's story. Although he protested his innocence, Nico was written up for sexual harassment and warned that another incident would cost him his job.

Nico determined to beat Brooklyn's sales record the following quarter to prove he'd done his share. In his quiet way, he'd built up trust with many of their clients, who often called him with questions. In addition, his father had a lot of connections and sent business Nico's way. Older couples gravitated toward him, and so did women who found Brooklyn's flirting with their husbands off-putting. In fact, many of the wealthier clients preferred his more refined manner.

He should have been prepared for Brooklyn's dirty tricks, but she blindsided him. First she sent out ads calling herself the top sales agent for the region, and in the office she boasted that she'd carried Nico. Next she contacted all his listings, indicating that she was taking over for him. She went out and replaced his signs with hers. She called his clients, saying she was from the agency and checking to be sure Nico was doing a satisfactory job. During the conversation she found out what the buyers were looking for and then sent them emails or flyers of houses that might suit their needs, particularly her own listings. What she was doing was unethical and even illegal, but that didn't stop Brooklyn.

Nico had an important commercial listing: A religious organization was selling hundreds of acres that had once been a campground, as well as its huge office building. The group planned to buy an even larger facility. Brooklyn called on the group to discuss some potential properties. They'd met her with Nico, so they didn't think it was unusual for one member of the team to contact them. Knowing that the group was very conservative, Brooklyn tearfully told her story about Nico attacking her. The religious leaders were horrified and immediately contacted the office to say that they planned to work with Brooklyn rather than Nico.

Nico had no idea why his client had suddenly turned on him. Other prospective buyers he contacted told him they'd already bought homes. He didn't understand what was happening until he started seeing Brooklyn's name next to the sales. He made sure to warn new clients about her. When people stopped falling for those tricks, Brooklyn resorted to cyberattacks.

Nico had a good following on his social network. Soon one or two posts daily popped up written by an anonymous poster, using the screen name "In the Know." This poster claimed Nico had cheated him. Other posts said that Nico was an imposter and that he was trying to take credit for someone else's sales, or that Brooklyn Goldstone did all the work to make him top salesman of the year. Most of the posts ended with this line: "If you want the real deal, contact Brooklyn Goldstone." Then it gave her contact information. The posts that hurt sales the most, though, were ones that asked, "Wonder why your mortgage rate is higher than your neighbor's who bought at the same time?" They connected Nico's name with his father's mortgage business and made it sound as if he were taking kickbacks. Or those that called him "the Italian Stallion" and indicated that he'd sexually harassed women. They ended with, "Don't spend time alone with this dangerous man. He might attack you, too." Facebook, Yelp, and online real estate media were flooded with messages like these. They began to hurt Nico's business.

At first Nico ignored the postings, hoping they would die down. Instead, the attacks only grew more vicious, and he had no way to prove Brooklyn was behind them.

Nico's Solution

Nico had recently read an article in a real estate publication about cyber-safety. He dug through back issues until he found the column written by Alexis Moore. He contacted SIA and soon worked out a plan to combat Brooklyn's underhanded tactics.

As SIA pointed out, anyone could post slams like these—a rejected lover, a disgruntled former client who'd lost his house to foreclosure, or one who'd lost a bid on a house. People often read postings like Brooklyn's and believe them. Others jump in and side with the negative comments without any evidence, or bring up complaints that may have nothing to do with the victim's professionalism or abilities. SIA representatives outlined this information for Nico's clients, using some similar examples from other businesses. They suggested that, before passing judgment, it's important to research the facts: Check a Realtor's license to see if he's been disciplined, check with the Better Business Bureau, look at his references, and contact former clients. When people took the time to find out the truth, it quickly became clear that "In the Know" had an ulterior motive rather than a legitimate claim.

Soon Nico's former clients, along with new clients who had researched his background, began posting rebuttals of "In the Know's" claims. Some of Nico's colleagues who were aware of what was going on also posted about his trustworthiness, his sales, and his awards.

Soon "In the Know" became the last person prospective clients would trust. Nico also stepped up his marketing campaigns and went to more networking events. The more people got to know him, the more they learned he could be trusted. After Nico showed he wouldn't back down or be intimidated, the attacks gradually stopped. Over time Nico proved himself a trusted authority in real estate and went on to become a top sales person at the brokerage. Brooklyn took a position at a different agency and often vied with him for regional awards, but he no longer dealt with comments from "In the Know."

What Motivates a Narcissist

Psychologists are divided on whether narcissists are emotionally insecure or have an overblown sense of superiority. But many experts believe a deep emptiness and lack of emotional connection underlie narcissism. Often these people did not have their needs met as children. They may have lived with an abusive, addictive, emotionally detached, or narcissistic parent. Often narcissistic parents praise children only when they perform in ways that stroke the parent's ego. Another possibility is that as children they were spoiled, never given rules or made to face consequences, or not taught to care about other people's feelings.

As adults these people are unable to develop intimate, mutually giving relationships. When they become emotionally distressed, rather than looking inward, they project the blame on others, refusing to see themselves at fault. They cannot tolerate losing arguments; they must defend their fragile egos and regain their self-worth at any cost.

How a Narcissist Uses the Internet

Narcissists love the Internet for broadcasting their deeds and soliciting praise. They love friending people and having large social networks, especially of people who adore them. Or, like Hadley, who appears in the story below, they may use the Internet or social media to promote themselves or their agendas.

But narcissists' love of social media and extensive connections can make them particularly vindictive if they decide you need to be "punished." As Nico learned, they may destroy your reputation, business, or other relationships. Posting anonymous detrimental messages, making snide comments, or openly disparaging you are some of their milder tactics; flaming and bullying are not uncommon. Narcissists also make it a point to know your weak spots and exploit these to hurt you or turn others against you. They are dangerous online opponents because they are determined not to lose, and they'll use any tactic—both legal and illegal—to reach their goals, and they'll do so without remorse.

Quinn's Story

Quinn attended a small conservative college and worked part-time at a clothing store in the mall. He and his coworker Alexandra did most of the work, while Hadley, the assistant manager, spent her time trying on the latest styles (often spending all day wearing new outfits with the tags tucked inside), preening in front of the mirror, or sitting in the back room with her feet propped up, texting her many friends. The only time she popped out of the back room was when good-looking men entered; then she was all over them, giving them extra-personalized service. And when the district manager arrived for his monthly inspection, she elbowed Quinn and Alexandra out of the way to stand at the cash register and ring up sales.

It sickened Quinn and Alexandra to hear Hadley brag about "her" high sales and act as if all they did was fold sweaters, hand out numbers for the fitting rooms, and vacuum floors. But part-time jobs were hard to come by, and Hadley was good about working with their class schedules as long as their sales remained high. They kept their mouths shut and didn't protest, even when month after month, Hadley won the top salesperson award. Neither of them could figure out how she'd surpassed their sales when they never saw her ring up any customers. Perhaps she worked harder on other shifts.

Then one day when Hadley was prepping the sales sheet for the district manager, Quinn walked past her desk and noticed she had her name next to his sales key number, and his name with hers. When he pointed out her mistake, she apologized and said she'd fix it, but it started Quinn wondering. Had she been taking credit for his sales all along? That might explain why she'd been top salesperson.

He started watching more closely and discovered that the few times she went to the cash register, she entered his code. And sometimes she put in his code before Alexandra rang up sales. If all these sales were being recorded under his number, he'd be winning that top sales award. Quinn waited until Hadley went on her dinner break to tell Alexandra his suspicions. They decided to confront her after closing that night.

At first Hadley laughed and said they were mistaken, but when Quinn warned her that he planned to contact the district manager and have the reports examined, she turned livid. She threatened that if either of them told anyone, she'd make sure they'd pay and see that they lost their jobs. Alexandra needed the job and she'd lost only a few sales, so she backed down. Quinn refused to be intimidated. He made it clear that he'd ask to see this month's sales report when the district manager came in two weeks, and the report had better have his name beside his sales number.

His only goal was to be sure sales were recorded correctly. He hadn't counted on Hadley's response. That night she began posting stories about Quinn hitting on her despite the store's "no fraternizing" policy. She bragged that she'd warned him about the violations and mocked Quinn for thinking she'd go out with him.

She alleged Quinn had sent her text messages, telling her how beautiful she was, how wild he was about her body, and describing what he'd like to do to her when they were alone. Hadley told her followers in Telegram that she had a crazy coworker following her around and making her nervous. She added details of what he supposedly said to her. She also reported the situation to management.

Quinn's low sales, which were actually Hadley's, combined with these reports of his behavior, led to him receiving a written warning a few days later. Now Quinn was furious. He demanded that they set up a meeting with the district manager right away. Instead, Hadley told him he'd just violated the company policy again by harassing her, and she fired him on the spot.

Many people, figuring it was a part-time job, might have let it go, but Quinn was infuriated at the unfairness. He contacted management to tell his side of the story. Unfortunately, Hadley had set the stage well with her texts, emails, and social media campaign. The district office believed Quinn was a disgruntled employee who'd been rightfully terminated, so they didn't do much to follow up.

Hadley had a flood of friends and followers confirm that Quinn had been harassing her, making her frightened to work with him. With that information, plus all their home office records indicating that Hadley owned the sales number Quinn claimed belonged to him, Quinn's story seemed even more suspect, and the case was dropped.

QUINN'S SOLUTION

Quinn, however, had a secret, one nobody on campus or at the store knew. A secret that would prove Hadley's stories completely wrong. A secret he was reluctant to share: He was gay. After a gay student was hazed on campus his freshman year, he'd kept his sexual orientation a closely guarded secret at school and work. Telling the truth would reveal Hadley's lies, but it also might expose him to serious repercussions on campus.

After agonizing over the situation, he decided to disclose the truth. He'd weathered the storms when he came out during high school. He'd have to do the same here. But he was frustrated that he had to make his private life public. In Quinn's mind the situation had become about more than recovering his job. He saw it as preventing Hadley from taking advantage of other employees.

After Quinn's revelation the district manager investigated the allegations against Hadley, and she was ousted. Still, Quinn was frustrated about his privacy being invaded. Then he read a news story about a workplace cyberstalking that mentioned SIA and a local lawyer who was a renowned civil rights and workplace attorney. He wondered if there was something legal he could do to prevent losing his job and having this happen again. After hearing his story, the attorney took on the case pro bono. Quinn successfully sued the store because he should not have been forced to disclose his sexuality and because the company had terminated him without first investigating the workplace situation.

Leaving a Narcissist

Because narcissists feel their needs are paramount, they may become furious if their partners try to leave. They may resort to manipulation, blackmail, or cruelty to keep friends, lovers, or coworkers in line. Because they have underdeveloped consciences, they have no remorse about wounding others or engaging in illegal actions to get what they want.

If you intend to leave a narcissist, plan your departure ahead of time, and take every precaution to protect yourself. (See chapters 11–13, along with appendix A, for both stalking and cyberstalking action steps.) Be on guard, because narcissists, when thwarted, may be vindictive. (See chapter 9 for more tips.)

Action Steps

Narcissists never see faults in themselves. Protect yourself from them with these tips:

- Never let narcissists get any personal information about you; they will be ruthless in using it to hurt you.
- It's better not to engage in battle with narcissists, but don't back down and let them win, especially if they're using underhanded tactics.
- If you are in a conflict with a narcissist, find others who will corroborate your story to your superiors or the public.

- Gather supporters who will vouch for your reputation and trustworthiness if your integrity is called into question.

- If your allies post online, request that they do not respond to the narcissist's messages or engage in any debate. After a while, as your only detractor, the critic will look foolish, and new visitors to the site will see the rants for what they are.

- Collect written evidence in a journal, documenting any incidents that reveal the narcissist's true colors; get supporting evidence from others, if needed.

Final Quick Tips

- **Keep records:** Document everything, maintain good accounts, and ask others to act as witnesses to keep the narcissist honest.

- **Be vigilant:** Monitor your social media accounts and online postings, and set up Google Alerts for your own name so you'll know if someone is misusing it.

- **Pay attention:** Watch for sneaky maneuvers and underhanded tactics. The more proactive you are, the better. It's much easier to get a potential problem eliminated immediately than to try to repair the damage after the fact.

CHAPTER 8

Competitive: I never lose. Never!

Competitiveness can have a positive side when it results in strong motivation, hard work, and innovation. Great athletes, exceptional students, and outstanding employees use their competitive natures to reach the top. It becomes a problem only when people need to be number one at any cost. Determined to outpace their classmates or coworkers, these hypercompetitors must be best or first in everything they do, and they may employ sneaky or devious tactics to secure their victories.

Recognizing a Hypercompetitor

As children hypercompetitors upset the game board if they were losing. If they couldn't win, no one could. As adults this behavior may be more covert; these overly competitive people may sabotage projects, start smear campaigns, or use other subtle underhanded tactics to get what they want.

Hypercompetitors are exacting with themselves and often adhere to strict diets, have rigid schedules, and work, train, or study long hours. They'll do whatever it takes to be at the top of their game, profession, or class. They may use their energy to subtly undermine others and maneuver themselves into positions of power. A close look at a person who is catty or snarky will often reveal a competitor underneath.

In a group, competitors, like narcissists (chapter 7) and attention getters (chapter 1), need to top others' stories. The hypercompetitor may be a parent whose child walked or talked first, a friend who has always faced a worse illness or loss, a student with a higher GPA, a former sports player who has won more awards, or a coworker who has overcome greater challenges. These claims may be exaggerated or blatant lies, but overly competitive people don't worry about the truth as long as they can shine.

In the workplace hypercompetitors exhaust others on their teams, browbeating them to work harder and faster, turning every assignment into a challenge, stomping on others as they move up the career ladder. They undermine others to make themselves look good. Many have no qualms about cheating or lying to get ahead.

In a relationship they want to stand out. They love to engage in activities where they can beat their partners. They're not out for a good time; they're out to prove their superiority. It's hard to relax and have fun, because they turn everything into a challenge. They tend to be overbearing and demanding. The drive to be number one makes them extremely critical. They feel better when they tear down others, so they spend a lot of time looking for what others do wrong and pointing it out.

Signs of a Hypercompetitor

Does the person you're with have any of the following characteristics? Using a scale of 0–2, rate each behavior as follows:

0-Never
1-Sometimes
2-Often

You can usually recognize overly competitive people because they:

____ need to win at any cost

____ want to be the teacher's pet or boss's go-to person

____ cause divisive feelings in the workplace

____ severely criticize those who are not performing well

____ stress "I" rather than "we"

____ like to put down others

____ are masters of sarcastic comments

____ steal others' ideas and pass them off as their own

____ quit games if they aren't winning

____ get ejected from games for rule-breaking and/or uncontrolled anger

____ turn "friendly" games into a blood sport

____ never let you forget they beat you at something

____ are sore losers

____ play dirty

____ are workaholics

____ always need to be the best

____ want things done yesterday

____ blame others for their mistakes

_____ take credit for others' work
_____ undermine others to look good
_____ keep tabs on what others are up to
_____ are hard-driving
_____ often take on a huge amount of responsibility
_____ drive others on the team to work harder and faster
_____ cherry-pick the work that allows them to shine
_____ love to be praised and recognized
_____ display their many awards in prominent places
_____ turn nasty or sulk when losing
_____ if criticized, are quick to point out the other person's flaws
_____ compare themselves to others
_____ are eager to find out "dirt" about others
_____ boast about their achievements
_____ often post about awards or accomplishments
_____ share all praise or congratulatory letters/emails they receive
_____ break up a game or change the rules if they're not winning
_____ hate to let others pass them on the road; may engage in road rage
_____ diet and/or exercise to an extreme

Scale
0–10
Strongly motivated people may fall into the lower end of this range. Look closely at the behaviors you've rated as 2s. If most of them are destructive or cruel, this person may have problems with letting others win or gain recognition. Especially if you're just getting to know this person, stay on guard; he or she may have a hidden competitive side that could prove dangerous.

11–29
The higher the score, the more cautious you need to be. Avoid revealing information—personal or work-related—because it may be used to hurt you later. Most likely you've already discovered that this person takes credit for what you do or downgrades you to others, either subtly or overtly. Keep a good record of your contributions to projects and have them validated, if possible. Also keep an eye on all online accounts for unusual activity. If you have a choice, it's better to work on a team with this person rather than as part of a competing team.

You may not get credit for your work, but at least your project won't be sabotaged.

30–74

Scores in this range are an indication of a hypercompetitive person who needs to win and may engage in sneaky or underhanded behavior to do so. The higher the number, the greater your concerns should be. Take all the precautionary steps mentioned above, and be prepared to defend yourself against online attacks. Keep a close eye on your social media accounts, your project files, and all personal information. It's highly likely this relationship could escalate into cyberattacks or other dangers. If it's a love relationship, take precautions against stalking (see appendix A and chapter 13) and revenge (see chapter 9).

Who Gets Hooked by a Hypercompetitor

Most employers love competitors; they'll work long hours, produce top products, and lead their teams to excellence. Although they may cause divisiveness, their output makes them valuable to the companies that employ them. Unfortunately, the people who report to them usually wind up frustrated, irritated, and burned out.

Competitors aren't found only in the workplace; they're also found in relationships. They share many of the same characteristics as the entitled, controlling, and narcissistic types (see chapters 4, 6, and 7). All of these types like to be number one and will do almost anything to stand out.

In personal relationships many people admire these strong individuals who are dedicated, hardworking masters of their crafts. Competitors are usually excellent providers, and many are intelligent and well-rounded. They may excel in a variety of fields or concentrate all their efforts on achieving recognition in one area, which makes them appealing to partners who value material goods, talent, and ambition. People who are shy or self-effacing, or who have low self-esteem may find themselves drawn to these goal-oriented, internally driven individuals.

Competitors often prefer quiet, unassuming types who aren't out to win, so they can stand out and easily dominate the relationship. Encouragers and positive people make competitors feel good about themselves, and these generous individuals don't mind giving the praise that competitors long to hear.

Sometimes hypercompetitors choose high-driving partners, which leads to clashes. Only one can be the best, so the whole relationship winds up being a contest, and every argument is one-upmanship. Because neither is willing to concede, these fights can escalate into physical violence. Every discussion, from who takes out the trash to who forgot to fill the gas tank in the car, explodes into an emotional confrontation.

Priya's Story

Priya, who was finishing her first year at an engineering firm, worked on a team with Airi, who pushed everyone mercilessly to turn in more and better work, to beat the other teams. Desperately needing her job to care for her elderly parents, Priya kept silent and did more than she was asked. She came up with great solutions to problems, but Airi took credit for all the outstanding ideas the team produced.

At the annual banquet the company presented Airi's team with the Top Team of the Year award. The CEO also announced that Airi was being promoted and commended her for four major designs, three of which had been Priya's. A colleague protested aloud that most of those were Priya's ideas.

The following week the CEO called the team into his office and asked who deserved credit for the designs. Before Airi could answer, both men on the team said they were Priya's. The CEO apologized for the mistake and praised her, while Airi sat fuming. Then he asked Priya to stay and invited her to work on a special project with him. Priya was excited by the idea he hoped to patent and even more thrilled that she'd get a share of the profits if it did well in the market.

Priya had always been reserved, and Airi used this trait to turn the other engineers against her, saying Priya was a snob who thought she was too good for the rest of them. Although it hurt Priya, she reminded herself she was there to do her job, not to make friends, and she was proud of the progress she was making on the prototype.

The project was top secret, but Airi slipped into Priya's office without warning, hoping to catch a glimpse of it. As soon as Priya realized Airi was there, she closed out the computer screen—but not before Airi had seen information about the project. Instead of her usual catty remarks, Airi acted friendly and questioned Priya about the project. Priya stayed as close-lipped as she could, but Airi was her superior, so Priya felt obligated to answer some of the questions. After that Airi often showed up and hovered over Priya's shoulder when she was working on the design. Several times when the CEO was out of town, Airi said he had asked her to check on Priya's progress.

The CEO was in Japan for two weeks when Priya finished the project. After he returned they prepared the patent application together and sent it off to an attorney. Priya was crushed when the attorney later informed them that another patent application had been filed more than a week before theirs. The similarities between the two were uncanny; except for a few minor details, the designs were identical. Priya was even more upset when the CEO accused her of selling the plans. Another engineer claimed he'd overheard her on the phone making a deal, and Airi had confirmed the story. The CEO hadn't wanted to believe it, but he said it was hard to fathom that someone had randomly come up with the exact same idea the same week she had. Reluctantly, he let Priya go.

Priya's Solution

Priya suspected Airi was behind the design theft but couldn't prove it. She searched online for information about hacking and computer crime and came across the SIA website. To her surprise, SIA contacted an investigator and a computer tech person in her area who agreed to assist her.

The investigator discovered the other patent application had been submitted by a Semir Jancic, not Airi. That information depressed Priya until further checking revealed he was Airi's boyfriend. Armed with that information, Priya and the investigator requested a meeting with the CEO. He agreed to have the tech examine the company computers. The tech discovered that Airi had sent the files from Priya's computer to her home computer. The CEO apologized profusely and offered Priya her job back, along with a huge raise. Airi was prosecuted and under questioning admitted that she had watched Priya log in. She'd used that login to steal the files.

What Motivates a Hypercompetitor

Hypercompetitors need external validation to make up for internal self-doubt. Many were raised by overly critical parents who set unrealistic expectations and never accepted anything as good enough, insisting their children strive harder, do better, and produce more. Some grew up as younger children in a family; no matter what they did, they never measured up to their older siblings. Children who grow up in home environments like this learn they must stand out to be loved and accepted.

Under their teeth-gritted, full-steam-ahead exteriors, hypercompetitors often feel insecure. They may be motivated by fear of being left behind, losing their jobs, or losing others' respect. Underlying all this is a strong sense of inadequacy, of feeling undeserving unless they're number one. They need to win because inside they never feel they're good enough. Being less than others is their greatest fear.

How a Hypercompetitor Uses the Internet

The Internet is the perfect medium for making competitors look good and/ or for destroying others' reputations. The competitor's main purpose for going online is to win—attention, fame, adulation, or recognition—so most online activity will be hype about accomplishments. Hypercompetitors share praise and compliments they've received and connect with people who can help them move ahead or ones they can use for name-dropping.

Everyone enjoys connecting with important people and sharing good news, but hypercompetitors try to outshine everyone else. If someone posts about an accomplishment, they're quick to comment: *I remember when I did that.* Or if someone's having a rough time, they'll say, *You think that's bad? Here's what happened to me.* Then they launch into a story about how they had it better or worse than the original posters. They may brag or position themselves online for maximum exposure.

In all those cases they're more annoying than harmful, but they can also use the Internet to sabotage their competition. They are not above hacking into emails or files to cause destruction or steal secrets, as in Priya's case. They also may post things that hurt others or ruin their opponents' chances of getting a raise, a contract, or a position. Those who work with a hypercompetitor need to be wary and watch all of their own online accounts, records, and social media to be sure no changes have been made.

In their desire to be first, hypercompetitors may turn to snooping. They may access files on colleagues' computers, rifle through their desks, or probe for information. They also like to gossip and find out as much as they can about others in the office. This gives them an edge, and they may even use information as blackmail if they're desperate.

When dealing with a hypercompetitor, always keep backup files for important projects. Use an online service and a flash drive you keep with you. Print out the information and store it in a locked file. That way, if vital documents are compromised, you have an original. Keep passwords secret and try not to give the competitor any clues to your plans or ideas. And if you receive a promotion or award that the competitor wanted, be especially careful. Overly competitive people are sore losers and may go to any extreme to sabotage you. They may use personal information you've given them to start a smear campaign, or they may even steal your information without your knowledge, as Noah discovered.

Noah's Story

Two law students, Noah and Eli, sat next to each other and chatted while filling out paperwork for an internship. Eli seemed quite friendly and inquired about Noah's law school and experience. He seemed surprised that Noah had already done a summer internship with a prestigious firm and questioned Noah about what he'd done there. As Noah recounted his experience, Eli nodded and said it sounded as if Noah would be perfect for this internship.

Noah hoped so. An internship at this prestigious firm would look wonderful on his resume, and the position was in the exact area he wanted to pursue in the future. After a little more conversation, Noah discovered that Eli had a lower GPA and much less work experience. Noah felt reassured that he was a better candidate than Eli for the opening.

A few weeks later, Noah was shocked to learn that Eli had gotten the position. He couldn't figure out why—until he took a break from his intense studying and logged into Tumblr. He was horrified to see his name come up with defamatory posts against women and various ethnic groups. He found similar messages on his other social media accounts.

Noah was sick. During the background screening the law firm would have seen these posts and decided he wasn't a suitable candidate. Noah had no proof, but he guessed Eli had planted this information to be sure Noah, his top rival for the job, lost the position.

NOAH'S SOLUTION

Although Noah's first impulse was to delete the posts, he remembered reading about Survivors In Action while researching a paper on cybercrime. He found the organization's contact information and emailed. The first thing they had him do was change all his passwords. Though he'd been warned against it, Noah had used the same password for all his accounts, an easy-to-guess combination of his initials and birth date. This time he entered different passwords for each, using a random combination of letters, numbers, and symbols to make it harder for someone to guess.

Usually the next step is to document the posts and delete them immediately, but in this case, SIA wanted the law firm to see that these posts were written in a different style and contained content that did not match Noah's previous posts or philosophy. Even more telling were the dates of the posts: They began the day after Noah had filled out his application and ended the day Eli learned he'd been chosen for the internship. Once the law firm had reviewed the posts and Noah had documented them, he deleted them.

The internal tech department at the law firm treated this situation as a security breach that could potentially cost the firm money if not detected and combated. Confidential client files, financial information, and more were contained on the servers. The IT team was uncertain whether Eli had hacked into their files, but if he'd done it once, he could do it again.

Meanwhile the human resources department at the law firm completed its own investigation, because something similar had happened to Brooke, another top candidate for the internship. Only in this case, the woman had gay-bashing posts on her blog, posts she'd claimed she hadn't written. After both sets of posts had been traced back to Eli, the law firm terminated him and awarded the internship to Noah, who originally had been their top choice.

Eli admitted his guilt, explaining that he'd gotten friendly with each of the candidates and questioned them to see if they'd be strong competition. Only Noah and Brooke had more outstanding qualifications, so he targeted them. He watched as they filled out their applications, then he surreptitiously jotted down their personal information and emails. Later he used that information to hack into their accounts. In Noah's case it was easy, because he had the same password for all his accounts—his initials and birth date.

Eli could have been charged with ID theft and/or cyberstalking. Because social media and blogs are online communities that cross state lines, Eli could have faced federal charges under the Federal Communications

Commission's Telecommunications Act. Noah's father, a prominent politician, could have pressured the firm to make it a criminal matter. He also could have filed a civil suit against the law firm for not taking the necessary steps to prevent a cyberattack. And both he and the law firm could have sued Eli. Because Noah's father didn't want his son's name in the news, he decided to let the matter drop, and the law firm didn't file charges.

Eli's school was a different matter. He was expelled for violating the ethics policy. Because Eli's father, a well-known attorney, contributed a large amount of money to the law school, he was able to get Eli reinstated the following year, after Eli had taken a series of ethics courses and agreed to do volunteer work for legal aid for two years.

Password Hacking Technique

The technique Eli used to obtain the passwords was simple. It took less than five minutes to crack Noah's password using simple JavaScript. Any password stored automatically on a browser can be accessed using this technique. The password is stored behind a series of asterisks (****). By typing in several simple codes, the hacker can discover how long the password is and how many numbers it has, and then through a process of elimination, discover what those numbers are. The same process is used for letters.

Knowing that Noah's password had six numbers and three letters, Eli tried Noah's birth date, which he'd seen on the driver's license Noah had secured on a clipboard. With that and Noah's initials—*Bingo!*—he had the password on his first try. All the passwords on Noah's social media sites were the same length, so Eli didn't need JavaScript to figure out the other passwords. Brooke's accounts were slightly harder to crack because she'd used random numbers and letters, but Eli wanted this internship, so he persevered until he had her passwords.

Leaving a Hypercompetitor

Dealing with overly competitive people can be difficult. They expect their partners, teammates, colleagues, and children to live up to their standards, which may result in impossible demands, constant criticism or ridicule, and fits of anger.

If you're in a relationship with such a person, you'll find that if you try to address a problem, your partner may go ballistic and start listing your faults. It's difficult to resolve issues because these attacks usually put you on the defensive, and the conversation quickly veers from the original topic into a litany of complaints about you.

If you're dealing with a hypercompetitor—whether a friend, spouse, or business partner—take precautions to secure your personal information. Competitive people may want revenge if you leave them or break up a business partnership (see chapter 9); some turn into stalkers, so follow the steps in appendix A and chapters 12 and 13 to thwart both online and physical stalking.

Action Steps

Hypercompetitors want to beat you—and they may manipulate your personal information to do so. Follow these important steps to protect yourself:

- Use different passwords for each account. Never use special dates, names, or initials; select a combination of letters, numbers, and symbols that isn't easily guessable. If you worry that you won't remember all your passwords, try an online service, such as Passpack (www.passpack.com) or LastPass (https://lastpass.com). Be sure you create a very difficult password for that site.

- Set up a Google Alert for your name. You'll receive notices of new posts by and about you.

- Check your name and variations of your name online to see what comes up. If someone with the same name has a shady reputation, try varying your name by using a middle name, a maiden name, or an initial to distinguish your blog and social media sites.

- Tell potential employers (or others who will be searching your name) to use the full name you've chosen when looking for you online.

- When filling out applications in public places, such as doctors' offices or schools, or at places of employment, always shield your information from the view of those around you, or better yet, sit in a secluded place; turn school IDs or driver's licenses facedown if you are near others.

Final Quick Tips

- **Switch it up:** Change your passwords frequently.

- **Be cautious:** Don't reveal too much information to strangers, even if they seem friendly and personable.

- **Search your identity:** Check your name online at regular intervals to be sure no misinformation comes up.

CHAPTER 9

Vengeful: Feel my pain.

One of the most dangerous of all the personalities is a person bent on revenge. Most will stop at nothing to gain the upper hand. They can be the controller, competitor, and narcissist all in one. They not only want to control you but also are determined to win at any cost, and even more importantly, they intend to punish you. These goals make them the most persistent and threatening personality type outlined in this book.

Recognizing a Vengeful Person

Vengeful individuals are determined, persistent, and positive they're right. Often these traits are difficult to detect early in a relationship. Some have learned to be charming manipulators; others may appear a bit rigid, never deviating from their strongly held beliefs and ideas. At times they may be bossy or overbearing, but many have learned to mask these characteristics to get along with others—at least at first.

Early clues may be touchiness, irritation, or anger, especially when criticized. Vengeful individuals may rant about pet peeves, insisting that their view is the only correct one. If they have trouble entertaining other viewpoints or become angry when challenged, those are definite warning signs. Watch their interactions with those closest to them—children, old friends, and employees. If people who know them well cringe or shy away, take that as a signal to avoid a close relationship. Other danger signals include their willingness to break things, get in people's faces during confrontations, or use physical violence of any kind.

Although most vengeful individuals are overt about their anger, some are surprisingly quiet and sneaky. Outwardly they're more controlled, but their fury is simmering below the surface. They find subtle and unexpected ways to get back at you. They may even plant clues to make it look as if someone else is responsible. Children who have been raised in households where they could not express anger sometimes learn more insidious ways of punishing others who hurt them. Those who use stealthy forms of revenge may find the Internet the perfect weapon.

When hurt badly enough, anyone can be goaded into revenge, but certain personality types are more prone to it than others. Be particularly watchful with those who are jealous (chapter 2), entitled (chapter 4), controlling (chapter 6), narcissistic (chapter 7), or competitive (chapter 8). Each of these can be the driving force behind revenge.

Signs of a Vengeful Person

Does the person you're with have any of the following characteristics? Using a scale of 0–2, rate the behavior as follows:

0-Never
1-Sometimes
2-Often

Vengeful people are often recognizable because they:

____ are touchy

____ have a hair trigger

____ get offended easily

____ cannot take criticism

____ are verbally abusive

____ have an all-or-nothing mentality

____ expect people to obey their commands

____ are narcissistic (chapter 7)

____ have a sense of entitlement (chapter 4)

____ are prone to jealousy (chapter 2)

____ retaliate for even the slightest offense

____ have little or no empathy for others

____ are easily irritated by small things

____ see themselves and their needs as most important

____ hate to look foolish

____ think people are out to get them

____ are unforgiving

____ drink or use drugs excessively

____ defy authority

____ blame others when things go wrong

____ destroy things when angry

_____ lash out physically and/or verbally when upset

_____ gossip about people who hurt or upset them

_____ have black-and-white thinking

_____ have prejudices against other groups (such as those of differing genders, ethnicities, or sexual orientations)

_____ are strict disciplinarians

_____ have to win at all costs (chapter 8)

_____ grew up in violent or abusive homes

_____ threaten others

_____ hold grudges

_____ are spiteful

_____ are prone to depression

_____ are moody

_____ dislike having their views challenged

_____ have physically hit or hurt you

_____ have physically hurt others

Scale

Note: If any of your score is from the last two choices, this is a sign to leave the relationship immediately. And remember, you are not to blame for someone else's temper in spite of what he or she tells you.

0–9

Anyone, given enough provocation, is capable of revenge, but being moody, prejudiced, or thoughtless doesn't necessarily lead to revenge. If it's early in the relationship, watch for additional warning signs as time goes on, and if the bad temper escalates or the person mistreats you, don't stay.

10–26

Most likely you've already seen the angry, unforgiving side of this person; perhaps it was even directed at you. The higher the score, the more likely it is that you feel as if you're stepping on eggshells not to irritate or offend. You need to ask yourself why you're staying with this person. Why do you feel you need to endure this pain and uncertainty? You don't deserve it. Deep down inside you know you deserve better. Take a look at the previous chapters to see if this person fits any of those profiles, and use those steps and cautions to guide you as you extricate yourself from this relationship.

The higher the score, the more dangerous this person is to you and others, both physically and emotionally. There's a good possibility you or someone you know has been hurt already. You may believe you can help or rescue this person, but you might be risking your life. This could escalate into more than just cyberstalking. Many crimes of passion are perpetrated because of revenge. Vengeful people destroy even those they love; they may turn into stalkers or even killers. Leave the relationship as soon as possible, but take every precaution for your safety. See if this person fits any of the personality profiles in the previous chapters, and use those as a guide when you leave the relationship. If at any time the vengeful person becomes violent or threatening, take safety precautions and enlist help from others, including school or work authorities, law enforcement, domestic violence organizations, and support organizations such as Survivors In Action.

Who Gets Hooked by a Vengeful Person

Because many vengeful individuals can mask their anger, most any person can be drawn in by their charm. Those who stay once the anger and cruelty are obvious usually tend to be of two types. The first are helpers, who see beneath the surface to the hurting child buried under the temper tantrums. They believe that if they give enough love, they can make up for the person's childhood anguish and change the revengeful person into a kind and loving person. As difficult as it is to accept, no single individual can make up for what the revengeful person faced. Unless that person seeks counseling and deals with the hurts of the past, he or she will not change. Helpers need to look at their own motives for staying, which may include a deep-seated desire to matter, to be needed, to be important in someone's life. All of these needs can be met in mutually satisfying relationships, where both people are emotionally healthy.

Others who get hooked by revengeful partners are those who endured abuse of their own. They have learned to expect it; some are filled with guilt and see it as the punishment they deserve. They may believe, or their partners may have convinced them, that they don't deserve anything better.

Although it's a lie, they have come to accept it as truth. As painful as the relationship may be, it feels familiar. They may not realize that relationships can be calm, rage-free, and mutually respectful, so they stay even when their partner's rages endanger their lives.

Sage's Story

Sage had dreamed of being an artist from the time she was a young girl. Soon after she'd transitioned from crayons to paintbrushes, her father abandoned the family, leaving her mom a broken woman. Money was tight, so Sage learned not to ask for the frivolous art supplies she desired. When she was old enough to babysit, she helped her mom with household expenses but always set a tiny bit aside for paints and paper. Any spare time she had, she spent painting.

Her mother discouraged Sage's dreaminess and artistic bent, telling her to get a practical degree so she could support herself. At her mother's urging Sage signed up for computer programming classes at the local community college. She hated every minute of it, but her mom insisted it was one of the fastest-growing professions. Always a people pleaser, Sage did what her mother wanted. She worked full-time as a waitress and put herself through her first year of college. That summer her mom developed cancer and was gone in a matter of months. Dazed and grieving, Sage started her second semester. She had a hard time concentrating on her studies, so she spent time wandering through the school's art gallery whenever she had time off from waitressing. The art soothed her and spoke to her soul.

Then, although it made her feel guilty, Sage did something very daring: She switched her major to art. In the studio she poured out her heartache on canvas. In spite of her sorrow, Sage was more content than she'd ever been. And when one of her paintings won first place in the school art show, she was thrilled. It was the best night of her life. Not only because of the award but also because she met Dina.

Dina bought Sage's prizewinning painting, and the two of them went out for coffee after the show and talked for hours. They had so much in common and became fast friends immediately. They both liked weightlifting, so they met at the gym the next morning to work out. Dina ran every evening and convinced Sage to join her. Soon they were spending all their free time together.

Two years older than Sage, Dina was attending the police academy training on campus. She had an apartment a few blocks away that she invited Sage to share. It was heart-wrenching for Sage to give up the home she'd lived in with her mother; however, Dina pointed out the benefits, including saving money on rent and spending more time together. The move would mean more money for art supplies. Sage was still a bit hesitant, but with Dina's prodding, she made the move.

Initially, Sage moved into the second bedroom until one night as they were watching a movie together, Dina slid closer and put her arm around Sage. Although Sage was a bit surprised, she didn't mind. Soon their relationship had progressed to the point where Dina suggested they turn the second bedroom into an art studio, and Sage readily agreed.

With that change in their relationship, Dina became more controlling. She demanded more of Sage's time and stopped asking Sage's opinion on what movie to watch or where to meet. Dina just announced what they'd do and expected Sage to comply. It bothered Sage, but her mom had been bossy, so she gave in to keep the peace. Most of the time she didn't mind. Until Dina started cutting into her art time. Soon Sage couldn't paint if Dina was home. Dina insisted on spending all their time together.

Dina's constant criticism hurt more. Before when they went running, Dina had been understanding of Sage's slowness. Dina would do speed bursts and then come back and jog with Sage. Now she yelled at Sage to keep up, calling her fat and lazy when she couldn't. During weightlifting Dina jeered at Sage's technique and mocked her for being a wimp. When they played video games, Dina wasn't content to beat Sage; she tried to destroy her and then gloated about her victories.

Sage tried to shrug it off. She knew Dina was under a lot of pressure at the academy and had been taking quite a bit of razzing from the guys. Sage hoped it was a passing phase and would soon get better. Instead, it became worse. Dina criticized Sage's cooking and cleaning, raged about her waitressing hours, and belittled her paintings. Sage tried harder to accommodate Dina and hid her hurt feelings.

The situation escalated the night Sage had to finish her final painting for the semester, worth one-third of her grade. She begged Dina to spend some of their time together in the studio. Dina grumbled, but she sat in the studio and kept up a running commentary, making it hard for Sage to concentrate. Sage was working on a tricky part when Dina asked her a question. Sage didn't answer. Instead, she angled her brush to add a small detail. The next thing she knew, Dina bumped her arm, making a huge slash right through the painting.

When Sage turned to her, shocked and speechless, Dina said through clenched teeth, "Next time I ask you something, answer me." Then she added, "It doesn't matter; the painting looked awful anyway." She stalked out, leaving Sage in tears.

Sage locked the studio door and stayed up all night trying to repair the damage. She ended up with muddied colors in the center of the painting. She was ashamed to turn it in and knew she deserved the low grade she received. What hurt more than the grade was that Dina had deliberately destroyed something that meant the world to Sage.

Then came the night Dina pulled a gun on Sage. "I could shoot you right now for practice." She said it in a joking manner, but after what had happened with the painting, Sage wasn't sure she could trust her. After Dina holstered her gun, Sage said that if Dina ever pointed the gun at her again, they were through. Dina whipped out the gun and said, "You mean like this?" She aimed at Sage's heart.

Sage tried to tell herself Dina had been drinking. But what if she joked around and pulled the trigger? Sage hoped the gun wasn't loaded, but she didn't want to take a chance.

The next morning after Diana left for the academy, Sage skipped class and loaded her car with everything she could fit. She had no idea where she'd go, but she headed into town to the restaurant where she worked. She asked if anyone knew of a place she could rent. The restaurant owner offered her the guest bedroom in her house temporarily while Sage looked for an apartment. With knowing eyes she suggested Sage unload her painting supplies in the garage.

Sage stayed there the rest of the day and ignored Dina's texts and emails. The next morning she deliberately went to class late to be sure she wouldn't run into Dina. At lunchtime she stayed in the painting studio.

Suddenly the studio doors banged open, and Dina stormed in. "Nobody leaves me. Don't think you're going to get away with this." After screaming threats and obscenities, she stomped out, vowing to make Sage's life miserable. And she did.

She showed up at the restaurant during Sage's shifts, demanding to be waited on and loudly criticizing the service, "accidentally" spilling food or drinks on Sage, leaving huge messes behind and no tip. She stalked into Sage's classes and caused uproars. She entered the painting studio and harangued Sage.

When Sage found an apartment of her own, Dina used her police contacts to find out the address. Then she came and banged on the door at all hours of the night, until the neighbors threatened to have Sage evicted.

Dina alternated between fits of rage and apologies. She sent emails begging Sage to come back, posted notes on her door, left roses on her car, and sent a singing telegram with a bouquet of flowers to her classroom. She continually called, texted, and emailed all of Sage's classmates and coworkers, asking them to pass on messages of love.

When that wasn't effective she turned to viciousness. The day of midterms, Sage came outside to find all four of her tires slashed. A neighbor gave her a ride to campus, but Sage was so shaken that she did poorly on her exams. She went to the art studio to find her latest canvas splattered with red paint. She almost collapsed in tears. She couldn't go on without help.

Sage's Solution

Sage asked several classmates for advice, and one recommended a domestic violence organization. She was turned away because her case wasn't severe enough. Then she heard about SIA. She was referred to a volunteer who lived a few towns away.

The volunteer came and met with Sage. They discussed getting a restraining order. Because Dina was studying law enforcement, she would lose her gun and the ability to be a police officer. Although that seemed like a good option, the volunteer advised against it, explaining that officer-involved cases tend to be high risk, meaning Sage might wind up a homicide victim. Knowing Dina's vengeful personality, Sage agreed that taking out a restraining order could be lethal, especially if Dina lost her future career.

Then the volunteer had Sage contact her cell phone provider to block Dina's texts and request a prepaid phone. Sage spoke with her carrier's fraud/security department to report the situation and restrict access to her cell account, so it couldn't be used as a weapon to stalk her (see Isaiah's story in chapter 2).

Next the volunteer accompanied Sage to meet with key people in her life. They started with the art department. After the SIA volunteer explained to the head of the department how dangerous a jilted lover could be, the professor agreed to lock the studio whenever an intern couldn't monitor it. Students who were used to coming and going at all hours of the day and night were annoyed at the new policies. Many blamed Sage. Most of her classmates were already avoiding her because they were sick of being involved in her messy breakup.

The SIA volunteer explained to them what was happening and gave them instructions on blocking calls, texts, and emails, which the majority had already done. She also requested that, if asked, they refrain from divulging Sage's whereabouts. A few rolled their eyes, but most of them were sympathetic once they understood the situation. Some of those who were reluctant to help changed their minds when the volunteer pointed out that, in refusing to help a victim, they were aiding and abetting a felon and putting Sage's life in danger. The volunteer also asked everyone to send a strongly worded message to Dina saying that they didn't want to receive any more calls, texts, or emails from her. Sage also talked to mutual friends of hers and Dina's, explaining that they had broken up and asking them to please not forward any messages from Dina.

The restaurant owner cooperated in working out new hours for Sage and came up with a plan of action for when Dina entered the restaurant. The hostesses were warned not to seat Dina in Sage's section even if she protested. While Dina was in the restaurant, the owner volunteered to work Sage's tables and let Sage help out in the kitchen. They needed to use the strategy only three times before Dina stopped coming in. It wasn't worth her time and money if her quarry disappeared into the kitchen the minute she arrived.

Sage's biggest fear, besides another possible car sabotage, was being at the apartment. Dina had come by drunk the previous Saturday night and threatened to shoot her way in. She hadn't pulled a gun, but Sage worried that sometime Dina might actually do it.

SIA suggested purchasing a security system, but Sage had spent all her savings on new car tires. The volunteer helped her find fake security cameras for her apartment and car for less than ten dollars. Both looked realistic enough to fool people. To make them seem even more authentic, Sage used her art skills to create a replica of car and house security signs that she taped in the windows. As soon as she had enough money, she planned to install the real thing, but for now she hoped they'd serve as a deterrent. As a student at the police academy, Dina wouldn't want to be taped harassing someone.

When Dina drove up the following Saturday night and started up the walk, she spotted the sign and camera and quickly retreated. She didn't get close enough to see if they were real.

But the situation with Dina had left Sage tense and fearful. She jumped at the slightest noise and had trouble sleeping. As she walked through town and on campus, she kept glancing over her shoulder, watching, worried, always on edge. The slightest problem or frustration had her in tears. She mentally berated herself for getting involved with Dina, and she doubted her own judgment about people, so she went into her shell and stopped talking to others. Worried that she might be having a breakdown, she discussed her reactions with the SIA volunteer, who assured her that they were normal. Many people experience similar symptoms or have PTSD following cyberattacks or stalking. The SIA volunteer suggested Sage seek counseling.

The mental health clinic on campus provided free services, and Sage took advantage of it. Because of her interest in art, the counselor suggested art therapy, which also helped Sage overcome her grief, both at the loss of the relationship and at her mother's death. It also decreased her anxiety and stress. At the SIA volunteer's recommendation, Sage asked to have all her sessions off the record so there was no chance Dina could access them. The therapist also introduced Sage to visual journaling (see chapter 15), which Sage could do at home every evening to reduce the day's built-up tensions.

To replace the running she'd done with Dina, Sage tried yoga and found it calming. At first she feared she'd run into Dina and always took a different and convoluted route to the on-campus studio. After a few weeks of not sighting Dina, Sage relaxed, but she never stopped being vigilant as she walked across campus.

When the yoga teacher mentioned retreats she was leading, Sage attended one. Knowing she wouldn't run into Dina at this secluded mountain cabin allowed Sage to relax totally in mind, body, and spirit for the first time since the breakup. She saved money so she could afford to do quarterly retreats. They helped restore her equilibrium and let her breathe deeply and freely, something she rarely did in town or on campus.

What Motivates a Vengeful Person

People who were raised in an authoritarian or strict religious atmosphere are often conditioned to watch for and punish those who get out of line.

They may even feel it's their moral duty. They see themselves as doing what's right and conquering what's wrong. If, however, those who mete out the punishment are operating from skewed or prejudiced mindsets, they can easily make it a vendetta against others who offend their personal morals.

Some vengeful individuals are driven by power and status. They can't bear to lose face, and if they do, they must retaliate. The most powerful motivators, though, are anger and shame. Consciously or subconsciously, vengeful people make others pay for their past pain. Most had abusive childhoods or have unresolved losses that fuel their anger and resentment. If their partners' actions trigger those distressful memories, they often over-react. The burning rage stored inside can explode whenever they feel an emotion, such as loss or hurt, that stirs up long-buried memories.

Everyone gets angry at times, but vengeful people go beyond anger; they'll hurt others or destroy property. They intend to make someone pay for their inner pain, and most will go to any lengths to do so.

How a Vengeful Person Uses the Internet

When their tempers get the better of them, vengeful people usually prefer in-person confrontations. Like Dina and Arden (in Kaleb's story on the next page), they stalk their victims and try to hurt them or their property. Individuals set on revenge will take advantage of any weapon at their disposal, and the Internet has the power to destroy people's lives. In addition to using all the cybercrime techniques described in previous chapters, they may steal identities and money, terrorize their targets, or stalk and even kill their victims.

They often aren't content to harass or humiliate; that's not their style or their main objective. They're out to destroy—not only reputations but also jobs, relationships, and even lives. They aren't aiming for power or prestige; their goal is punishment. They intend to mete out retribution for the pain the victim has caused them. In their minds any means justifies the ends: making sure the person who hurt them pays. In extreme cases they can shoot someone in cold blood and convince themselves that the person deserved it. Ruthless and relentless, they won't stop until they've achieved their goal, or gotten caught.

Alexis Moore's story in the Introduction is an example of the cruelty and cunning of a vengeful person. Using the Internet, her ex emptied her bank account, trashed her credit rating, closed out her utilities and insurance, caused her to lose her jobs, and stalked her. Kaleb, too, experienced cyberattacks after his relationship ended that later escalated to stalking.

Kaleb's Story

Kaleb dated Arden for a year, but eventually her frequent rages and temper tantrums got to him. When she wasn't irritated about something, Arden was fun to be around and had a great laugh. But if she got upset, she went ballistic, screaming and swearing. She'd even socked him on occasion, usually on the arms or chest. He was a bodybuilder, so it mainly stung rather than hurt, but it bothered his pride. The longer they were together, the more frequent her fits became, until Kaleb wanted out of the relationship.

When he first told her, Arden caused a scene. She accused of him of cheating on her and pummeled him until he immobilized her wrists. Then she kicked him, bit his arm, and even spat at him. Finally, he shoved her so she stumbled backward and fell onto the couch. Then he raced for her front door. He got out and partway down the street before she reached the doorway. She stood there shouting obscenities and threatening to report him for abuse.

He hadn't made it home before his phone started dinging. Arden demanded to know who he was seeing on the side, telling him if he didn't stay with her she'd go to the police and he'd be sorry. Kaleb ignored the texts and the strings of emails, except to say that he'd taken pictures of his bruises and the bite mark on his arm, so he'd be happy to talk to the police. That ended those threats, but Arden remained convinced Kaleb had another girl. She swore she'd find out and make the bitch pay.

As time went on Arden grew even more determined to get revenge. She not only cyberbullied Kaleb via phone and email but also stalked him. This progressed to even more dangerous physical attacks. As he sped off to work on his motorcycle one day, he skidded and couldn't gain control of his bike. He wound up in the hospital with a broken leg and ribs. The highway patrol took his bike, and the investigation showed the tires had oil or something slick on them. They asked if he had used any tire treatment, and when he said no, they determined the tires had been sprayed with Armor All. When the police questioned him about who might have tried to hurt or kill him, Kaleb had a pretty good idea, but he was reluctant to give Arden's name.

The police were still investigating the case when Kaleb went back to work on crutches. One of his coworkers lived near him, so Rosita offered to drive him. Instead of working the counter, Kaleb sat on a stool at the drive-through window. Rosita was especially helpful about running orders over to him. She also walked him out to her car after work, holding the doors for him, helping him into the car.

A few nights later as Kaleb and Rosita emerged from the restaurant laughing about an odd customer they'd waited on, Arden jumped out of the bushes with a knife. She slashed at Kaleb and knocked him to the ground. He tried to ward her off with his crutches while she stabbed at him with the knife. When Rosita tried to throw herself in front of Kaleb and block the attack, Arden turned on Rosita and slashed her arm. Rosita's screams brought several employees running. Two of the men grabbed Arden and wrestled the knife away from her. They had to pin her facedown on the ground until the cops came to prevent her from biting and scratching them.

When the police arrived Arden resisted arrest and screamed at Kaleb and Rosita that she'd get them both. The Armor All was tied to her, and she was charged with attempted murder, which was pled down to felony battery. Along with court-ordered counseling, Arden spent several months in jail and was required to pay restitution for Kaleb's medical bills and bike repairs. When she was released, one of the conditions of her probation was to have no contact with Kaleb whatsoever. That didn't mean Kaleb could relax. He never knew when Arden might be waiting around the corner to attack.

Female Violence in Interpersonal Relationships

Many men brush off physical assaults from the women they're dating, because their first instinct is to deny or ignore these attacks. They may believe they're not in danger because they can easily overpower their irate dates. Most feel ashamed or as if they're less of a man if they complain about or report the abuse. This primal instinct to remain stoic and silent is extremely dangerous. Any type of physical violence needs to be taken seriously. A woman who scratches, bites, or hits needs help as much as a male batterer. Quickly end any relationship in which a partner becomes violent or physically abusive. Or like Kaleb, you may wind up risking your life.

Leaving a Vengeful Person

All planning needs to be done in secret and ahead of time, if possible. Unless you're fleeing from an abusive situation, take time to find a place where vengeful individuals can't locate or influence you. You'll need to make sure you've cut off all possible avenues of communication, including phone numbers and social media that they can use to reach you, control you, or hurt you. Often they'll try to blackmail or threaten to get you to return. If they do contact you, stay calm and end the conversation if they become abusive. If that doesn't work, they may stalk you.

Never try to deal with this type of person alone. Many crimes of passion are motivated by revenge. Sage stopped Dina before things went too far, but the situation could have escalated to physical violence. Make plans to protect yourself. Get a restraining order. Notify the police immediately if you spot the stalker. Follow all the tips in chapter 3 for dealing with stalkers as well as the action steps in appendix A and chapters 11–13 for both stalking and cyberstalking.

Action Steps

If you're facing an emergency situation and have no funds or you are waiting for a security company to install a device, fake devices can sometimes deter stalkers. You can purchase these very inexpensively, and they may help to keep you safe. If you're in a life-or-death situation, check with SIA. Sometimes they can help you find security devices free or at a reduced cost.

Here are a few simple tricks to fool a stalker temporarily:

- Look at pictures of security devices online and see if you have anything with a similar shape or style. Sometimes an alarm clock, old camera, electric pencil sharpener, or other small appliance can look like a security device from a distance. One woman placed an alarm clock with the numbers facing down on her car dash. Enough glow came from below the clock that, in the dark, it looked as if it were a security device.

- Another possibility is to buy small nightlights and hang them from the upper corners of windows. One woman even draped a string of Christmas lights around her window, took out all the bulbs except one blinking red one in the upper corner, and angled it so it looked as if it were part of a security system.

- Your device may look even more official if you have a security sign. Sage designed stickers that looked like security company logos. Don't use the logos of actual companies, but design your own. You can look at samples for ideas on the usual wording. Anything that warns, "This property protected by ____ Security Service" could serve as a deterrent.

- If you don't have the time or materials to create a sign, consider posting a note on the door. One stalking victim took a small piece of paper and wrote a message that looked as if it were from the police or a security company, saying that they'd received her call and wanted her to know they had her property under twenty-four-hour surveillance. In another situation a woman posted a note that said, "Got the film and am reviewing it now for identification." Her stalker bolted and never returned. This may not work for the more determined stalkers, but many don't want to get caught. They want the revenge but not the consequences.

- Think creatively. Use the materials you have on hand and your knowledge of your stalker. None of these measures is a guarantee against a determined stalker, but these homemade devices may buy you some time and ward off an attacker temporarily until you can protect your home or apartment properly.

Final Quick Tips

- **Repeat this: There's no excuse for abuse of any kind.** No one has the right to treat you with disrespect or cruelty. You don't deserve abuse; recognize that the vengeful person's behavior is wrong.

- **Don't blame yourself:** Keep in mind that the cruelties directed at you are not related to you or what you've done; they are motivated by the abuser's past pain.

- **Get away:** Never stay in an abusive relationship. Get out and stay out, no matter how much the other person begs you to return or promises to change. Unless abusers address their problems through therapy, they will soon revert to old habits.

- **Enlist help:** It's difficult to get away without outside help; find trusted friends, relatives, or agencies who will support you.

- **Protect yourself:** Do whatever you need to do to stay safe. Check out the strategies in part II. In some cases you may even need to go into hiding (see "Going Black Ops" in chapter 13).

CHAPTER 10

Exploitative: Sooner or later, I'll get you.

Exploitation can take many forms, but it almost always occurs in situations where one person has power over the other. Whether it's a boss, teacher, parent, or mentor, that person uses a position of authority to force another person to comply with his or her will. Because minors are dependents, children and teens are often at the greatest risk for this type of exploitation. In some cases an exploiter may use blackmail, threats of violence, or other forms of coercion to get a victim to comply.

Recognizing an Exploiter

Often, particularly in the case of strangers, exploitation begins on the Internet in chat rooms, through gaming or other online activities, or through social media. Most predators start out by being friendly and appear innocent. They single out victims by complimenting them, encouraging them to talk, and being kind and understanding. After they've established the friendship, they gradually move to slightly naughty comments, jokes, or suggestions, usually accompanied by coaxing and sweet talking. Over time their suggestions progress to more risqué requests. Thus victims get sucked in gradually and continue to comply with requests for fear of losing the friendship, attention, and connection they've established. By this time victims have often revealed secrets about themselves that the predator can use to blackmail them.

In-person exploitation may follow a similar pattern, with an exploiter coaxing a victim and rewarding compliance. In most cases, these types of exploiters are difficult to spot early in a relationship because they appear to be caring individuals. Not until later do they begin making their demands. Most victims are taken by surprise when someone they've learned to trust abuses them.

Not all abusers take the time to lure their victims. When there is an imbalance of power, exploiters may use their superior position to force their victims to submit to their will. These abusers are easier to recognize because they like to control others. They issue commands and expect obedience.

Many have short tempers and are quick to punish or retaliate. Some see themselves as better than certain groups, and justify their actions on this basis. Situations like these, in which the exploiter has a hold over you, can be the most difficult to escape.

Signs of an Exploiter

Does the person you're with have any of the following characteristics? Using a scale of 0–2, rate each behavior as follows:

0-Never
1-Sometimes
2-Often

You can identify exploiters because often they:
____ are charming and thoughtful at first
____ empathize with your problems
____ use flattery to get you to do what they want
____ tell sexual jokes or stories
____ ask very personal questions
____ ask you to describe your body
____ provide rewards in exchange for favors
____ talk you into doing things that make you feel uncomfortable
____ do things that are morally wrong
____ hurt or take advantage of you
____ make you feel bad or dirty
____ warn you not to tell others what they're doing
____ force you to do things you don't want to do
____ hurt you physically or emotionally

Scale
0–8
If all the points are from the first four options, it's possible that this person is not an exploiter. But if it's early in a relationship or friendship, be wary and watch for the other signs listed here. If any points are from the final seven choices, see the following page.

9–28

This person is an exploiter. The higher the score, the greater the danger. No one, not a parent, teacher, boss, or anyone in a position of authority, should ask you to do something that hurts you, causes you emotional distress, or is illegal or immoral. If this is happening to you, you are being exploited. See the section on leaving an exploiter for information on getting out of the relationship.

Who Gets Hooked by an Exploiter

Anyone can become a victim. Exploitation is possible anytime there's an imbalance of power. If exploitative people have control of your welfare, your paycheck, your grades, or your spiritual life, they can use that to manipulate you. Likewise, if they're physically stronger or have information they can use to blackmail you, they may use it to control you. Most people in positions of authority do not misuse their power, but some do.

It's also possible to be exploited by strangers. Teen runaways or online gamers can be at risk. Exploiters look for innocent, gullible, or vulnerable victims. They also prey on those who are lonely, isolated, or ostracized. Anyone who is going through a rough time emotionally—whether from an abusive home life, low self-esteem, a recent breakup, the death or divorce of a parent, or even normal teen angst—makes a good target. By providing the caring and empathy these sad or hurting teens need, exploiters gradually groom their victims to be dependent on them. They can then use this dependency to manipulate and get their way.

Amy's Story

Amy had a limp and one of her arms hung uselessly at an odd angle. All through school, she'd been teased and mocked. Although she was a good student, Amy dropped out, got her GED, and then spent most of her time alone in her room with her computer. She'd learned how to type one-handed and was a whiz at video games. She made friends with many of the guys who played with her online. One in particular always complimented her abilities, and they soon teamed up for several games.

They chatted about themselves as they planned their strategies. When he learned that Amy was sixteen, Gavin told her he was eighteen and had just graduated from high school. He lived just over the state border, about two hours from Amy's home. He said it would be fun to meet someday, and Amy agreed, except she was embarrassed by her arm and limp. Finally, she confessed this to Gavin, and he insisted she take a picture of herself and send it to him. Amy hesitated, afraid to lose the budding friendship if he mocked her. But he kept insisting until she eventually complied.

Amy was totally unprepared for Gavin's response. He told her the people who had mocked her were crazy; she was a stunning beauty. He praised her gorgeous eyes, her beautiful hair, and her lovely smile. Then he added, "I hope you won't be offended, but I think you have a sexy body and great legs, too. All that, plus you're a super gamer."

Amy basked in the compliments, something she'd never received. Every time they talked he called her nicknames like Pretty Eyes and said he couldn't get her picture out of his mind. Amy, who had never dated, enjoyed the flirting. Gradually, Gavin introduced sexual innuendos into the conversations. Then one day he mentioned that thoughts of her in a swimsuit had given him a wet dream. Amy was a bit shocked by that but also secretly flattered when he asked to see a picture of her in a swimsuit. She was worried about doing that because her dad, a fundamentalist minister, monitored her phone and Internet use. He often checked her history to be sure she wasn't doing anything she shouldn't be. Gavin suggested she use Snapchat so there'd be no record.

Amy changed into a swimsuit and sent the picture. Gavin's compliments grew even more fulsome. It wasn't long before he told her he was falling for her and asked to see her in her underwear. Gavin mentioned how much he liked lace, so Amy bought some lacy bras and panties. Then he talked her into some topless photos. After she sent Gavin some provocative pictures, he praised her body and insisted he'd never been so attracted to anyone in his life. He couldn't get enough of her photos. Hungry for more compliments, Amy sent the totally nude pictures he begged her to take.

Next Gavin talked her into making some videos of herself masturbating. Each time she sent one, he admired her body. And when he told her he was dying to meet her in person, she agreed to go to his apartment. She lied to her parents and said she was going on a weekend retreat at a church with one of her former classmates. Gavin had printed up and mailed her a flyer to use. The phone number was his cell. When her father called to find out details of the retreat, Gavin posed as the minister in charge and answered all his questions, reassuring Amy's dad that the participants would be well supervised.

Feeling guilty, Amy took off for Gavin's apartment, shaking with anticipation and nervousness. She stopped along the way to change into a more provocative outfit, along with her lacy underthings. As she neared the apartment building, Amy debated turning around and going home. Perhaps she'd made a mistake. But the elaborate lie she'd constructed to get here meant she'd have to explain to her dad why she'd left the retreat. And he'd insist on calling the minister to discuss the situation. She had no idea whether Gavin would cover for her. Reluctantly, she parked and walked up to the apartment. She pressed the buzzer, and Gavin told her to go up the stairs to apartment 3-D and come right in; he was waiting for her and he had a surprise.

The minute Amy walked into the apartment, the door slammed and locked behind her. She whirled around to find a man blocking her exit. Rather than the eighteen-year-old she was expecting, Amy was shocked to discover that Gavin was in his fifties.

Along one wall he'd taped every one of her nude photos. Amy had assumed that the Snapchat photos would instantly disappear. What she didn't know was that Gavin had snapped photos of those pictures, so he had copies of all of them. Even worse, his computer was on, playing a video of her masturbating.

Gavin threatened to post the photos and videos online and send them to Amy's father and church members. During their conversations she'd told Gavin how strict her church was, so he knew the devastation it would cause.

Amy couldn't let that happen. Their church took the verse in 1 Timothy 3:5 very seriously: *If anyone does not know how to manage his own family, how can he take care of God's church?* If anyone found out what she'd done, her father would lose his job.

Sickened and scared, Amy did what he asked. After that weekend Gavin continued to blackmail her. She met him at a local hotel for a few hours whenever he came to town. And he scheduled periodic "church retreats" and "mission trips," when she had to go to his apartment. Terrified of her family finding out, Amy searched online for a way out. She had to be careful her dad didn't see what she was looking for, so she made trips to the local library, coming home with Bible study books and Amish romance novels, which her father allowed her to read. And she had plenty of time to read because she stayed offline and didn't play any of her favorite games. Once or twice she'd gone online to see that Gavin had paired up with another girl. She debated about warning the girl, but was too humiliated by what had happened to share her experience with anyone else.

Amy's Solution

Amy found the SIA website and was relieved to see an organization that didn't require parental permission before providing services. She couldn't tell her mother, who believed that being submissive to her husband was her main duty in life. Her mom would immediately report Amy's sins to her father. Besides fearing that her father would lose his job, she didn't want to hurt her parents. Although they were extremely strict and overprotective, she loved them and could never confess the awful things she'd done.

SIA representatives offered Amy counseling and encouraged her to go to Planned Parenthood and get tested for sexually transmitted diseases. They also enlisted the help of a private investigator, a former police detective who had worked sex crimes. The volunteer who worked with Amy did all she could to empower Amy and honor her wishes. Amy's fear of retribution from her family, friends, and church was real, and, having dealt with situations like this before, the volunteer discussed this with her. Their talks were uncensored and honest. SIA would do whatever it could to help and protect her, but no one could guarantee that her parents and church wouldn't find out, especially as the detective moved forward with the case. The SIA volunteer believed it was important for Amy to weigh all the facts and consider possible scenarios.

Once Gavin was arrested, the media would likely discover the case and make it public. Because of her age, her name should be kept out of the news, but her identity might still leak out. SIA and Amy discussed the pros and cons of telling her parents, including the possibility that her parents might kick her out of the house when they found out. Amy agonized over whether to tell them, as well as whether to move forward with the case, which would mean she'd have to testify. She didn't have long to decide because they needed to catch Gavin before he grew suspicious.

The volunteer also explained that there was no guarantee that Gavin would be prosecuted and convicted, or even go to jail for any length of time. Knowing that up front might keep Amy from feeling revictimized if Gavin didn't receive the punishment Amy felt he deserved.

After the investigator discovered that Gavin was victimizing two other girls, Amy made her decision. She would stand up to protect others who were victimized, but she'd need her parents' help and support if she were to go to court. The SIA volunteer went with Amy for emotional support when she told her parents. Having a stranger there might prevent tempers from flaring out of control.

The scene was as terrible as Amy had imagined. Her father went ballistic and screamed at her. If the volunteer hadn't been there, he might have beaten her with a belt. Having the SIA volunteer by her side helped Amy cope. Meanwhile Amy's mother sat in the corner, hands over her face, crying as her husband raged. The SIA volunteer tried to talk to the father, to get him to see Amy's side, but his fury only increased.

Then Amy stood and said that she was leaving. Because she had prepared for this, she remained strong on the outside, although she was falling apart on the inside. For the first time, her mother spoke. She begged Amy not to go and pleaded with her husband to show God's forgiveness to their daughter.

"She's no daughter of mine," Amy's father said and stalked from the room.

In a tear-choked voice, Amy's mother suggested that perhaps Amy could stay with her aunt until things settled down. She called her sister, who agreed to take in Amy. Amy's aunt supported her when the case went to trial, but her parents had nothing more to do with her. Her father forbid her mother to have any contact with their daughter, and because of her religious beliefs, Amy's mother submitted to her husband's will.

As the SIA volunteer had predicted, Gavin received a light sentence. After a brief jail term, mandatory counseling, and probation, he was free. It seemed so unfair after he'd ruined three lives. Amy vowed to keep other girls from falling into the same trap. She spent time online warning others about her experiences.

Other Cases

Girls aren't the only ones who fall victim to exploiters. Boys, too, are lured in. Sexual predators target them the same way Gavin reeled in Amy. And sometimes peers exploit each other, which was the case for Sawyer, who was attending a Canadian boarding school. One of the older boys forced him into a sexual relationship that was secretly taped. The video went viral. Sawyer was humiliated and wanted to commit suicide, but one of his friends stopped him. His friend helped him have the video removed by following the steps on NeedHelpNow.ca, and they reported the exploitation to Cybertip.ca, a service of the Canadian Centre for Child Protection. The picture-removal tips on the Need Help Now site are also applicable to other countries.

What Motivates an Exploiter

Exploiters may believe that the person they're hurting isn't worthy of respect. Some see other races, genders, or ages as inferior, which gives them the right to use those they think of as lesser beings. Yet others convince themselves that those they're abusing are not harmed by their actions; they may disassociate from their feelings completely. Exploiters are generally narcissistic (see chapter 7) and put their own needs above those of their victims.

Those who sexually abuse children are considered to have personality disorders. Most are willing to spend time "grooming" their victims and will use gifts, attention, threats, blackmail, or violence to accomplish their ends. More sadistic types will lure or force children into submitting, and these abusers are more likely to kill their victims.

How an Exploiter Uses the Internet

Keep in mind that on the Internet people can be whomever they want. Exploiters can choose their age, gender, and personal details. Like Amy, you have no way of knowing their true identities. Many predators join groups specifically to target their prey. They choose gaming sites, chat rooms, or other social forums that allow them to make friends.

Once they've established friendships, they set about making you dependent on them in some way, usually by providing emotional support and understanding. If you're struggling, they listen sympathetically. They may offer encouragement and advice along with compliments that raise your self-esteem. They say things that make you feel good about yourself.

Over time they ask for things, usually small requests at first; later they raise their demands. Very gradually they lead you into their trap. By the time you realize you're being exploited, they often have a strong hold over you. Perhaps you're even in love with them, so you justify doing what they ask, even if it feels wrong or immoral. If you balk, they generally have some form of blackmail to ensure you become compliant. All the personal information you told them when they were empathetic listeners now comes in handy.

If they've chosen a strong enough motivation, you're forced to give in to the blackmail and do what they say. Sometimes without your knowledge, they take information about you or photos of you and sell them or make them public. If anyone has distributed child pornography with you in it, you are entitled to compensation.

Financial Exploiters and Identity Thieves

Two additional classes of exploiters deserve special mention. Financial exploiters use your information to gain access to your money or bank accounts. These can be strangers who hack into a bank or credit card company, or it may be someone you're in a relationship with or someone you've recently left. Without your knowledge, they can clean out your accounts or harm your credit rating. Before leaving or divorcing, be sure to protect all your assets, and keep a close eye on your accounts afterward. (See chapter 12 for more information on safeguarding your finances and credit rating.)

Anytime you do business or store any personal information online, you're at risk of someone stealing that information. Hackers can access public records, break into banks and government files, and take over your identity. Following the safeguards in part II will help keep you safer online. It's also important to keep an eye on your records, bank balances, credit rating, and personal information to see if changes have occurred that you didn't make. Any unusual transactions or records that don't belong to you need to be investigated promptly. Identity theft can take years to clear up, especially if it has been going on for a while.

Most people think of exploitation as a problem with strangers. They believe that if you protect your information (whether online or on paper) from unknown contacts, you'll avoid predators. That's always a wise idea, but you need to be aware that people you know can exploit you as well. Those closest to you likely know your Social Security number, birth date, and other data that can give them access to all your records. It may be that, like Ryker, you've been taken advantage of by someone in your own family.

Ryker's Story

Ryker grew up dirt poor in a home with an abusive, alcoholic mom. His deadbeat dad, who had been arrested multiple times for petty theft and assault, rarely paid child support. At age sixteen, while attending an alternative high school, Ryker got a full-time job, intending to seek emancipation.

He had worked part-time at a neighborhood grocery store for two years as a bagger and proved himself reliable and willing to work hard. The owner hadn't bothered with a background check for the full-time job because Ryker had been a model employee and was willing to work evenings, weekends, and holidays. The grocery store pay wasn't quite enough to cover monthly expenses for an apartment, utilities, and food plus car payments, so Ryker applied for a job cleaning office buildings several evenings a week. Because janitorial employees had access to empty buildings, he needed both state and criminal records checks along with a credit check. His Goth look and nose and eyebrow rings made him appear scary, but Ryker was happy to comply. Although he'd been sent to the alternative school for truancy, he'd stayed out of trouble with the law.

When the records came back, they showed outstanding arrest warrants from several states, three civil judgments against him, and many credit cards in arrears. Ryker was shocked. That was impossible. He'd never been out of the state and never borrowed money. They must have made a mistake. He double checked the reports, and all three had his Social Security number, full name, and birth date. The janitorial company refused to hire him.

Ryker was afraid to go to the police; they might arrest him for the warrants. He hurried to the grocery store, hoping the owner would vouch for him. He pulled up the work schedules for the past year, and on three of the five arrest dates, Ryker had been working. The owner shook his head and said it must be identity theft. Someone was impersonating Ryker, but he had no idea how he could he find out who it was or manage to stop that person.

As Ryker was leaving the store, one of the older cashiers called out to him. Betty was a bit of a gossip, but she had a good heart and always tried to mother him. Between customers, she told Ryker she'd overheard him talking to the owner. Her daughter's ex had stolen her credit cards and stalked her; she'd been helped by SIA. Betty pulled up the information on her phone, handed it to him, and insisted he enter his information on the SIA inquiry form.

RYKER'S SOLUTION

The next afternoon Ryker trudged over to the library before work to check for an email from SIA. He wished he had his own computer, but if he couldn't get this situation straightened out, maybe he'd never own anything—not a computer or the car he'd dreamed about for years. He wasn't holding out much hope that any organization would help him, especially with him being only sixteen. They'd probably need his mother's permission, and she'd never sign anything.

Ryker was surprised to find an email saying that SIA was connecting him with a volunteer in his city, one who happened to be a private investigator. SIA also offered to help him seek emancipation. Ryker couldn't believe they'd do all this for free.

It took almost two years to get the issues resolved. The investigator first had to track down the person who'd stolen Ryker's identity. Whenever they started closing in on the suspect, the illegal activity would cease, only to start up later in another city or state. Each time, the pattern was the same: The criminal opened bank accounts in Ryker's name with a small amount of money and then wrote bad checks. After getting arrested for illegal gambling, assault and battery, or drunken driving, he fled to another town.

Meanwhile, because the credit bureau had Ryker's new address, bill collectors came after him. His phone rang day and night with demands for money. Process servers showed up at his door. When Ryker tried to explain that he wasn't the criminal, the process servers would say, "Yeah, right, kid. That's what they all say. You're served." Letters and notices arrived from police departments, banks, and collection agencies as well as from the government for tax evasion. The SIA investigator helped Ryker file police reports and send notarized statements to all of the credit bureaus and data-furnishing companies, explaining the identity theft, but the warrants and bills continued to pile up.

On one of Ryker's rare days off, he drove to the beach. As he headed home the police pulled him over for burned-out taillights. Because the officer discovered a warrant in his name, she arrested him and had his vehicle towed. No one believed his protests until the investigator arrived to bail him out.

This should have been the happiest time in Ryker's life: He was now emancipated, he'd graduated from high school, the grocery store owner was letting him work overtime hours, and Betty had gotten him a part-time job with a landscaping company. He loved that work so much, he planned to start his own business. For the first time in his life, he ate three meals every day, he'd made enough money to buy a beat-up car, and he even had a computer and stacks of computer games. All his dreams had come true, except one: clearing his name.

A break in the case came when the identity thief managed to get a driver's license in rural Louisiana. An SIA detective in that state followed up on the lead and nabbed the criminal. Finally they had their man, a man who turned out to be Ryker's father.

Once his father had been arrested and charged with identity theft along with all his other crimes, Ryker and the investigator went to work clearing Ryker's name. Now they had the proof they needed to back up their claims. Through the police in Louisiana, they also discovered the reasons behind the identity theft.

After his parents divorced, his father had taken Ryker's Social Security card and used it to avoid paying child support and taxes. But as his gambling addiction and drinking increased, warrants for his arrest piled up. He began his itinerant lifestyle, moving to new cities to stay one step ahead of the law and his creditors. When he was flush he lived well. But more often he was broke. He'd either steal what he needed or use Ryker's name to open a bank account and write bad checks.

Because this had been going on for a while before Ryker discovered it and his father had accumulated so many debts and warrants, the case was complicated. But eventually the investigator succeeded in getting Ryker a clean record.

Ryker's case was one of many that SIA was handling in which teens had been deprived of their identities. Unfortunately, parents stealing children's identities is not uncommon. Parents use children's names to avoid taxes, alimony, or child support. In other cases parents collect death benefits for their children. Because these victims are reported dead, as teens or adults they cannot open bank accounts, get credit, or collect tax refunds if they are working. Like Ryker, many discover that crimes have been committed in their names. And teens are not the only ones who face identity theft.

SIA has worked with a range of victims (many of whom also were cyber-stalked) to find attorneys through the National Association of Consumer

Advocates (NACA). These lawyers will take identity theft cases on contingency. In some cases data-furnishing companies and credit agencies were also sued, and the victims won large settlements.

Because Ryker had filed police reports and sent a notarized affidavit of forgery to the credit bureaus and collection agencies, the creditors and banks should not have been pursuing him for debts that he did not owe. Two collection agencies, in particular, had violated state and federal credit-collection laws by threatening him on the phone. One had even threatened that they knew where Ryker lived and his deadbeat ass was going to get a beating if he didn't pay.

Following SIA's advice, Ryker contacted NACA, and an attorney took his case on contingency. The attorney sued the data-furnishing company, which had continued to give out his information to creditors despite the affidavit, as well as the collection agencies that had used illegal procedures to harass him. Ryker won a settlement, and that helped him completely restore his credit.

Several months later, Ryker walked out of the bank after securing a loan for his fledgling landscaping firm. First he called to thank the NACA attorney and the SIA investigator, and then he went to the grocery store, where Betty and the store owner had a party waiting for him in the employee break room. Ryker continued to work at the grocery store while he built his company and took business management classes at a local university.

Leaving an Exploiter

Exploiters usually use some form of blackmail to keep their victims compliant. It may be emotional blackmail—threatening to reveal secrets or to destroy an important relationship—or physical blackmail, using private photos or other evidence. They also play on the sense of guilt and shame a victim feels. Most victims fear letting others know what they've done. Often they believe they are to blame, that they caused the abuse, or that they deserve to be treated this way. Shame keeps them locked in an abusive relationship. If the relationship is with a family member or relative, the situation is further complicated by the need to keep the family relationships intact, by a sense of obligation, and even by an underlying love for the abuser.

Getting out of relationships with exploiters is difficult because, in most cases, they hold some authority over you or are blackmailing you. Ministers, teachers, bosses, and family members can take advantage of their positions to abuse you. Often you're at their mercy because you have no place to go and no way to support yourself; leaving will only put you in a worse situation.

Reporting Exploitation

If the exploiter is a stranger or someone outside the family, reporting this individual (even if he or she has threatened you) is usually the best option. Don't let the exploiter know you plan to do this, and try to act as normal as possible once you've submitted the report. If there's a way to avoid physical contact, do so. If your main contact has been online, give an excuse for not contacting the exploiter for a while so he or she doesn't get suspicious. Maybe you have a big test to study for, your parents limited your Internet time, or you're grounded for a week or two with no gaming allowed.

If the abuse is sexual, minors can file a report online at the Cyber-Tipline (www.missingkids.com/cybertipline). Run by the National Center for Missing & Exploited Children (NCMEC), the tipline investigates leads on suspected sexual exploitation. The Rape, Abuse & Incest National Network (RAINN) has online resources for children and adults available at www.rainn.org. Counselors at the National Sexual Assault Hotline (800-656-HOPE) can assist with any type of sexual abuse. (Appendix D lists additional resources.)

If you're afraid of repercussions, try to find a safe place to escape from your abuser. Sometimes the exploiter's threats are bluffs, but he or she may turn violent at the thought of being exposed. For minors or others in dependent relationships, getting away may seem difficult or impossible. Try confiding in someone you trust. Perhaps a school counselor, teacher, doctor, therapist, or family member can help you find a safe way out of the situation. Also try domestic violence assistance providers, child protective services, and other support groups in your local area. These organizations may help you find a safe place to stay and offer other protective services. Also contact SIA for support and assistance in planning strategies. Go online at a library and set up a free email account so there's no record of your contact. And delete all records before signing off. Never use a phone or computer that the abuser can access or check.

Minors may find that some organizations require parental permission before providing services; if the abuser is a parent or guardian, this can seem impossible. Ask to be referred to groups that help teens, and keep in mind that SIA has no age limits and does not require parental permission.

Protecting Others

You may be staying in this destructive relationship to protect someone else. Parents may sacrifice themselves for children; older siblings may give in to save younger siblings. In that case, first find a way to safeguard the others' welfare. Contact SIA or another organization to help you develop a plan to take care of yourself and those you love.

One final difficulty can arise when you think of leaving an exploiter. You may care for this person, or deeply love him or her. This emotional bond may make you reluctant to leave.

Loving an Exploiter

It is not uncommon for victims to refuse to leave abusers. They love their abusers and believe their abusers love them. Called *Stockholm Syndrome*, these emotional ties cause people to remain in perilous relationships and endure great cruelty. The name was taken from a famous case in Stockholm, Sweden, where bank robbers held four people hostage for five days. Although the robbers strapped dynamite to their captives' chests and locked them in a bank vault, the hostages wound up fearing the police rescue and empathizing with their captors. After her release one woman started a defense fund for the criminals; another got engaged to one of the robbers. Amazing as it seemed to outside observers, these hostages had bonded with the criminals.

Police officers have reported similar situations during domestic violence incidents. Victims sometimes turn on the officers and defend their abusers. Children's service workers see abused children clinging to their parents and begging not to be separated. People who have left abusive relationships sometimes say, "I know what he did was wrong, but I still love him," or "She was a nasty bitch, but I can't get her out of my mind," or even "He's beating his new girlfriend, but I can't help being jealous of her." Outsiders find it difficult to understand these strong psychological bonds, but it can be a struggle to leave an exploiter you care about.

Stockholm Syndrome

People do not have to be locked up to experience this syndrome. It can occur anytime individuals feel threatened and trapped. If victims or their loved ones are in danger and they have no place to flee and no way to support themselves if they do, or if their abuser is blackmailing them, a natural reaction is to cooperate.

Many exploiters use occasional rewards to increase the feeling of closeness and make victims more compliant. Apologies or flowers follow a beating. Gifts or compliments accompany sexual favors. Hostages receive food or water. These kindnesses stand out in stark contrast to the previous behavior, making victims grateful and leading them to believe the abusers have had a change of heart.

Over time victims come to identify with their exploiters, to see things through the abusers' eyes. Particularly in situations where they have little contact with others, it's easy for victims to accept the abusers' point of view, especially if they see no way out. To protect themselves, they disassociate from reality. Victims bond with their exploiters, empathize with them, and grow to care deeply for them.

Many believe themselves or their actions are to blame, and they make excuses for the mistreatment. Victims point to stress, alcohol or drug habits, financial troubles, overwork, or childhood abuse to excuse the exploitation. They consider their own hurts negligible when compared to the emotional traumas their abusers are enduring.

Do It for Love

If you truly love an abuser and are concerned for his or her welfare, the best thing you can do is leave. Being understanding and compassionate does not mean staying with an exploiter. It means not providing abusers with a target to blame, hit, or hurt. Whenever abusers use you, they avoid facing their problems or getting help for their pain. Psychologists have found that individuals who take revenge or hurt others wind up feeling worse and adding to their internal distress. Exploiters cannot change or lessen their emotional pain through hurting someone else. You aren't helping by submitting to them; you're preventing them from healing. Show your love by getting out of the relationship.

Action Steps

Reestablishing an identity can be a long, time-consuming process, as Ryker learned. It can often be difficult to prove your identity to the authorities' or creditors' satisfaction. Here are several precautionary steps to follow after your credit has been cleared:

- Set up a credit freeze. Request that companies put a fraud alert on your accounts. Add a consumer statement to all credit bureau records that says: *My name is X, and accounts have been opened without my permission using my Social Security number. Do not open accounts without first contacting this consumer at the following phone number: XXX-XXX-XXXX.*

- Try opening a new line of credit to see if the credit bureaus are sending your message. If the creditor opens the account without calling you, contact the credit bureaus again.

- Monitor credit reports every six months to be sure that no old or inaccurate information is included. Even after successful lawsuits against credit bureaus and collection agencies, one or two accounts could reappear. Past information may be inadvertently added when accounts are researched and updated.

- If these companies continue to give out incorrect information after they've been notified of the situation, contact an attorney or get in touch with NACA (see appendix D).

Final Quick Tips

- **Be wary:** People can create any identity they choose online. Safeguard your personal information and use screen names that don't give away your real identity or location.

- **Avoid sexting:** Never post sexy or nude pictures of yourself, not even if the person you're dating begs for them. Remember that whatever you put online will be there forever. And even if you use a site that claims to delete pictures quickly, the person receiving them can snap photos of them and later post them online.

- **Be patient and persistent:** If you've been a victim of identity theft or financial fraud, recovery takes time.

Part II
Savvy Survivor

CHAPTER 11

Don't Be a Victim

If you've reached this chapter after identifying your relationship with one of the personality types, you may need some practical advice for getting out of the relationship. Perhaps you started with this chapter because you want to arm yourself with strategies to keep yourself safe online. Or you've recently left a bad relationship and need to stay safe in the future. Some action steps at the end of the chapter can help you avoid being a cyberstalking victim, and appendix A provides additional checklists, but changing your beliefs about yourself can be one of the most powerful steps in protecting yourself both online and off.

Staying safe is not only a question of following safety measures, it's also an attitude. One of the first steps to avoiding being a victim is to identify your own tendency toward it. If you see yourself as a victim, others will too. Even if you find that you have a victim mindset, you can change it. Once you've accomplished that, you can better protect yourself and avoid dangerous relationships.

Are You a Likely Victim?

How many of these statements are true for you? Using a scale of 0–2, rate the sentences as follows:
0-I never feel this way.
1-I sometimes feel this way.
2-I often feel this way.

____ I'm stuck and see no way out.
____ Life has always been hard for me.
____ I've never gotten a good break.
____ The person I'm with will never let me go.
____ I'm at this person's mercy.
____ I have no money or resources.
____ No one cares about me.

_____ I've been cut off from friends and family.

_____ The person I'm with is more powerful than I am.

_____ I don't deserve any better.

_____ My life sucks.

_____ Nothing I do makes a difference.

_____ I have no other options.

_____ I'm under someone else's control.

_____ Life away from this person would be even scarier.

_____ I can't trust myself to make wise decisions.

_____ I'm not bright enough or strong enough to get away.

_____ Life is gray and depressing.

_____ Sometimes suicide seems the only way out.

_____ Life is overwhelming most of the time.

_____ I'm not pretty enough, smart enough, talented enough, or good enough.

_____ This is the way life is.

_____ There's no sense in wishing for something better.

_____ My needs always come last.

_____ Others' needs and feelings are more important than mine.

_____ Life's a bitch, and then you die.

_____ God (if there is one) never seems to hear my prayers.

_____ I tried praying/asking others for help, but it didn't work.

_____ I have a lot more bad luck than good luck.

_____ Exciting things happen to other people, not me.

_____ Whenever something good happens to me, something awful soon follows.

_____ I can't depend on anyone else.

_____ People can't be trusted.

_____ Dreams don't come true.

_____ If something bad is going to happen, it happens to me.

_____ My problems always seem worse than other people's.

_____ I fantasize a lot but know that what I wish for will never happen.

_____ I rarely get what I want, and if I do, it's soon taken away from me.

_____ In my family I was the scapegoat

_____ I have more life challenges than anyone I know.

_____ Few people know all the things I have to put up with.

_____ Things might work out for other people, but not for me.

_____ If life is a bowl of cherries, I wound up with the rotten one in the bottom of the bowl.

_____ I see no way out of my present situation.

_____ All my life, people have mistreated me.

_____ I feel guilty and ashamed.

Scale

0–8

Your outlook may be tinged with gray from time to time, but overall you avoid a victim mentality. You see options and opportunities where others see challenges. If you're in a relationship with one of the personality types outlined in part I, reading this book has empowered you to take action. You're clear-headed and can come up with a plan, and you know how to execute it.

9–27

You have a tendency to pity yourself and perhaps even blow your problems out of proportion. Instead of looking at what's wrong in your life, try looking at what's right. If you're in a bad relationship, you may spend more time fantasizing about getting out than acting on that goal. You're quite capable of taking action if you don't let apathy stand in your way.

28–42

Life appears hard, and you often struggle to cope with everything that's going wrong. If this is a temporary situation or you've just experienced a great loss, your view may be colored by this sadness. Or you may be trapped in a situation that you need to escape for your own well-being. If that's the case, don't allow negative thinking to keep you stuck. If your mind is too fuzzy to think straight, reach out for help. Having some support as you get out will give you the added strength you need.

43–92

If your score falls into this range, there's a strong possibility you're depressed. It may be situational, meaning that it's tied to a recent sad or overwhelming life event and that your mood and feelings will improve over time. If it isn't recent, then it's important to see a health professional. And if these statements and beliefs are accompanied by suicidal thoughts, call (1-800) 273-TALK (8255) immediately. (See chapters 13–14 for additional help.)

You may see no way out of your situation. Perhaps you've been stuck for a long time. If your total is on the high end, you may have endured emotional, physical, and/or sexual abuse in childhood—a pattern you seem to be unable to break. You may view yourself as worthless and undeserving; you may also be carrying a load of guilt and shame. The world appears sad and depressing because that's the way it has always been. At this moment in time, you may not have the strength or willpower to get out of the situation. Contact SIA or one of the other groups in appendix D. Someone there can assist you with a plan. You do deserve better, and reading this book is the first step to getting there. Making a call is the second.

Moving Out of a Victim Mindset

If you scored high on this quiz, don't despair. It only means you need to work on taking control of your life. You may feel as if you're trapped and there's nothing you can do about the situation. You may be fearful or have nowhere safe to go, no one to turn to, no help, and no money. Although you may feel hopeless, people in your situation—or even worse ones—have escaped.

One of the first steps to getting out of the victim mindset is to realize you are deserving—worthy of happiness, love, respect, and peace of mind—despite what others have told you, and to be convinced that you are not to blame for the abuse. You may have spent a lot of time anticipating others' actions, trying not to anger or upset them, and feeling that if you did, you were at fault. But the truth is that no one deserves to live in fear. There's no excuse for abuse.

You've already taken the very first step toward eliminating a victim mindset by reading this book. And you now know help is available. Begin by contacting SIA or one of the other groups listed in appendix D. The people there have been trained to deal with crisis situations. Most of the hundreds of SIA volunteers and supporters have been in situations similar to yours. They've been abused, stalked, and terrorized both online and offline, so they know what you're going through. If they got out, you can, too. Often when you're in the midst of a bad situation or operating in panic mode, it's difficult to see other options. They can help you explore new possibilities.

Learned Helplessness

Research studies show that when animals are caged or fenced in and receive occasional shocks when they try to get out, they learn to stop trying, even if the door is left open. Circus elephants, for example, are often chained by one leg when they're babies. They quickly discover that no matter how hard they try, they can't pull up the stake that's holding them. When they're adults that same chain keeps them in place, even though they're capable of escaping. They've learned to believe that chains keep them stuck.

Something similar happens to children who grow up in an abusive environment or who live with emotional trauma. They come to see themselves as helpless because when they're young, they are; they have no way out. When they're grown they still believe they have no control over their circumstances because being independent or acting on their own behalf was too painful or even impossible in the past. Thinking they have no choice, they accept the role of victim, never realizing that they now have the power to pull that chain out of the ground and set themselves free.

Beliefs are extremely powerful, and they influence how much control you believe you have over life. Individuals may remain stuck in a situation because they've lived with it for so long that they can see no alternatives. This book is about offering solutions and new ways of looking at situations, and about getting help to get free.

From Victim to Victor

Alexis Moore's story is an excellent example of a victim who learned to take charge of her life. Alexis grew up in an abusive home, and in her early twenties, she wound up in an abusive relationship. It was not until her ex almost killed her that she gained enough courage to flee. Once she did, he stalked and cyberstalked her, which is recounted in the Introduction. Only when she reached the brink of suicide did Alexis finally break free of him and gain the courage to take control of her life.

Your situation might be more desperate than hers; your pain and abuse may be much worse. Right now your cyberattacker may have you living in fear. If your life is threatened, your physical safety is paramount. Follow the checklists in this chapter, chapter 12, and appendix A, and also read chapter 13, which suggests some radical ways to deal with stalking or to escape. Although you may not see it yet, there is a way out of your situation. After you are physically safe, return to this chapter to learn how to avoid being victimized again.

Harper's Story

Growing up the oldest child in a chaotic family, with a father who was a drug addict, Harper learned to mother her four younger siblings. Her mother was in jail, and the parade of women through the house frequently abused her. She did her best to protect the other children from their cruelty. Starting when she was ten, her father made her fulfill his sexual needs whenever he was between women. Harper wanted to run away, but she couldn't leave her siblings. She sacrificed herself over the years to prevent her father from harming her two sisters.

When she got pregnant at sixteen, her father beat her and accused her of being a whore, although the baby was his. She endured his verbal abuse and shaming of her in public, fearful that if she told the truth, child protective services would take her away. As much as she wanted out, she had to protect her sisters. After one sister graduated and the other ran away, Harper set out on her own with her daughter and her brother. She worked as a waitress and did pole dancing on weekends to make enough money to feed them and keep a roof over their heads.

Her boss at the club showed an interest in her, and they began dating. He showered her with gifts and bought her extravagant meals. She always ate only a small portion of them and saved the rest to take home. When Cesar offered her an apartment in exchange for sexual favors, Harper agreed. The new apartment was larger, cleaner, and in a much safer neighborhood. Cesar bought Harper a cell phone, a laptop, a TV, and plenty of jewelry.

Whenever Cesar came to call, Harper's brother took the baby to the park or wandered the nearby mall until Cesar left. Then one evening Cesar asked Harper to service a special customer who'd arrived from out of town. They had their first fight, and Cesar hit and choked her. Fearful for her life and afraid of losing her job, Harper gave in. Soon taking care of Cesar's cronies became a regular occurrence. Harper complained that he was treating her like a prostitute, and Cesar backhanded her and told her she was one—she'd been eager to hook up with him for money.

Next Cesar wanted to tape her sexual encounters; he could make good money from selling amateur porn videos online. Another fight ensued, and this time Harper's injuries were so bad that she required hospitalization. She knew she had to get out. She waited until Cesar was away on a business trip to pack. She pawned the jewelry, found a job at a restaurant in another city, and rented a cramped apartment that smelled of mold.

A short while later, the cyberstalking began. *Get back here, bitch* turned into nasty, obscene texts and emails. Harper had made a fatal mistake: She'd brought along the cell phone Cesar had given her. He terrorized her by sending messages that said he knew where she'd gone that day. She varied her route, but he always knew exactly where she'd been. Cesar had ties to the mob, so his threats to have her killed and her body dumped into the freshly poured concrete of a city building were only too real. New at her job, Harper had made no friends yet, so she walked alone to and from the bus station to get to work. She lived in fear that each step might be her last.

Realizing she had to do something to keep her brother and baby safe, Harper contact SIA. One of the first things the SIA investigator realized was that Cesar was using Harper's phone to track her.

Predators can track victims using the GPS coordinates of the phone with an app that texts that information to them. Cesar may have put the app on her phone early in the relationship to keep tabs on her (jealous individuals are highly likely to do something like this), or he may have installed it remotely after she left, sending the app via email, the same way spyware is installed.

One crafty perpetrator reported his ex-girlfriend's phone stolen and requested updates on the GPS location. The carrier continued to update him, so he was able to track her to her new location.

Harper's Solution

Although Harper followed SIA's advice to get a new phone, Cesar now knew where she lived. Some weekends he parked his car outside her apartment building, while she cowered inside with the curtains drawn, too terrified to run errands. Several times he left dead animals on her doorstep along with notes telling her that's how she'd end up if she didn't return. He also stole her mail, including her bank statements.

The SIA investigator helped Harper set up a sting operation. Harper wrapped her old phone in a fancy package, addressed it to herself, and set it outside her apartment door. The investigator notified a friend who was a cop, and when Cesar took off with the package, they followed the phone signals to track him down. The officer arrested Cesar for petty theft, but they couldn't hold him unless they had more substantial charges, which Harper could provide.

Over the years, she had been privy to Cesar's dealings and had slept with some of the mob bosses. This valuable information could bring down Cesar and several of his cronies. There was only one problem: The city cops were being paid to look the other way. The investigator contacted the FBI because some of the deals took place across state lines. In exchange for testifying, Harper was put in the witness protection program. After a lengthy trial Cesar was imprisoned, and Harper was free.

In a new city thousands of miles from her old life, Harper had a new identity, a new job, and a nicer apartment. Things were going well. Her daughter had started school, and her brother was in the vo-tech program at his new school, learning engine repair. He was also working part-time at a local garage.

Harper, now called Sylvie, had met a new man and enjoyed his attentions. He also loved her daughter, and she was thrilled when he offered to babysit whenever her brother couldn't do it. They talked about moving in together. Then one day Sylvie got sick at work. She rushed home and discovered her boyfriend sexually abusing her daughter.

Sylvie started to call the cops, but he beat her until she screamed for mercy. Then he told her he'd seen porn videos of her and tracked down her real name. If she reported him, he'd make that information public. He was sure the mob would be happy to know where she was. After he left, a shaking Sylvie bundled up her daughter and took her to the nearest clinic. Tears streaming down her face, she told the truth when asked, knowing she was putting her life in danger. She might be a victim, but she would not let her daughter become one.

Sylvie wished she could contact the investigator who'd helped her before, but she'd needed to cut all ties with the past. She did contact SIA, however, and they provided a new volunteer to help her during the arrest and trial that followed. Before Sylvie moved and changed her name again, the volunteer strongly urged her to get counseling for herself and her daughter. Sylvie hadn't listened to that recommendation the last time. She was too ashamed of her past to tell anyone, even a therapist. And she couldn't be totally honest about her past. But she'd see that her daughter got help.

This time Sylvie chose the name Victoria, and determined to live up to her new name, she went for counseling. Following SIA's recommendation, she insisted that no records be kept of the therapy. The SIA volunteer explained that records could be broken into and made public. And in some cases those records are kept in places that are not particularly secure. For her own safety and that of her daughter, Victoria called around until she found a counselor who agreed to her terms.

During counseling Victoria discovered how her childhood abuse had set her up to be a victim. She clearly saw that she had moved from being abused by her father to being victimized by Cesar and then by her latest boyfriend. And her daughter had joined that cycle of abuse. Victoria intended to break out of that old pattern, for both their sakes.

The counselor, Anna, had several techniques that she said were a bit unconventional but she believed would be effective. She began with the Emotional Freedom Technique (EFT), which involves tapping. Anna explained that lightly tapping on certain places on the body can reduce stress and trauma. These points are meridian points used in acupressure, and they not only calm the nerves and reduce the distress signals being sent to the brain but also can also help heal emotions related to trauma.

Following Anna's lead, Victoria mirrored the tapping sequence and repeated phrases Anna suggested. She felt foolish when she did it, but she kept going and was surprised to discover that her anxiety level dropped. Next Anna had her picture her most vivid memory of early abuse, tapping while she did so. Victoria stopped talking when bad feelings overwhelmed her but continued tapping along with Anna. After her emotional distress decreased, she went on with the story. When they were done tapping together, Victoria could think of that particular memory without pain. EFT also considerably reduced her trauma level related to the recent events with her ex-boyfriend. (More information on EFT/tapping can be found in chapter 15, and links to tapping scripts are included in appendix C.)

Anna assured her that this was the first step in freeing herself from the cycle of victimhood. They also worked on some forgiveness techniques to help Victoria let go of anger and blame, both toward herself and toward her abusers. Anna explained that holding onto these negative emotions caused Victoria to subconsciously view herself as a victim and attract victimizers into her life. Victoria also worked on writing a new personal story that moved her from victim to victor. (See the section on mythmaking in chapter 15.)

Releasing Negative Emotional Energy

As Victoria discovered, when you're holding negative emotional energy about events, you can wind up repeating the same cycle. The first step is to recognize your feelings—rage, fear, grief—and own these emotions. Most victims have learned it's not safe to express feelings, and they may have learned to distrust their emotions.

Emotions as Signals

Seeing emotions as flashing warning lights often takes away this negative charge around expressing them. Anger is a signal your rights have been violated. Fear lets you know you're in danger. Sadness may be a sign of unfairness, helplessness, or loss.

Each of these is a valid message informing you that something is wrong. You may have blocked or repressed these emotions if you were unable to express them in the past. Owning your feelings and realizing that they are a reflection of how you view a situation frees you to accept them without judgment.

Acknowledging and releasing feelings is scary, especially if you've tamped them down for years. If you're afraid of what might come up, do it with a trained counselor or a victim support group. Victoria spent some time in Anna's office screaming and raging at those who had hurt her; then she allowed tears to flow that she'd been holding back for years. That brought a deep sense of relief.

Letting Go

In addition to emotions, victims have negative energies tied to these traumatic events, such as blame, self-loathing, guilt, and shame. Releasing the emotions is a start, but it's also important to release the beliefs that the events engendered. Separating the facts from the beliefs is the first step.

Once Victoria had lowered her anxiety and expressed her feelings, she could view the situation more dispassionately. Anna helped her see what the facts were: Her father had sexual relations with her, he fathered her child, his girlfriends hit and screamed at her, Cesar asked her to service his customers, and so on. Each fact was listed without any accompanying judgment as to whether anyone was right or wrong. Although this sounds as if it's letting the abusers off the hook, the intent was to free Victoria from judgments about herself.

Next Victoria listed the beliefs she associated with each fact: My father was wrong; what he did was evil; he had no right to do that; I was bad; I provoked him; it was all my fault; I deserved it; I'm unworthy of love; I'm worse than my mother; if my own father couldn't love me, then no one else will; all men treat me badly. Victoria's list was long, and as she looked at it, she saw that she blamed her father and the men in her life, but her negative judgments about herself were much worse. She also clearly realized that she was repeating the same litany of beliefs in each new relationship.

The beliefs Victoria added to the facts were charged with emotional energy. Anna asked if Victoria was willing to let go of all the beliefs she had added to the story. Together they tapped on these negative beliefs, and when they were done, Victoria burned the list. By releasing these emotional charges and forgiving herself, she removed the shame and pain she'd carried for decades. She also let go of the blame she'd heaped on those who had wronged her.

Understanding the Releasing Process

Victoria worried that she was agreeing that the abuse was acceptable. Anna assured her that this was not the case. Victoria was letting go of all emotions that tied her to the abusers and freeing herself of any power the abusers held over her.

Anna made it clear: *No one deserves abuse EVER, not for any reason. You are not agreeing with or justifying their actions. You may feel sorry for them that their inner pain caused them to hurt you, but that doesn't mean you allow them to do it again. Getting out of their lives and staying out is usually the best solution. If you still care for someone in spite of the abuse, the best thing you can do is to leave and find a way to help them get therapy.*

Once Victoria had cleared the old patterns and released her wounded-ness, she was free to find a relationship with someone who would love her. No longer a victim, she met a wonderful man and married him. He encouraged her to go back to school and get a degree as a counselor. Today, she works with women in abusive relationships. Her clients trust her because she's been in their shoes and she found a way out.

Emotion-Clearing Action Steps

If you're being cyberattacked, you may have endured some abuse in your past that gave you a victim mindset. Clearing that will allow you to think more effectively and strategize. Even if you aren't presently a victim, you can use Victoria's steps to ensure you don't become one or to clear any emotional pain you may have.

- Tap on a specific emotional trauma to release the distress (see appendix C for links to tapping scripts and to illustrations of tapping points).
- Express your emotions about the incident (grief, anger, and so on) in a safe environment. Pretend the abuser is sitting in front of you, mute and paralyzed, if it helps.
- Separate facts from beliefs. Write down the beliefs you formed because of the events. Give yourself permission to release all negative beliefs and reclaim your energy.
- Create a new myth for your life story, one that empowers you and allows you to move on (see chapter 15 for more information).

How to Avoid Becoming a Cyberattack Victim

Here are some action steps that can prevent you from becoming a victim of cyberstalking. They may take a few hours to implement, but that pales in comparison to the hundreds of hours it takes to undo the damage of a cyberstalker.

- **Don't give out personal information offline or online.** Keep your home address, location, names of family members, phone number, and all other identifying information private. Teens, especially, should be wary about giving out any personal details, particularly to any friends they make online.

- **Install spyware protection** and keep your settings high on your firewalls. Be sure the spyware protection is from a reputable company, and be extremely careful that you are downloading it from the company website, not a third party.

- **Create a junk mail account.** Use this for online ordering, signing up for social media accounts, and registering for events. Give it as your contact email to strangers, salespeople, or acquaintances. It will help protect your personal account from spam, hackers, and spyware.

- **Use special screen and email names.** Choose a different name for your social media persona. Making it gender neutral can help keep you safe. Also be sure that your photo doesn't reveal your location or name, or better yet, use an avatar.

- **Do not fill out all the fields when registering online.** If something is not required, don't provide it. Avoid filling in birth dates and locations. Also consider entering safer addresses (for example, a business or school address rather than your home address). If the account you are registering for has no reason to require this information and no need to contact you, you may want to fill it in with *Not Applicable* or *100 Anywhere Street, Anytown*.

- **Guard your email and social media account** logins the same way you do your credit card information. All it takes is one person knowing your login and password for the rest of the world to learn it.

- **Read and monitor privacy policies.** Always read the privacy policies before you sign up for a site. If it has options for sharing information, make sure you opt out of third-party sharing. Many online sites change their privacy policies frequently, so keep up to date on the changes.

- **Watch what you're sharing** on social media, on Twitter, or in chat rooms. Strangers can learn a lot about you by the places you visit, the pictures you post, and the things you enjoy.

- **Ask friends and family to be cautious.** Tell them your concerns about privacy and request that they not post information that violates your privacy. Also give them information about protecting themselves online, so they aren't targeted.

- **Check the privacy policies of your ISP (Internet service provider), cell phone carrier, IM (instant messenger) or IRC (Internet relay chat), and other online services.** Make sure they prohibit cyberstalking. If they don't, change providers.

- **Protect all accounts,** including cell phones, landlines, emails, bank accounts, and credit cards, with secure passwords that would be difficult for anyone to guess. Change these at least twice a year. Do it more frequently if you've ever been hacked or been the target of cyberstalking.

- **Choose unusual answers for your security questions.** Select answers that belong to someone else. Instead of using the name of the street you grew up on, use the street name of your childhood enemy. For the name of your favorite pet, substitute your neighbor's yappy dog. For favorite food, write "peanut butter" if you're allergic to peanuts. Make sure they're answers you'll easily remember, but that other people (even spouses and family members) will never guess.

- **Be suspicious of any incoming emails, telephone calls, texts, or messages that ask for your identifying information.** The caller ID spoof can mimic your bank's caller ID. It is very easy for a cyberstalker posing as a banking representative, a utility worker, a credit card representative, or your cell phone provider to obtain your personal information. Most institutions do not contact you to ask for this information; they already have it. Hang up and call the institution directly to be sure that you were not a target of a cyberstalker.

- **Never give out your Social Security number unless** you are absolutely sure of who is asking for it and why. With your "social" in hand, a cyberstalker has access to every part of your life.

- **Don't open emails or click on links from strangers.** This is one of the easiest ways for people to install keylogger programs, viruses, and other malware on your computer. If a message comes from someone you know, but it has a strange subject line or no subject at all, and it contains only a link, don't open it. Email your friends or relatives to ask if they sent it. If they didn't, their accounts may have been hacked.

- **Conduct an Internet search for your name and phone number every few months.** Be sure nothing damaging has been posted. A cyberstalker may have created social media accounts, web pages, or blogs about you. Only you can stay on top of how your name is being used online. Always do a search like this prior to applying for jobs or colleges.

- **Make your real name unique online.** If someone with the same name as you has a shady reputation or espouses views that are not your own, change your name to make it different. Add your middle initial or middle name, use your maiden name, go by a nickname, or revert to your full name. Make sure everyone knows which person is you, particularly potential employers or others who might be checking your reputation. It will also prevent you from being targeted by someone who is after the other person with the same name.

- **Sign up for Google Alerts** on your name and any screen names/ pseudonyms you use online. You'll receive a message when someone posts something about you.

- **Check your credit reports regularly.** You can request a free copy of your credit report once a year directly from the three credit bureaus: Equifax, Experian, and TransUnion (see appendix D). If you have a reason to be concerned, check the report more frequently. It is worth the additional cost to be sure you have not been a victim of identity theft. You will not damage your credit rating if you obtain a copy directly from the bureaus. Avoid paying third parties to obtain copies of the report because they usually charge more than the credit bureaus, and you'll wind up on another mailing list.

- **Inform your bank and credit companies that no one is allowed to make any changes to your accounts,** no matter what the reason. You can have special instructions placed on your accounts that all changes need to be verified via a call to you first. This is particularly important following a breakup. Even if you are reasonably certain that your former partner is trustworthy, this is a good practice for moving forward on your own.

- **Use only a secure, designated PC for online banking** and other private transactions, if you can afford to do so. Switch to a different device for surfing the web, gaming, and accessing social media. This practice helps prevent you from picking up viruses and maintains a more secure cyber environment.

- **Be proactive if you encounter something suspicious**—a weird phone call, unusual activity on an account, or a dwindling balance that can't be explained by your bank. It could be a cyberstalker, so act accordingly. Change all of your account passwords immediately, close the account and reopen another one, or as a last resort change banks. Check your credit report. Note anything else that appears strange. Document and report all incidents.

- **Have your PC checked by a tech professional** if you're having problems or think you may be a target. If you're experiencing cyberstalking incidents, your computer may have been compromised. Have someone in the know check it for spyware, viruses, and unauthorized hardware.

- **If you think you have a cyberstalker, move fast.** Most people don't take action because they think they're crazy or imagining things. Record incidents—time, place, event. Victims of repeated attacks tend to become paralyzed with fear. The faster you take action and block the attacker's ability to hurt or harass you, the sooner that person will lose interest in the abuse.

If you have a blog, website, professional profile, or business account online, follow these additional steps:

- **Protect your privacy when registering your domain name.** The information you use to sign up is public record and easily obtainable online. Domain proxy services offer some protection but can be pressured or forced into revealing the information. Use a business address, preferably a post office box that does not reveal your home location. And set up an email that is used exclusively for managing the domain.

- **Never discuss private or family business online.** This rule is extremely important for professionals, especially those who are highly visible.

- **Use your work address for correspondence or rent a private mailbox.** Unless people need to come to your place of business or mail items to you, never post your home address online.

- **Create a separate persona** under a different name (for example, your nickname or maiden name) or use a pseudonym for public appearances, if you're a celebrity.

- **Don't post your email address.** Instead, create a simple contact form where people can post and submit their information. It not only keeps your email safe but also allows you the freedom to decide if you'll respond. And you can choose when and how to make contact.

- **Require people to sign up for an account to post comments on your site or blog.** Or activate the option to track commenters' IP addresses. Blogs and websites usually have settings to filter spam, but they can't filter out cyberattackers who are personally targeting you. Most cyberattackers will avoid sites where they can be tracked or identified.

- **Establish a policy for acceptable postings.** Guidelines can help to eliminate negative or flaming comments.

- **Set up an approval process for comments.** Either you or someone you designate should read each comment before allowing it to be posted. Check your comments regularly and delete any that are unacceptable.

- **Use web counters or other free registry dashboard services** to record all incoming traffic to your blogs and websites. This will allow you to identify who is viewing your site, because the registry records the IP address, date, time, city, state, and Internet service provider. These records are useful for marketing, but more importantly, they provide valuable information in the event that your website or blog is targeted by a cyberattacker.

All these steps will prevent you from becoming a victim. If you're already experiencing attacks, the next chapter and appendix A can help.

CHAPTER 12

Thwarting a Cyberabuser

Getting out of the victim mindset and deciding to take charge of your life can be the single most empowering step you can take. Always begin by following all the action steps listed in the previous chapter to secure your personal information and maintain your privacy.

Cyberabuse runs the gamut from simple annoyances to bullying and harassment to cyberstalking and cybercrime, which includes financial and identity theft as well as terrorism and other violent acts. Different methods of defense are needed for each type of attack, and every case is unique, so one solution will not fit all situations. By reading the case studies in part I, you can find a variety of ideas for stopping cyberattackers, and you can contact SIA or some of the organizations listed in appendix D for help.

Be Creative

In addition to obtaining support and assistance from others, devise your own creative solutions. Once you get out of the victim mindset and reclaim your power, you will be amazed at how inventive you can be. Unless the attacker is a stranger, you know quite a bit about this person and can use that knowledge to thwart him or her. Make a list of any weak points, dislikes, and fears. Also list the ways people have stopped your attacker in the past. The goal is to figure out what would upset the cyberattacker most and use that knowledge to stop the abuse. For example, if the attacker thrives on attention from peers, try to prevent the cyberharassment from going viral. If the goal of the cyberabuse is to make you squirm or live in fear, try to maintain an outer calm and poise that will frustrate his or her efforts. If the attacker thrives on secrecy or works in a high-profile industry, particularly one that would frown on abuse, find a way to go public with the information.

These strategies won't always work, and depending on the attacker, they may backfire and cause an increase in the abuse, or the attacker may come up with new methods. It can help to discuss your plans with an SIA volunteer who can help you evaluate how effective the plan may be.

Remember C-S-D-N

No matter what type of cyberabuse you're facing, use the letters C-S-D-N to help you remember the most important steps. This simple mnemonic—based on the initials of the phrase "Cyber Self-Defense Now"—contains the four basic steps for online safety in any situation:

- **C—Call or Contact:** Seek help from 911 or other emergency services, SIA, your service provider, and/or any other appropriate organizations (see appendix D).

- **S—Secure:** Protect your accounts by changing passwords, getting tech help, and blocking the abuser; this also includes taking measures to secure your physical safety, if needed.

- **D—Document:** Keep copies of all evidence; take screenshots, save phone messages, and print out emails.

- **N—Notify:** Report the abuse to authorities, which may include law enforcement, Internet service providers, school principals, teachers, coaches, bosses, and others.

By acting quickly and following these simple steps, you can protect yourself and stop the cyberabuse. Each category of attack needs a different approach, but **C-S-D-N** is vital for any abuse, whether physical or cyber. The sections below detail additional strategies that can help you combat the various forms of cyberabuse.

Cyberbullying

Physical bullying usually leaves behind outward signs, but in cyberbullying those scars are internal. The pain is often not evident until the victim makes the devastating choice to commit suicide. What kids do as a joke or to be accepted as part of the group can have terrible consequences. If you're on the receiving end of teasing or cruelty, you know the pain, the humiliation, the shame firsthand. If you're an observer, you've likely thought about the pain that bullying causes. With the Internet you can't always see the results, so it's easy to go overboard with cruelty. But whether the abuse is occurring online or offline, there's one main rule: **Speak out!**

The number one issue with bullying and cyberbullying is the silence surrounding it. Kids, teens, and even adults who are being bullied don't tell anyone. Their reasons range from being macho to not ratting on others. They may be ashamed of what's happening and not want anyone to know. But the first and most important step is to tell someone.

Break the code of silence. The unspoken rule that you should never snitch on your peers is one of the reasons cyberbullying, and bullying in general, is so rampant. Many people see what's going on. Perhaps some even join the harassment so they don't become targets. But the only way to stop bullying and cyberbullying is to SPEAK OUT. Tell the truth. Let authorities know what's happening. Inform parents, school administrators, coaches, or anyone in charge of the group. If you're afraid of the repercussions, do it anonymously. Send a letter, make a call from a public phone and disguise your voice, or go to the library and set up an email using a fake name. Not everyone will listen, but keep speaking out until someone hears and helps.

If you're a youth who is being cyberbullied:

- **C—Call or Contact:** Tell your parents, teacher, school counselor, or another trusted adult. If the site you're using has a button to report abuse, use that.

- **S—Secure:** Change passwords and security questions. Be sure to block the abuser.

- **D—Document:** Take screenshots, print out emails, and save phone messages. After you have a record, delete the negative messages.

- **N—Notify:** Use this evidence to have social media sites and Internet service providers remove the messages. In some cases they may even block the cyberbully from using their services. Also show this evidence to your principal, school board, coaches, counselors, and other authority figures who can take action to help you; depending on how threatening or severe the abuse is, you may need to inform law enforcement.

In the past some schools or organizations didn't take bullying or cyber-bullying seriously. Their attitude was "Kids will be kids" or "It's all a part of growing up." Few educational systems or groups have that attitude now. With the increasing number of teen suicides, most have strong policies in place to prevent abuse of any kind, either online or offline. Federal policy is mandating that schools institute rules to protect students from being bullied.

If someone else is being bullied:

- **Speak out.** Whether it's you or someone you know who is being bullied or cyberbullied, tell someone immediately. Let people know. Inform the authorities, such as the school principal and administration, a boss, a club leader, or a coach.

- **Don't participate.** Sometimes you know bullying is occurring and you're pressured to join in. Taking a stand against it may be unpopular and may even make you a target, too. If you're not strong enough to just say "No," make an excuse for not participating. Avoid the bullies for a while or find different online activities. There's no excuse for abuse.

- **Don't hit "like" or "send."** If you see a message or picture that will hurt someone, don't like it or pass it on. Instead, respond to the sender, saying you don't agree. Don't get caught up in arguing or judging; just point out that it's hurtful, illegal, or against social media policy. You can word the message so that it sounds as if you care about the bully and want to prevent him or her from getting in trouble. Also send a message to the person being bullied to show that not everyone agrees with what's happening. Sometimes that one message of support can help victims hang on and stop them from harming themselves.

- **Go against the crowd.** Sometimes all it takes is for one person to say "No" or "Stop" or "Let's do something else." It's easier to go along with everyone else if they've singled out someone to bully. Everyone just follows the lead of the person who came up with the idea. Everyone wants to be part of the "in" crowd rather than one of the victims, so it takes guts to step out and say, "I'm not going to participate." You may find that others in the group agree and will join you. Many people become silent but unwilling participants out of fear. When one person has the courage to declare "Enough," others who have been afraid to speak up will follow that lead. Be the brave one, the one willing to set limits.

- **Identify the bullies.** The goal is not to shame or punish them, but to get them help. Many bullies are abused at home, so they need counseling to deal with their own issues. Kids who feel good about themselves have no need to bully others.

- **Educate the group.** Ask to have speakers visit the school, workplace, or organization to talk about bullying. Invite trained experts who can emphasize the effects and consequences of cyberbullying.

- **Get parents and other adults involved.** The more adults who take a stand against bullying and set limits on it, the less likely bullying is to happen. Parents who monitor their children's Internet and cell phone use can deter bullying and detect when their own children are targets.

- **Campaign for antibullying policies.** If your school, job, organization, or sports team has not set a policy for dealing with bullies, push to institute one. Make sure it includes help for the bullies, not just punishment. It should include both online and offline rules.

Additional Strategies

Following all the usual rules can be helpful, but sometimes a little creativity can bring fast results. One teen set up an automatic response to let the bully know her messages were being forwarded to the school principal and the bully's parents.

Here's a sample of the notification Kenley sent: "I'm unable to read or respond to your text [or email] at this time, but copies of your message are being forwarded to Mr. Steven Jefferson at Central High School, Ms. Mahalia Kennedy-Jones, and Mr. Rutherford Jones. They will be in touch with you." Without reading the offending messages, Kenley forwarded them to the appropriate parties.

The autoresponse proved effective. No more messages were sent. If that hadn't worked, she also could have forwarded the texts and emails to local law enforcement, an attorney, and any other authorities the bully might fear.

After following all the suggestions in chapters 1 and 11 for securing her social media accounts, making copies of the posts, and deleting any nasty or cruel comments, Kenley also placed announcements in the header of each account that said, "Due to reports of inappropriate postings, all activity on this site is being monitored. Anyone who posts derogatory or defamatory comments in violation of site policy will have their account terminated (see section 3a of site policy)."

Sometimes messages like the ones Kenley sent will be enough to stop the cyberbullying. Bullies want their peers to laugh with them, but few are willing to have their texts exposed to authorities. Messages like those also have another advantage. Bullies are out for a reaction. In Kenley's case they got no response, which was disappointing.

Online Gaming

Gamers, especially newbies, are often cyberbullied by "griefers," who cheat, taunt, or swear at them. Griefers may deliberately thwart other players or block access to domains. Anyone can be a target, but griefers usually select vulnerable players and exploit their faults and mistakes. In some cases cyberabusers have attacked online characters and even virtually raped them. Because players have their identities tied up in their virtual lives, any of these attacks can be mentally and emotionally devastating.

If you've been targeted, you may be feeling sick or upset from the attack, but if at all possible, try not to react. If they get no response, most griefers will find another victim. Be sure to report all attacks to the site administrators; most gaming sites have acceptable use policies, and these bullies need to be banned from the site. If you feel violated or emotionally shaken up by the cruelty, talk with a trusted adult or counselor.

To stay safe while gaming, it's always best to play with friends you know and trust, only play in private areas, and never add people you don't know. Buddy up with a trusted friend; it's easier for cyberattackers to gang up on a lone player, so having backup helps. And, as with all Internet sites, never share private information, logins, or passwords.

Always remember that people you meet online may not be who they claim to be. As Amy discovered in chapter 10, adults can and do pose as teens, hoping to lure vulnerable victims. One young boy agreed to meet a fellow gamer at a local fast-food restaurant, figuring he'd be safe in public. Although the gamer was older than he'd expected, they hit it off well, and the preteen followed him out to his vehicle under the pretext of seeing an amazing development in gaming. The teen was shoved into the vehicle, pinioned by a man in the back seat, and they drove away. He was forced into a human trafficking ring for two years, until the FBI found him.

Tips for Parents

Is your child being cyberbullied? One of the best ways to find out is to observe his or her behavior. Common signals that someone is being cyberbullied include the following:

- Spending a lot of time alone
- Not engaging in favorite activities
- Appearing listless, sad, withdrawn
- Decreasing Internet use
- Bullying younger siblings or others
- Changing eating habits
- Pretending to be sick to avoid school
- Getting lower grades than usual
- Avoiding friends and favorite activities

If you spot these warning signs, act quickly. In addition to the damage it does to self-esteem and self-confidence, one of the greatest dangers of bullying is that it can lead to suicide. Researchers at the Yale School of Medicine found that "bullying victims were two to nine times more likely to report suicidal thoughts than other children were."[1] Recent studies have shown that cyberbullying victims are much more likely to take their own lives than other teens. Recent news reports of teens and preteens committing suicide as a result of cyberbullying have made it clear that this type of bullying can have tragic results.

The first step is to talk to your children. Open the conversation with a general observation. You might mention that you've been reading a lot

---

1 Yale University, "Bullying-Suicide Link Explored in New Study by Researchers at Yale," *Yale News*, July 16, 2008, http://news.yale.edu/2008/07/16/bullying-suicide-link-explored-new-study-researchers-yale.

about cyberbullying and ask if they know anyone who's experienced it. Sometimes that's enough of an opening to get them talking. If they do tell you about their experiences, listen carefully and don't overreact. If they don't confess to any personal problems, keep the discussion general, focusing on a case study you've read or "friends" they bring up in conversation.

Ask if they have any thoughts or ideas that could help victims cope. Offer your own suggestions and get their opinions as to how effective those strategies would be. Also find out what sites are most popular with their friends. Even parents who monitor their children's phones and Internet usage often aren't aware of the latest sites, so they miss those posts.

Also watch for signs that your teen is bullying someone else. One mom was shocked when school authorities questioned her son about cyberbullying some of his classmates. She insisted she'd checked his phone and Internet accounts on a regular basis. What she didn't know was that her son had Kik and Tango accounts (both cell phone messenger apps) that she had no idea existed.

If you haven't already done so, set rules for using all electronic gadgets, discuss online safety precautions, and take time to monitor what your teens and children are doing online. Some Internet security companies offer parental controls, blocking, and usage information. See what security measures your company has. Also be sure your children know and follow safety rules for online gaming. It can be tempting to play with strangers, especially if the teens' gaming skills outstrip those of their friends, but insist they stick with people they know.

If your children admit to being bullied, make sure they know you'll keep everything they tell you confidential and empower them to seek their own solutions rather than telling them how to handle the situation. Offer suggestions and ask, "Will this work?" Solutions that seem logical to you can cause more harm than good.

Do speak with your children before reporting any incidents. Sometimes when parents stand up for their teens, their children experience even greater harassment. So plan all strategies together. Also consider what might happen to the bully. It's natural to want bullies to pay for the harm they've caused, but if the bully will be hurt or abused at home as a result, try to work with the school counselor and other authorities to stop the bullying without jeopardizing the bully's safety. Many times bullying is a cry for help, and counseling and other measures are more effective than punishment or revenge.

It's also critical to ensure that your children have the emotional support they need. See that they get evaluated and receive counseling, because cyberbullying often affects them more deeply than anyone realizes. The cruel messages can destroy their fragile self-esteem and make them question their value and worth. Parents who thought their children were unaffected or were over the bullying are devastated when their children later commit suicide. Even if the cyberbullying seems mild and ends quickly, don't overlook the emotional impact. Insist on professional help while continually reassuring your children of their importance and of your love.

Cyberharassment

When cyberbullying takes place among adults, it's usually termed cyberharassment. These attacks can be mildly annoying, or they may be so intense they disrupt your career and/or personal life. Cyberattacks can originate with friends, acquaintances, ex-lovers, or even relatives. Strangers also can become cyberabusers. If your harasser threatens or follows you, use the additional strategies found under "Cyberstalking" later in this chapter and in chapter 13.

One form of harassment that is the hardest to combat is **cybervengeance,** which frequently involves revenge porn. Emails with lewd photos can destroy reputations and careers. This type of harassment has been unleashed against politicians and other public figures, and sometimes leads to them leaving office or dropping out of a race. It has cost ministers their pulpits, newscasters their jobs, and spokespersons their platforms. For more information on dealing with this type of attack, see Avery's story in chapter 6.

Dealing with Cybervengeance

Be relentless about getting the porn or humiliating pictures or information taken down; report it to the websites. If you're a minor whose pictures have been circulating, anyone who has the picture on their phone or computer can be charged with possession of child pornography.

You may also want to try this technique to have images removed from people's phones or computers and prevent the photos from going viral. Using an email account other than your own, send a message to anyone who received copies of the photos that says: *WARNING: Law enforcement is investigating the dissemination of pornography. Anyone with copies of photos of a minor will be charged with possession of child pornography, and anyone who forwards them will be charged with distribution of child pornography. Violators will be prosecuted to the full extent of the law.*

If you're an adult and your state has revenge-porn laws (see appendix D), you can post a similar message, citing the law title, number, and date.

Once again, these are the main steps for dealing with cyberharassment:

- **C—Call or Contact:** Let as many people know about the harassment as possible. If it occurs in the workplace, make sure the boss is aware of it. If it is ongoing and interfering with your life or work, contact the resources in appendix D.

- **S—Secure:** At work discuss the situation with members of your IT department. They can monitor the messages and may be able to suggest additional security solutions. This is particularly important if you are being harassed by someone outside the company, as Jennifer was in chapter 3. If you have concerns for your physical safety, follow the action steps in chapter 13 and appendix A for preventing stalking. At home follow all the rules for online safety—changing passwords, security questions, and accounts. Also have your computer checked for viruses, spyware, and other security breaches. Get a new phone number or email account.

- **D—Document:** Keep records of all emails and phone messages. Have a third party collect and verify the messages. This will keep you from seeing them and give you an additional witness to the ongoing problem.

- **N—Notify:** At work send copies to those who are in positions of authority. At home report the activity to the webmasters of the cyber venues where the harassment is taking place. Often the offensive material will be removed and the user banned.

Stopping Cyberharassment

The faster you address the problem, the easier it is to combat it. The following steps will help you protect yourself if you are cyberharassed:

- **Take all harassment seriously.** It's easy to brush off early attempts as someone being in a bad mood or being mistaken. But keep a record of any messages that are cruel, unkind, or contain threats or sexual innuendos. Later these may be needed as proof of an ongoing problem.

- **Take time to think.** Don't overreact or shoot back an immediate response. Consider whether to answer. If you're harassed on the phone, don't respond. Instead say, "Excuse me, I need to hang up now." If the harasser calls back, let it go to voice mail. A natural reaction is to say something nasty on the phone or online, but this could result in your getting in trouble rather than the harasser. Keeping yourself in the role of innocent victim will make it easier to prove that you're being harassed.

- **Let others know.** The natural tendency is to keep quiet about nasty messages, but the more the abuser gets away with the harassment, the more likely it is to escalate. One employee who received several emails from a colleague that were particularly nasty in tone took action by answering one email and copying their boss on her reply. She wrote: *I don't have that particular information yet, but I've copied our supervisor so he'll know that you need those statistics as soon as they become available.* Her colleague, knowing that what she said might end up being copied to their supervisor, immediately changed her tone in future emails.

- **Report incidents to a third party.** If your boss is harassing you, alert his or her supervisor. If your company uses My Safe Workplace, you can report incidents anonymously at www.mysafeworkplace.com or by calling (1-800) 461-9330. (The site also includes international dialing instructions.) All forms of harassment or discrimination can be reported to the Federal Trade Commission's Equal Employment Opportunity counselors at (202) 418-1799 or to the US Department of Labor's Civil Rights Center at (202) 693-6500.

- **Reveal the cyberharasser's identity.** Some harassers hide behind a screen name and avatar. Try to find out who they are. Often the IT department at work can help with that. One reporter, whose articles appeared online, was harassed by several regular readers. She investigated, found out their real identities, and posted their names and pictures online. She also added a message to her signature line on all articles, stating that people needed to use their real identities when commenting and warning that, if they didn't, she would make their identities public. A threat like this may be enough to stop some harassers who hide behind pseudonyms to express their opinions, particularly when their comments are derogatory toward certain ethnic groups, genders, sexual orientations, or political parties.

- **Get a third-party monitor.** Ask for help with documentation. Having a neutral party view and collect the messages can help you avoid being affected by them. Another person will also be better able to judge when the tone becomes dangerous or threatening.

- **Set up an autoresponder.** Most cyberabusers are reluctant to leave messages that might be overheard. If they do, make sure to replay them on speaker phone so that others hear them. If you can time it so a boss is walking by, do so. You can also use the autoresponder strategy suggested under "Cyberbullying," but change the forwarding message to suit your particular situation. Kai used this method to stop her ex-boyfriend from cyberharassing her. Because Bradon was running for city council, Kai put an automatic responder on her phone and email saying that all messages were being forwarded to a reporter at the local news. Bradon stopped immediately because his political career was more important to him than harassing Kai. Be sure the message will be an actual deterrent to the harasser. If the threat to the cyberabuser's reputation and well-being is stronger than the desire to cause harm, this can be an effective way to stop the problem. Be sure to follow up and forward any future messages to the news or whatever authority figure your cyberabuser fears.

- **Counteract the negative.** If, like Nico in chapter 7, someone is flaming you or posting defamatory messages on a site over which you have no control, ask colleagues and friends to balance the messages with positive ones. Be sure your supporters don't engage with the harasser; they should ignore what was said and post only positive messages. Keep going until the positive messages outweigh the negative ones. Often this will spur others to write positive things about you as well. Sometimes seeing that you get more praise each time they criticize you will frustrate harassers enough to stop. If the complimentary posts come from a variety of people and the derogatory comments are from the same source, people reading the messages will conclude that your detractor must be wrong.

Cyberstalking

People who move into cyberstalking are usually extremely vengeful and persistent. In many cases, destroying their victims is more important to them than not getting caught. They're willing to risk their lives to get back at the victim. Threats of law enforcement rarely deter them; many see themselves as above the law. Cyberstalkers may be mentally unbalanced, which makes them especially dangerous.

Cyberstalkers fall into two main categories: those who only use the Internet to keep track of and terrorize their victims, and those who also physically stalk them. The stalkers may issue online threats as well as use electronics to help them locate their prey. If your cyberstalker is physically threatening you, following you, or intimidating you in any way, take precautions for your physical safety and use some of the strategies in chapter 13 to throw them off your trail.

Basic C-S-D-N steps for cyberstalking include the following:

- **C—Call or Contact:** Dial 911 or other emergency services if you're in danger. Let your IT department at school or work know. Alert social media sites and/or the phone company. If the stalking is physical, talk to your local police department, campus security, company security guards, or anyone else who can keep an eye out for the stalker. Also inform your friends and colleagues, so they don't inadvertently give out information that allows the stalker to find you.

- **S—Secure:** Have your computer, phone, and vehicle checked for tracking devices or other data-logging software. Once these have been removed, establish new online accounts and/or change all passwords and security questions. If the stalking is physical, follow the safety precautions in chapter 13 and appendix A. Hire an investigator and use security equipment to protect you and your property.

- **D—Document:** Keep an incident log of all correspondence and contact you have with the cyberstalker. Note the date, time, and details of each incident. As with cyberharassment, ask a third party to document incidents when possible.

- **N—Notify:** Reach out to law enforcement and an attorney, if needed. If the stalking is physical, use the incident log to get a restraining order.

Additional Tips

Search your name online to see what information is available. Several Internet aggregators provide detailed information about people based on their phone numbers, email addresses, and names. Viewers can see your address, an aerial picture of your house, the cost and size of your home, your place of employment, your salary range, your hobbies, your social networks, and names of family members and relatives. Much of this data is free, but paid services give even more detailed information. All of this can provide valuable clues for your stalker.

To protect yourself, find the company's privacy policies and get this information deleted. Spokeo is an example of one of these services. To clear your information there, go to www.spokeo.com, and run a search for your name. Copy the URL of the results page, and then click on the "Privacy" link (bar along lower edge). Scroll down. When you click on the "Opt Out" button, it will ask for the URL. Check your name to see if it's associated with previous addresses. You can clear other family members' data as well. Also do this on other aggregate sites that appeared during your search.

Enlist witnesses. Find friends or coworkers who can back up your story. Include their information in your incident log. Some law enforcement personnel tend to dismiss claims of cyberstalking or may not know how to deal with them. Having witnesses who corroborate your story along with a detailed log will verify that you aren't just hysterical, overwrought, or imagining things.

If the cyberstalking includes financial fraud or changes to your accounts, bills, or appointments, follow the steps listed in the section below (also see Ryker's story in chapter 10). If you are also experiencing physical stalking, see chapter 13 for additional help.

Cybercrime

Sometimes cyberattacks exceed harassment and stalking to encompass criminal acts. These may include online fraud, identity theft, sexual exploitation, and terrorism. If you are dealing with a cyberabuser who is using any of these techniques, you need outside help, including assistance from law enforcement. Again, follow the C-S-D-N steps for cybercrime:

- **C—Call or Contact:** Call 911 or other emergency services if you're in immediate danger. If the cybercrime is sexual and you had physical contact, go to a doctor, hospital, or clinic immediately. Whether the sexual exploitation was physical or online, if you're a minor, call the National Center for Missing & Exploited Children's CyberTipline at (1-800) 843-5678 or file an online complaint at www.missingkids.com/cybertipline. Both youth and adults can contact RAINN for rape, incest, or sexual assaults at www.rainn.org or (1-800) 656-HOPE (4673).

  For financial fraud or identity theft, immediately call financial institutions, credit card companies, credit reporting agencies (see appendix B), and any other parties involved. Set up a credit freeze and fraud alert. Contact an attorney through NACA (the National Association of Consumer Advocates).

- **S—Secure:** Change passwords and security questions, and block the abuser; also follow the steps in chapters 11 and 12.

- **D—Document:** In cases of sexual exploitation, make copies of all photos and videos, print out emails, and save phone messages. If you met in person and had any sexual contact, list those incidents. In cases of financial fraud or identity theft, keep copies of all records, get notarized statements, and secure proof of your identity.

- **N—Notify:** Report all cybercrime to the police. Continue to stay in contact with the agencies that are dealing with your case to update them on any new developments. If needed, hire an investigator to track down the criminal.

In cases of consumer fraud, file a complaint with the Federal Trade Commission (www.ftccomplaintassistant.gov). Outside the United States, complaints can be filed at econsumer.gov. Also report online scams to your state attorney general (www.naag.org/current-attorneys-general.php).

If the cyberabuse has crossed state lines, the FBI may need to investigate, depending on the severity of the crime. File an online complaint with the Internet Crime Complaint Center (IC3), run by the FBI and the National White Collar Crime Center (www.ic3.gov/complaint).

Additional Steps for Financial Fraud and Identity Theft

If the cybercrime involves monetary or identity theft, you will need to take several additional steps to combat it. Use the following checklist to protect your finances and reestablish your credit.

- **Switch banks.** This prevents the cybercriminal from gaining access to your account. It also allows you to start fresh with a clean record.

- **Have all account information sent to a safe location by mail.** This may mean renting a post office box or using a friend's or relative's address if your attacker is monitoring your mail or has access to it. Do not give out an email address, even a brand-new one, in case the criminal has access to your computer.

- **Have all electronics scanned** for spyware, viruses, keylogging, or other software that would allow a cybercriminal to collect your information.

- **Report all credit cards stolen and notify all creditors.** The credit card issuers should send new cards with new account numbers. Use a different email address, password, and security questions. If the cyberabuser has access to your mail, be sure to have cards mailed to another address—a post office box or a friend's or relative's house.

It's better to keep the account open with new contact information, because closing it can negatively affect your credit score.

- **Set up a fraud alert on every account.** This alert should state that absolutely no changes are to be made to your account without first calling you at a certain number. No one, even those who call in and have all the account information and can answer the security questions, should alter the information. After you've done this, try calling the various accounts to see if they're implementing the alerts. If they aren't, switch to a different company, if possible. If it's not possible, ask to speak to someone in authority. Move up the chain of command until you get someone who will ensure that security procedures will be followed. Having a lawyer or law enforcement contact them can also reinforce the seriousness of the situation.

- **Constantly monitor all accounts** as well as your credit rating and bank statements for any changes you didn't make.

- **Be patient and persistent.** Of all the crimes, financial fraud and identity theft take the longest to clear up. Problems may haunt you long after the perpetrator has been sentenced. Credit reporting companies receive old data and reenter that faulty information in your file. Some of the creditors who were defrauded may refuse you credit based on previous history. And the old records may be on file in places you didn't notify. It can take years, sometimes even a decade, before your financial history is clear.

CHAPTER 13

Staying Safe in Dangerous Situations

Cyberabusers can be divided into two categories: those who operate solely via electronic means and those who use electronics to physically target or track victims. Cyberattacks may escalate to physical stalking. The stalker uses phones, computers, and other electronic devices as weapons. If your cyberattacks have moved from virtual to physical, you'll need additional means of protection. The most important steps are to stay safe and elude the stalker.

Try the tips used by Jennifer in chapter 3 and Sage in chapter 9. Think about your safety at all times: Avoid poorly lit, isolated areas; establish safe zones; travel in groups; install surveillance equipment; vary your daily routines; take different routes to work and appointments; learn self-defense techniques; and keep a log of all encounters with your stalker (see appendix B). Continue to report all incidents to law enforcement. If the stalker has hurt or abused you in any way or is using technology to stalk you, get a restraining order (see appendix D).

Begin with What You Know

If you already know your stalker, you are at an advantage in several ways. First of all, you know what this individual looks like; it's easy to pick him or her out of a crowd, so you can tell when you're being pursued. Second, you know the places your stalker frequents, and you can avoid those. You may know your pursuer's work hours and schedule. All of this information can be valuable. Spend time writing down everything you can. Include the stalker's relatives and friends, their addresses and contact information as well as the stalker's, his or her extracurricular activities and acquaintances, employment history and colleagues, car make and model, favorite restaurants and activities, and any other personal details, along with a detailed description, any pictures, and credit card/bank account/Social Security number if known.

You may have one additional advantage. If you've dated or lived with this person, you know a lot about what motivates him or her. Add this information to the file. Often this knowledge will spur ideas for slowing or stopping the predator. It also gives you insight into character and motivation, which means you can more easily predict the stalker's patterns, thoughts, and plans. You know what upsets him or her, and how far this person will go. All of this can help you plan your strategy.

Collect all the information in a file or keep it online. Give a duplicate copy of this information to at least one person you trust. The police or an investigator will find these records invaluable. And if something happens to you, the file will be useful for tracking down the perpetrator.

If you're being stalked by a stranger, find out as much about this person as you can. Hire an investigator to gather data, and keep track of any details you discover, including email addresses, phone number, and the times that stalking usually occurs. If the stalker sends gifts or letters, try to trace them back to the sender. Sometimes even the slightest detail can provide clues to the person's identity. Putting a face and name to the faceless entity stalking you makes it easier to protect yourself. The more you know about your stalker, the more easily you can elude him or her.

Foiling a Stalker

Stalkers are devious, so you need to be even more wily to stay one step (or more) ahead. If the stalker frequently shows up at places you're going but doesn't seem to be physically trailing you, it's likely he or she has access to your phone and/or email accounts. Begin by changing all passwords. Also try making plans with friends using a different phone (calling from work or a relative's phone) and opening a new email account on someone else's computer or at the library and emailing from there.

Turn all electronics over to an experienced tech and take your car to a mechanic. Tracking devices on your car, a GPS locator app on your phone, and keylogger software on your computer can give the stalker access to your movements. Removing these along with frequently changing email and other passwords can help you keep your location secret.

Not all stalkers are easy to escape; some have access to other sources of information, as in Alexis Moore's case.

Alexis Moore's Story

When Alexis fled from her abuser, he stalked and cyberstalked her relentlessly, bent on revenge. As a skip tracer who tracked down debtors and fugitives, he had access to databases and information that allowed him to trail her every movement. Using his contacts and skill, he drained her bank account, closed out her utilities, cut off her insurance, turned off her phone, canceled her appointments, bought things using her charge cards (sinking her into debt), and harassed her at home and work. She lost two jobs after he cyberharassed her colleagues and supervisors; friends and family avoided all contact with her after he threatened their lives. Bill collectors sent by her ex, some brandishing guns, pounded on her door day and night.

But nothing compared to the terror of her ex's phone calls describing what she was wearing and where she was standing right that minute. Her ex had told her repeatedly that he'd have someone throw her in the trunk of a car and tow the car to his father's scrap metal business. There they'd crush her inside the car and add it to the salvage piles, and no one would know.

Alexis knew he was capable of it; he'd almost killed her when they lived together, and several times after their breakup, cars had attempted to run her off the road. She needed to throw her ex off her trail, but with his access to all her personal information, that seemed impossible. Using her creativity, she came up with a plan to confuse her predator—the red-herring technique.

Red-Herring Technique

In mystery stories red herrings are clues that distract or mislead readers. They cause readers to jump to false conclusions. Determined to make her own life a mystery to her ex, Alexis employed this new technique to redirect the stalking.

Knowing that her phone records, emails, and credit information were in her cyberstalker's hands, she created a fake life. She played tricks on him so he could never be sure he had the right information on her whereabouts. She frequently called phone numbers that had nothing to do with her life or plans—doctors' offices she didn't plan to visit, hair salons she didn't use, attorneys she didn't know, restaurants she never intended to frequent. She applied to rent apartments she would never live in and requested credit cards she would never use. This way, her ex didn't know where she was all the time. He had no clue. Constantly following wrong leads kept him busy and frustrated. Meanwhile, Alexis used prepaid disposable phones to make her real appointments.

But she was still trapped, never knowing if or when her ex might choose to attack. For all she knew, he might get so angry that he'd break into her apartment and drag her off. And her life was a mess. Friendless, penniless, jobless, and depressed, she struggled through her days.

She stayed confined to her small apartment most of the time. Formerly an avid jogger, she gave up her daily runs. Too frightened to attend classes, she applied to finish her college degree online. Her social life nonexistent, she was gaining weight, and she was miserable.

She'd made stalking difficult for her ex, but he'd made life even harder for her. The years stretched before her, a desolate, unbearable life with no way out. She couldn't go on like this. She even considered suicide (see chapter 14). Then an opportunity came her way that would offer her a way out, although she didn't realize it at the time.

Speaking Out

Despondent, Alexis sat watching TV; the grim news stories flashing past matched her bleak mood. Then the local station aired a plea from an assemblywoman who wanted abuse survivors to support legislation she wanted to introduce. She asked to meet with victims who were willing to speak out against domestic violence. The request seemed aimed directly at Alexis, but if her ex learned of her plan, he'd put an end to it—and to her.

Although it meant putting her life at risk, she had to do this. She had to speak out, to tell the truth of what life was like for victims. Even if she couldn't help herself, perhaps she could help others. Trembling, Alexis picked up her latest disposable phone and dialed.

Although she'd used the red-herring technique to lure her ex in the opposite direction, Alexis drove to the briefing, hands clenched on the wheel, petrified that any minute her ex's vehicle would appear in her rearview mirror. She didn't know her way around downtown, so she'd have trouble getting away. Vulnerable and exposed in the parking garage, she regretted coming. The only thing that kept her going was the thought that her testimony might convince lawmakers to protect victims.

Reaching onto the seat beside her, she lifted the thick file on her stalker. She'd brought all her incident logs, police reports, and the other data she had gathered. Palms sweaty and heart pounding, she hugged the files to her chest, knowing they'd do little to stop a bullet.

Alexis and another survivor told their stories at the assembly hearings, but the other woman refused to take the podium at the press conference afterward. Glancing around the room at what seemed like hundreds of news cameras, all Alexis wanted to do was hide. But she knew she had to speak out and take back her life, or she would live in fear forever. In a shaky, hesitant voice, she recounted her story.

Afterward one of the police officers told her, "Today is probably the luckiest day of your life. Nobody will ever forget you. All of those news cameras in the press room have your story, and they know your name. Most predators, they want easy prey—you are no longer easy prey."

Alexis didn't realize it then, but she'd taken her first step that day toward becoming a leader—a leader in the movement to encourage everyone to speak out and not be afraid. And she'd also established a new strategy for stalking victims, a technique she later dubbed *hiding in plain sight*.

Hiding in Plain Sight

For those with a strong presence in the community, hiding in plain sight provides an option to remain visible and connected while neutralizing the stalker. Over the next few years, Alexis leveraged that initial TV appearance into dozens of interviews on TV as well as in magazines and newspapers. People recognized her face and knew her story.

She made a name for herself in her community, in her state, and across the country by speaking out on behalf of victims. She worked with law enforcement and lawmakers around the nation to change laws to protect those who were abused, stalked, or cyberstalked. Her message gradually took hold, and laws were passed to help others who were trapped as she once had been.

Her ex continued to harass her online, and he attempted to sue for defamation of character. But the power had shifted. Alexis set up an answering service and directed all messages he sent via phone or email into her ever-growing incident file. Eventually, the messages tapered off when her ex realized she was unaffected by them. With law enforcement knowing his name and face, it was unlikely that he'd hurt her. If he did, everyone would know where to look.

Later, Alexis helped an aspiring political candidate use this technique to free himself from the grip of a persistent stalker and cyberstalker. She encouraged Alejandro to do what she had done for the past few years—get his face and story out to the press.

Alejandro's Story

After Alejandro ended a relationship, his ex-girlfriend Cassia wrote disparaging comments about him on social media and took out ads in the newspaper, attacking his integrity. Her smear campaign was costing him his career, and soon he was trailing far behind the other candidates. Cassia even followed him on the campaign trail and stood up in public meetings to challenge him, trying to damage his reputation.

About to drop out of the race, Alejandro contacted SIA, and they suggested he go public about the situation. Alejandro preferred to appear strong and in control, but at this point he had nothing to lose, so he called a press conference.

Alejandro had expected negative press following his announcement of being stalked and cyberstalked. Instead he was shocked at the groundswell of support. Reporters interviewed him about the situation. People picked apart Cassia's messages on Facebook and in the ads; many left supportive posts or pointed out flaws in her information. As the media dug deeper into the story, they tracked down Alejandro's colleagues, college professors, and others to get more information on Alejandro, and all of them had only good things to say. The media investigation kept Alejandro's name in the public consciousness throughout the campaign. Soon his cyberabuser, whose reputation and credibility were torn apart by the press, moved to another state to escape the notoriety, and Alejandro won the election by a landslide.

Going Black Ops for Greater Threats

The hiding-in-plain-sight technique works well with stalkers who care about their reputations, are fearful of being caught, or can be hindered by public opinion. Some stalkers, however, care little what others think and are driven by rage so great that they'll stop at nothing to destroy their victims. They may have personality disorders or are so consumed by fury or the need to control that they will even kill.

Abusive spouses, scorned lovers, or vengeful employees intend to make the victim pay, even at the cost of their own lives. They're on a mission to kill and destroy; prison is no threat. If your stalker is in this category, you may fear for your life if you escape. Going black ops may be your only choice for survival.

Used only in the most dangerous situations, going black ops means taking on a whole new identity. Choosing this method of escape is always a last resort, and you must be certain you're ready. You must leave behind everything you own and everyone you love to start a new life with a brand-new name, so it's usually only done to prevent homicide. The black-ops approach requires as much determination and passion as hiding in plain sight, but with the caveat that you will be starting over from scratch. If your life is at risk, however, it may be your only option.

Gideon's Story

Gideon, an art show director, evicted a woman from the apartment building he owned. Zoe was furious and cyberstalked him. It began with hang-up calls, nasty emails, and rumors that he'd made sexual advances. Gideon ignored all of it, assuming it would soon go away on its own. Instead it got worse. Much, much worse.

Zoe tracked him via his art gallery's online calendar and traveled to every event to make his life miserable. She also hired private investigators to trail him and take pictures for her, claiming she was upset by her lover's infidelity. Then one night, after an art opening, she shot him twice as he exited the gallery.

Gideon survived and testified against her, but the jury did not find her guilty of attempted murder. Instead, she was convicted only of a misdemeanor, which meant she spent no time in jail. After the trial she told the news media that she was the real victim and fabricated a story of his abuse, making him out to be the guilty party.

Her emails and phone messages grew more irrational, and her veiled threats indicated she planned to finish the job this time. Going out in crowds and taking all the usual precautions for stalkers were no help for Gideon. He lived in fear, never knowing when she would strike again.

While he was recuperating he read a magazine article about identity changes and contacted the author, Alexis Moore. SIA helped him go underground with a changed name and a new Social Security number. Gideon sold his property, moved to another state, and had plastic surgery to change his appearance. He lost everything—his career, his MFA degree, his credit rating, all his friends and art contacts. He can never contact his father or sister again, and he had to start over in a new job without prior experience or qualifications. Yet he was willing to give up everything to stay alive.

Life-Changing Decision

Going black ops is a serious decision with far-reaching consequences. For those who have to leave family members behind, it can be gut-wrenching. Making this choice means never seeing or contacting them again. It might mean not watching nieces and nephews grow up. Not being present at your parents' deathbeds. Never knowing if your best friend married or had a baby.

It means losing years of experience and training at a job and needing to start over at a menial level. Everything from college to medical school degrees is wiped out in an instant. It means retaking a driver's test, having no credit rating, having no "next of kin" to fill in on applications. Having no medical records, prescriptions, health insurance.

It is used only as a last resort. But if you must choose between losing your possessions or losing your life, go black ops.

Tips on Going Black Ops

Many victims have utilized the black-ops approach and are living abroad or in new locations within the United States. Changing your identity requires the support of law enforcement, prosecutors, advocates, and public officials. (See appendix D for information on contacting the Social Security Administration and other advocates for assistance.)

Be aware that black ops is not foolproof. In this cyber age, determined predators or skilled hackers may break into government records and protected databases. It's also possible that credit bureaus and other agencies may comingle credit records from your past and present, which can open you up to accusations of identity theft.

If the Social Security Administration (SSA) denies you a Social Security number change, citing "lack of ongoing abuse," appeal this decision by engaging your local political representative, assemblyperson, or senator. Bring your documentation and seek their support in forwarding your application to SSA along with their recommendation. More than half of all abuse and stalking victims are denied a Social Security number change on the first attempt. Don't be discouraged; continue to reapply and pursue your goal until you have the tools you need to become a survivor.[2]

---

2 Asking public officials to intervene on your behalf is a good option whenever you run into a problem with law enforcement, prosecutors, or any agency as you're trying to protect yourself from stalking or cyberstalking. Most officials are willing to help constituents, in the hopes of getting reelected.

CHAPTER 14

Dealing with Depression and Suicide

The emotional trauma of dealing with cyberstalking or stalking can leave you exhausted and depressed. So can the related problems of broken relationships, lost jobs, and damaged reputations. Maybe you can't face another day of relentless bullying, cruel taunts, and terrorizing threats; maybe you've received messages telling you that you should die. When you can't see any way out, sometimes suicide appears to be the only option. If you are considering suicide, please call or contact someone immediately. And take some time to read this chapter. Perhaps it will give you a glimmer of hope in the midst of your unbearable pain.

In the United States: **1-800-273-TALK (8255)**
National Suicide Prevention Lifeline
www.suicidepreventionlifeline.org
1-800-SUICIDE (784-2433)
National Hopeline Network
These toll-free crisis hotlines offer twenty-four-hour suicide prevention and support. Your call is confidential.

Outside the United States: Contact the International Association for Suicide Prevention (www.iasp.info) or Suicide.org for a helpline in your country.

Many people who are being stalked or cyberstalked think about taking their lives. Alexis Moore was one of those people. Today she has an international business helping people recover from abuse, stalking, and cyberstalking. But she was once a victim herself, so she knows what it feels like. What many people don't know is that when her life reached rock bottom, Alexis chose to commit suicide. She couldn't go on. There was nothing left for her. She'd escaped the physical abuse but couldn't endure the ongoing stalking, the loss of jobs and friends, the terror of being hunted. She had no way out.

Unless she took action, her life would remain in a downward spiral forever. The action she chose was to end it all.

Alexis's Suicide Attempt

After learning that her beloved grandmother was dying of cancer, Alexis reached the darkest point in her life. She had nothing left to live for. When she'd fled her ex, she'd left behind her two dogs, her car, her job, and her friends. Since that time, her ex's cyberharassment had cost her two jobs, destroyed her credit rating, cut off her utilities, and drained her bank account. She had no money to pay bills, and bill collectors, some brandishing guns, were hounding her day and night.

Everyone had abandoned her except for her grandmother. Friends and family wouldn't risk their lives to spend time with her. The lawyers she'd hired to fight her ex quit when they received death threats. Her ex had also threatened to kill her, so she lived in constant fear. Alone and trapped in a never-ending nightmare, Alexis could see no escape. Suicide appeared to be the only option.

The phone rang incessantly in the background, but she paid no attention as she prepared to die. While she sat on her bed with a bottle of pills and some vodka, someone pounded on her door. Again, she ignored it and unscrewed the cap on the pill bottle. Outside her bedroom window a face appeared. A former work colleague, aware of how despondent she'd been over her recent job loss, had panicked when he couldn't reach her by phone. Now he was signaling to her to let him in. When Alexis didn't respond, he started removing the window screen. Her plans interrupted, Alexis let him in.

Her rescuer sat beside her on the couch. He didn't do anything special, only listened without judgment. That was all she needed. After talking for hours she realized she'd been about to give up her life for her stalker. That made her angry, and she determined to do whatever she could to beat this predator rather than be his prey. Once she made that decision, she never looked back.

That simple decision set her on a path to a future she could never have imagined. When she made the choice to overcome stalking and cyberabuse, she had no idea how she'd accomplish it. She still had nothing—no money, no job, no resources. Only her determination.

That proved to be enough. Alexis had no idea that someday she'd be helping victims from around the world. If anyone had told her that in a few years she'd be a sought-after speaker and expert, she never would have believed it. At that time she was terrified to leave her house or to go out in public. She had no reason to think that she'd soon be stepping onstage to speak to thousands of people, giving TV interviews, or contributing to magazines.

Instead she focused on taking charge of her life. One step at a time, she fought her way free. She developed strategies that have helped thousands of other victims escape from abusers, stalkers, and cyberstalkers. And by telling her story, she has saved countless people from committing suicide. Her message to anyone who only wants to end the pain is this: Tell someone first.

Tell a trusted friend, a relative, a colleague, or a neighbor. If there's no one you can trust, call a hotline. Don't hint around. Speak the truth; say what's in your heart. Talking saved Alexis's life, and it could save yours.

Seeds of Greatness

Most people only want the pain to end; they don't want to die. Your life is precious, and you have no idea what your future will hold. You may not see your potential or the gifts you will someday give the world, but others can.

Like Alexis, you too have seeds of greatness buried in your life, although you may not realize it. Alexis thought she had no future. But that awful moment in time when she'd reached her lowest point turned out to be her greatest asset.

You may have reached your lowest point, the winter of your soul. Your seeds of greatness, like the seeds of all plants, need time underground in the darkness before they germinate. Everything may appear bleak, but it is only part of the greater cycle of life.

That low point in Alexis's life allowed the seeds to sprout into what eventually became her greatest gift to the world. Deep inside you, a seed is buried. A seed that one day will become *your* greatest gift.

It may not feel like it now, but you and your life matter to others—if not in your present situation, they will in the future. You may have more than you can cope with right now. Reaching this point doesn't mean there's something wrong with you. Perhaps you have no support, nowhere to turn, and the pain seems endless. Suicide will end the pain, but it also will end your precious life—and that beautiful seed, your great potential, will be lost to the world.

It may take courage, more courage than you believe you have right now, to reach out for help. But if you do, you will be giving the world a gift. If you don't believe this is true, imagine telling someone who loves you that you're about to commit suicide. What would his or her reaction be?

Your life is so important that if you told perfect strangers your intentions, they'd try to stop you from dying. Because your life matters. People have climbed out on ledges to talk down jumpers. They know the jumpers have much to offer the world. And you do, too. Someday you will look back on this moment and be glad you chose life.

Reasons People Choose Suicide

People commit suicide for reasons as varied as the individuals themselves, but they may be motivated by one of the following factors. Whatever their motives, they all have an underlying need—to end their pain—and they see death as their only means of escape.

Feeling Overwhelmed and Hopeless

Often cyberabuse reaches the point where victims feel so much despair that they lose all hope. They may feel they're alone in the world and that no one cares. Some see themselves as a burden to others and think everyone would be better off if they were dead. Perhaps that's how you've been feeling.

At this moment your life may not seem valuable or even worthwhile, but that's only because you cannot see the future. You have no idea what your future holds. People who have reached the bottom usually have the greatest empathy for others and go on to do amazing things. Even if you can't believe this is possible in your situation, it can happen. In fact, quite a few famous authors, artists, inventors, and movie stars attempted suicide early in life. Think how much richer they made the world by choosing life.

Shame and Humiliation

Few people can handle facing others after they've been humiliated or been exposed online. The natural reaction is to hide, to not show your face in public, to become a recluse. The ultimate way to hide is by taking your own life. The sad thing is that suicide is permanent, whereas humiliation isn't.

If you've done nothing wrong, then be proud of yourself. Remind yourself that the one at fault is your abuser; you have no need to be ashamed. If you've done something that violated your own moral code, try to forgive yourself, or if your religion has a ritual or prayer for forgiveness, use that. Everyone is worthy of forgiveness, including you.

DEALING WITH HUMILIATION

If you're feeling worthless and useless, ashamed and humiliated, get angry. Not at yourself, but at the people who have done this to you. Often that's enough to change your entire mindset. Determine not to let them win. If they do, they'll do it again and again. You have the power to stop them. If you can't do it on your own, call SIA or another self-help organization. Let them take on the battle with you.

Suppose you'd never read those messages, you didn't know they existed, you had no idea those pictures had been passed around. How would your life be different? Try writing about this using the journaling methods described in the next chapter.

Put the situation in perspective. Who are the people who are making your life miserable? Should they have the power to control your life? What have they done to deserve the right to hurt you? Are they really better than you, especially deep down where it counts? Do you have to accept their assessments of you?

Project into the future. Five years from now, will anyone know who these bullies are? Will you even remember them or have any contact with them? Will these incidents still affect you? You never know where you'll be in the future. Someday you may be in a position to deny the bully something important—a job, a loan, or an autograph.

One movie star admitted that while she was growing up, she'd been mercilessly bullied by a gang of girls who mocked her and had beaten her up in the school restroom. Years later, after she was famous, she was in a restaurant when two of those bullies approached her for her autograph. Now the power was reversed, and she reminded them of what they'd once done to her. She could even choose to deny their request.

Check your posture right now. Are you slumped, curled inward, hanging your head, biting your nails? Shame results in physical reactions: curling up, averting the eyes, hiding. Even small children, when they feel ashamed, cannot meet someone's eyes, so they often run and hide. Embarrassment makes us want to pull the covers over our heads, to cower.

Take the opposite position: Stand up straight, shoulders back, head held high, looking straight ahead. Imagine meeting the person or group who's abusing you while you're in this position. See yourself meeting their eyes and saying, "I have nothing to be ashamed of; the one who should be ashamed is you." Practice claiming your power.

Chances are if you're reading this book, the cyberabuse or stalking isn't occurring right at this moment. Yes, your cyberattacker may be posting new messages right now or your stalker may be trying to track you, but right at this moment in time, you're *here*, not there.

With the computer turned off, the only place those messages or photos exist is in your mind. If they're bringing you pain right now, it's because you're torturing yourself with the memories, imagining what others are thinking. Erase those thoughts from your mind by concentrating on the present.

Breathe deeply and concentrate on how your breath moves in and out of your body. Mentally tense and then relax every muscle group in your body from your toes up to your face and head. Pay attention to the details around you. Count the veins on your plant leaves or study the weave of your clothing, trying to isolate each tiny thread. Find something you love or something beautiful and examine it closely.

Fear and shame can't exist simultaneously with deep concentration on something you love. These emotions aren't real; they don't exist in this moment, because right now, you are safe. Practicing this mindfulness can help you learn to appreciate how often you are free from your stalker and cyberattacker.

Even if your cyberabuser sends ten messages in an hour and they each take two minutes to read, in an hour you'll have spent twenty minutes on them. What did you do with the other forty minutes? Worry about how many more messages the cyberattacker would send? Think negative thoughts about this person? Feel sick thinking about all the people who have seen the messages? Cringe in embarrassment?

Why not pull your forty minutes of attention away from the cyberabuser and use it for something that's important to you? Once you start practicing this regularly, you'll reclaim huge blocks of time that previously were lost to negative thoughts. Count how many letters are on this page, or count your blessings, a challenge that can keep your mind occupied for a long time.

Mindfulness has an additional benefit beyond soothing you. It allows those fight-or-flight hormones to dissipate, leaving you calmer and more creative, and better able to generate solutions. You'll also find that the less you think about your attacker, the freer you'll feel.

PTSD and Depression

Many victims of cybercrime or stalking report an ongoing sense of terror, nervousness, sleep disturbances, fear of being alone or in dark places, jumpiness, and inability to relax—symptoms associated with post-traumatic stress disorder (PTSD). Although PTSD is often associated with returning military personnel, it can affect anyone who has been through a severe emotional trauma, particularly if it involved the threat of injury or death. Continual cyberattacks have the same effect on the body and mind as physical threats; the constant fear and tension take a toll on both mind and body. Often these symptoms persist long after the situation ends.

As a victim, you live with trauma and fear. To combat the perceived danger, your body prepares to defend itself by flooding your system with chemicals so you can stay on high alert. Usually when adrenaline courses through the body in response to a dangerous situation, it provides a much-needed boost of energy, enabling you to run faster or fight harder to escape. Once the situation is over, your breathing calms and your heart rate returns to normal. Gradually, the chemicals that allowed you to deal with the emergency dissipate, and your body relaxes.

If the attacks are ongoing, however, your body never returns to normal. You remain in that state of high arousal, on constant alert, with fight-or-flight chemicals flooding your body continually.

Sleep is one of the ways your body and mind process and heal from traumatic experiences. If you are unable to sleep or are restless during the night, your brain has less time to work through the distress. Over time lack of rest takes a major toll on your body. Negative emotions increase, causing the release of large amounts of stress hormones, leading to anxiety, weight gain, depression, digestive upsets, and memory problems. Stress can also suppress the immune system, making it more likely that you'll get ill.

Depression drains you physically, emotionally, and mentally, leaving you with little energy to act. You feel listless and apathetic, as if nothing matters. This lethargy is usually accompanied by a sense of helplessness and hopelessness. Life seems overwhelming and difficult, and everything looks bleak.

OVERCOMING DEPRESSION

If your depression is ongoing, it's important to see a doctor or a therapist. It's possible you have a chemical imbalance that needs to be corrected. Counseling is important, especially if you're feeling suicidal.

To help with situational depression, review the techniques in the next chapter that may help you lower your stress levels and help you cope. Here are a few additional ideas for self-help.

Feel love. Close your eyes and take several deep breaths. Place both hands over your heart and feel their warmth. Now recall a time when you felt totally safe and loved. You may be with a person, a pet, or in a group. If you can't recall a loving memory, imagine a scene that fulfills all your dreams. Let these feelings of love wash over you, fill you, and surround you. Stay in this secure, peaceful place for at least thirty seconds.

This exercise will physically calm you, reduce stress, and retrain your mind to think positive thoughts. Try to repeat this exercise a minimum of three times a day. The more you do it, the greater the benefits you will receive.

Let go of the past. One of the ways to let go of the past is to forgive those who have harmed you. It's understandable if you feel this is impossible. You've been through some unbearable pain, pain you may have kept hidden for years or decades. Forgiving may feel as if you're excusing their actions, saying they don't need to pay for what they've done.

Forgiveness is seeing clearly that what they did was wrong but deciding that you won't give them or the situation the power to hurt you anymore. Until you let go of past hurts, you will attract similar negative circumstances into your life. Each time you remember those wrongs, you re-inflict that pain on yourself, living it over and giving yourself fresh wounds. Dwelling on the past makes it more likely you'll draw similar mistreatment in the present. And those old memories tie you to your attacker. They allow that person to still hurt you, long after he or she is gone from your life. Letting go of the bad memories frees you to live fully.

Stay healthy. Getting proper sleep, exercising daily, and eating well are good not only for your body but also for your mind and emotions. Avoid drugs, alcohol, and cigarettes, which can add to your depression.

It's also important to stay mentally healthy. Don't dwell on the negative. Stop reading the cyberattacker's messages. Skip sad movies, music, and books. Refrain from rereading old love letters or thinking about things that make you depressed.

Instead do things to make yourself happy. Make a list of things that you once thought were fun. Try to spend time each day doing at least one thing that makes you feel better. Take up a new hobby or interest; find something absorbing that will keep your mind fully occupied.

Plan for the future. Think about what you'd like to do two years, five years, and ten years from now. If that's too far ahead to think about, plan for next week or for tomorrow. Set an intention, a schedule, or an appointment and plan to keep it.

Instant Relief

Deciding to commit suicide may make you feel calmer, possibly even happier. But that relief comes from deciding to act rather than stay stuck. This sense of relief may make it seem as if you've made the correct decision. You may even experience a burst of energy, enabling you to divvy up your possessions, write notes, make plans, and procure the suicide weapon. But you would feel the same sense of relief if you made another decision: the decision to call someone who can help. There are other ways to end your suffering besides suicide. In your present distress you may not be able to think of any, but others can help you find solutions.

The only choice Alexis made when she decided against suicide was not to let her abuser win. If that's the only intention you have the strength to make, that's enough. You'll be astonished at how powerful that simple decision is. And if you don't even have enough strength to make that choice, dial a suicide hotline or email SIA. Someone there can give you the support you need until you're able to make a decision.

Suicide survivors say that at the last minute they regretted what they'd done and didn't want to die. Don't take a chance you'll regret. Call someone NOW.

Final Quick Tips

- **Stop:** Do not take action if you are feeling suicidal. Give yourself a timeframe to reconsider your decision, even if it's one day. During those twenty-four hours, you may change your mind. Keep returning to this step each day.

- **Call someone:** Contact a friend, a neighbor, even a stranger. A suicide hotline, counselor, clinic, church, and SIA are all options.

Tell them what you plan to do, and tell them why. Listen to their advice.

- **Make a decision:** If you're feeling overwhelmed, paralyzed, or trapped, decide on one step you can take to help yourself feel better. If your mind is too cloudy, ask the person you've contacted to suggest a next step. Once you've taken one step, it will be easier to take others.

- **Forgive yourself:** Be loving and gentle with yourself. This pain was not your fault; you didn't deserve it. So don't blame yourself. You deserve love and support, so surround yourself with people who will give you what you need.

- **Visualize the future:** You can build a future without pain. Look for a ray of hope, for something positive you can or will do a few weeks or months from now.

CHAPTER 15

Recovery: Reclaiming Your Life

Your healing—both emotional and physical—is paramount once you are free from a cyberattacker. It's even more vital if you are trying to escape from one. Panic makes it difficult to think, assess the situation, protect yourself, or make sound decisions. The techniques in this chapter can help lower your fear level and restore your inner balance and strength, so you can face your situation with confidence. They can also assist you in reframing your experiences so you can make wise choices and move on with your life.

Breaking Old Patterns

Leaving an unstable person or being the target of cybercrime can leave you feeling as if you're somehow at fault. You may think if you'd been a better or different person, this never would have happened. You may even think the perpetrator is right about you. You buy into all the negative things your cyberattacker said about you and see yourself as worthless. You come to accept that you'll never have a healthy, loving relationship. You feel you don't deserve one, not after what you've done.

All of these feelings—worthlessness, unworthiness, inadequacy, shame, guilt, and many other negative emotions—are normal if you've been in a relationship with an abuser. You may not believe it now, but these are lies you've been told. They may even echo criticisms you heard in childhood. But they aren't true.

As long as you believe them, you'll continue to repeat the same patterns of being victimized, because deep inside you feel you deserve it. At this point, if you've followed the action steps in the previous chapters, you may be free from the cyberattacker—but unless you can heal those old wounds, you may wind up in another bad relationship, which is what happened to Simon, the software developer from chapter 5.

Simon's Repeating Pattern

Simon established a new life in a town far from his old troubles and from Oliver. He erased his debt and began putting his life back together. After receiving a grant to fund the development of his video game, he rented a home and gradually became involved in the community. He tried out for a local theater production and won a part in an upcoming musical.

His life as a recluse was over, and Oliver had moved on to a new relationship. Simon was free. Free of the horrible nightmares, free of the constant stress, free of looking over his shoulder, expecting something awful to happen.

Now that he had his life back, he considered dating again. Remy, who played the lead in the musical, seemed to be eyeing him. Simon made a tentative approach the next time the cast went out for drinks after rehearsal, and it wasn't long before they were in a relationship.

Soon Remy gave up his tiny studio apartment to move into Simon's house. With Simon's encouragement Remy quit his part-time job to concentrate on his playwriting. Remy made no money at it, but it made him happy, so Simon gladly supported both of them. Remy drank too much and cheated on Simon from time to time, but he cooked and cleaned when the creative muse wasn't gripping him. Sometimes he secluded himself in the office for days or weeks at time as he poured his heart into a new play. Then he'd emerge, triumphant and cheerful, and spend several days being loving and kind. Simon lived for these brief interludes, which grew more infrequent as time went on.

After Remy received a series of rejections on his work, he started drinking excessively and raging at Simon. Within three years Simon had contacted SIA again because Remy had turned physically abusive and the cyberharassment had begun. SIA helped Simon extricate himself from his latest relationship, but he needed something more, something that went beyond the action steps in the previous chapters, something to help him turn his life around completely.

These are some ideas that helped Simon and may help you avoid repeating the cycle.

Changing Your Life Story

Myths and fairy tales have endured for thousands of years because they have a universal element of truth. They reveal people in circumstances that occur over and over in life. We may not be gods or goddesses, but we've all experienced betrayals, triumphs, loss, and love—the pain and joy of being human. So myths tug at our souls, as do great movies and books.

Many people create myths about their own lives, and they continue to act them out without realizing it. You may not be aware of it, but you likely have a favorite story—one that rings true for you. It might be a fairy tale you love, a movie you adore, a book you've reread many times. Often you're drawn to that particular story because it parallels your own life, or because you wish it did.

Examining that story can help you get in touch with some of the deeper beliefs that are influencing how you're living your life. Try to recall your favorite story, if you have one. Many times it's a story you loved as a child. Then look at how you may subconsciously be re-creating that story in your own life.

Making Your Own Myth

Intention is powerful. And the stories we tell ourselves can keep us stuck in grief and pain, feeling as if we do not deserve better. Or they can turn our lives around and take us to new heights, moving us far beyond what we expect or perceive as our current reality. Dreams do come true.

When Alexis chose the motto "Victim to Victorious" for her story, she began reclaiming her power. She refused to be cowed by her stalker and instead took back her life. She not only became victorious but also moved into the role of empowering others. She went from being homeless, alone, and scared to being a champion for victims around the globe. What fueled the change was switching her mindset to one of victory. Once she viewed herself in that new light, she was able to achieve remarkable results.

Think about the story you've been telling yourself about your life. Perhaps you've chosen the Cinderella story, where the poor girl is abused, made to do all the work, and not allowed to go to the ball. You may love the part where her luck magically changes and she gets her heart's desire, but you've remained stuck in the early part of the story, enduring abuse and mistreatment.

Even if you don't have a favorite story, you can still benefit from this mythmaking exercise. Choose an empowering story, one in which you'd love to be the hero or heroine, one that speaks to all you desire to be. Or make up your own. Let your imagination run wild.

When Alexis was about to commit suicide, she couldn't see any story but the relentless pain, fear, and tragedy surrounding her. She envisioned it continuing forever and saw no means of escape. But her decision to not give up lit the spark that later grew into a flame. Perhaps all you have left right now is a tiny ember, a small flicker of hope or anger or strength. That's all it takes to free yourself.

Sometimes just recognizing the story you've been telling yourself is enough to break the spell. But even more powerful is to create a new myth. If the story you love has a happy ending, picture yourself moving past the tragic parts to the happy ending. Imagine yourself successfully navigating through the pain to reach the joyous, triumphant end.

If your life story is filled with pain, heartache, or terror, you can fashion a new story, one that allows you to move beyond present circumstances and become the triumphant star of your own imagining, the way Nathaniel did.

Nathaniel's Myth

Once there was a little boy who was born into the wrong family, a family of cruel, evil magicians who used their power to imprison and torture him. Whenever he refused to do what they said, they beat him mercilessly. One day while they were out hunting a new victim, Nathaniel escaped. He rushed through the deep, dark forest alone, heart pounding and legs trembling. He was free, but as darkness fell he realized he was lost.

Suddenly a beautiful woman appeared in front of him and offered her hand. She led him to a lovely cottage, where she fed and cared for him. But he soon discovered she was a wicked witch who'd disguised herself. Now he was trapped by her cruelty. Whenever he tried to escape, she found him and tormented him with her evil powers.

One day he tricked her and fled. After a long, treacherous journey, he reached a glade where fairies were dancing. When he stepped into their magic circle, the witch's hold was broken forever. He was free at last. Nathaniel stayed in the magic circle until he had gained enough power to create his own magic circle. Then he traveled to distant lands and used his magic circle to heal others.

In the threads of Nathaniel's story, you can read the truth of his abusive childhood and disastrous marriage to a woman who stalked him relentlessly. For him SIA was a magic fairy circle of protection, and now that he's free from his stalker, he lives far from his family and his ex. As you can tell from his story, he's become an SIA volunteer.

The Power of Stories

One of the reasons stories are so powerful is that they stay with us long after facts and resolutions have disappeared. They speak to the core of us. This is why we used so many real-life stories in this book. You may forget the action steps, but we hope that you'll remember the stories, and that one or more of them will give you the strength to find your own solution.

Push aside that doubt, uncertainty, and previous disappointment for a short while, and let yourself fantasize about a new life with a happy ending, one where you are in charge of your destiny and have everything your heart desires. Fill your mind with the new story and start to live as that person.

Nathaniel could have become a knight, a warrior, a prince, or whatever his heart desired. And so can you. Try writing your own story. Turn those who caused your traumas and heartaches into ogres, dragons, witches, or other creatures. Slay them, chain them, imprison them, rise above them—whatever it takes for you to overcome their power. Make yourself the hero of your myth.

Use a myth or religious story in which the hero triumphs, or invent your own. Your story doesn't need to be set in ancient times. You can make yourself whatever your heart desires: a movie star, politician, famous artist, FBI agent, bird, or bear. Confront your past trauma alone, with an avenging army or ravenous beasts, or magically make it disappear. You're the director of this movie.

EMBED THE STORY DEEPLY

If you can suspend disbelief long enough to adopt a new story, you'll be amazed at how your life changes. To help that story become a part of you, try this technique to not only embed it in your mind but also feel it in your body.

Choose a time when you know you'll be alone so you'll have the freedom to act out the story. Using your body makes the story become even more real. The more sensory details you add to your experience, the stronger it will be. Put on music you love. Choose a song that you listen to often, because from now on your subconscious mind will associate that music with your new story. Each time it plays, the story will be reactivated deep inside. If the song has lyrics, be sure they support your intention. Sad songs or those that downgrade you will be counterproductive.

Select your favorite fragrance. If that's coffee or perfume, a spice or incense, fill the room with the scent. You may also want to have a physical object you love or use often with you—a piece of jewelry, a hairbrush, a coffee mug, or anything you use regularly. You can also choose a stone or any small object that you can carry with you. This will be a physical symbol to help you remember your intentions.

Once the stage is set with your favorite aroma and music, act out, or better yet, dance your story. Make sure you have plenty of room. You may want to start curled up on the floor as a baby and let yourself grow and rise from there. If, because of physical problems, you're unable to move, bend, or dance, do as much as you can, even if it's only waving your arms or tapping your toes. Vividly imagine yourself doing the other movements. Studies have shown that the same areas of the brain are stimulated when you use your imagination as when you actually engage in the physical activity.

Perform each part of your story, dancing through the pain, fighting off your enemies, escaping from your tormentor. Allow yourself to be powerful and triumphant. Then continue the dance into the future. Act out where you want to go, who you want to be. Let your body move into that dream, those longings, the hopes you've kept secreted in your heart and soul. Keep dancing until you've reached all your goals, become all you've ever dreamed of being. Let yourself face the world strong and unafraid, powerful and triumphant. This is the real you, the person you deserve to be, the person you are becoming.

Then pick up the physical object and imagine storing all these new memories and feelings in it. The next time you put on that watch, pick up that mug, or finger that stone in your pocket, all these feelings will come flooding back. Whenever the scent of coffee or lemon or perfume wafts through the air, your subconscious will remember. Each time that song plays, you'll have another reminder of your new story.

One final suggestion is to choose a motto. Make it short and easy to remember, like Alexis's "Victim to Victorious." Write it down and keep it in a place where you can see it. If you're still with an abuser, be sure to keep it hidden or just memorize it. Use it to remind yourself of where you're headed.

Be sure to set a timeline for yourself. You may believe that all this could happen in the distant future but think it's impossible in the here and now. Let your imagination soar and believe that this story—the good part, the empowering part—is happening now, this very minute. Each time you hear that song, sniff that aroma, touch the physical object, claim that dream. Act and live as if it's already true, and it will be. Not next week, next month, or next year, but NOW.

Journaling

Many people find journaling therapeutic. Research has shown that writing about a traumatic event for fifteen to twenty minutes a day for four days can reduce emotional distress and improve physical health.[3] By expressing your feelings in words, you help the brain process what happened, and often by the fourth day, you'll find you have new insights and ideas.

Describe an upsetting event and your deepest emotions surrounding it. Put your pen to paper, and let the words flow in a stream-of-consciousness style without stopping or editing. Don't worry about spelling or punctuation. Don't stop to think or censor what you're writing. Keep going until your fifteen or twenty minutes is up.

Some people save their writing to read later; others shred it or burn it. If you keep it, be sure you have a private place to store it, where no one will read it. Knowing that it's for your eyes alone will allow you to come to the page with more honesty and openness.

Another journaling exercise that might be helpful is to tell the same story from a different point of view. Often stepping outside yourself and viewing the situation from another angle allows you to obtain some distance from it. Reviewing it as an outsider can neutralize some of the distress surrounding the situation.

If it's not too traumatic for you, also try telling the story from your cyberattacker's point of view. Sometimes that can give you amazing clarity about the situation and even inspire understanding of the cyberabuser's motivation, which can help you better prepare for, or possibly prevent, future attacks.

Visual Journaling

Visual journaling combines art with words. You do not need any art skills to complete the exercises. You can scribble, collage, cut and paste, or finger

---

3 Karen A. Baikie and Kay Wilhelm, "Emotional and Physical Health Benefits of Expressive Writing," *Advances in Psychiatric Treatment* 11 (2005): 338–46.

paint. The goal is to get in touch with your pain and release it onto the page. Use any art materials you have—a pen, crayons, markers, paints, or torn paper will work.

Close your eyes and access a physical or emotional pain. Or ask: *How am I feeling today?* Then open your eyes and draw or scribble your answer. Or cut pictures from magazines and glue them on the page. Some therapists suggest using your nondominant hand, but try it both ways to see what you prefer. Keep going until you've completely expressed that feeling.

Then sit with your art for a short while, asking what it's trying to tell you. Take a few moments to freewrite your answer. As with the journaling above, don't censor your writing; just keep the pen flowing on the page. You might find some surprising insights or new angles you hadn't considered.

It can be helpful to follow this up by setting an intention. Select a change you wish to see in your life or circumstances. Speak the intention aloud, then ask how you can accomplish it. Without thinking or judging, pick up your crayon, pen, or other art supplies, and scribble or draw the answer. When you're finished, again freewrite whatever the art has brought to mind.

People who engage in this as a daily practice find that many of their dreams and intentions come true. Regular use of an art journal also has been shown to reduce stress, lower the heart rate, boost the immune system, and alleviate depression.

Tapping Down the Distress

EFT, or the Emotional Freedom Technique, is a simple technique you can use by yourself to alleviate suffering, both mental and physical. Often called *tapping*, it is easy to learn and is quick and effective for reducing distress. Although it may look odd at first, it has proven quite beneficial for many people. Tapping has been used for everything from healing diseases to losing weight to overcoming traumas.

The technique was developed by a psychiatrist, who based it on acupressure points. Tapping on those pressure points often gives rapid and effective relief. Most of the studies on EFT have been anecdotal, but with the great success people have had overcoming all kinds of difficulties, it's well worth a try. It works especially well for ridding yourself of old beliefs, such as *I'm not worthy, I'll never get out of this situation, I don't deserve to be loved*, and other negative thoughts. But it has also proved helpful for PTSD.

Appendix C contains links to online information and videos by experts in the field so you can watch and follow along. Even if this seems strange, give it a try. Choose one of the stress-reducing scripts and tap along. Reducing stress, panic, and fear allows you to think more clearly and take action to help yourself.

Exercise, Creativity, and Spirituality

Running, yoga, writing, singing, dancing—any physical or creative activity can help restore your equilibrium. When you immerse yourself in an activity and get into the zone, things that were bothering you disappear. All of these activities counteract the negative effects of stress and are wonderful forms of self-therapy. Try all of these techniques, or choose the ones that resonate with you and help the most.

Some people also find that a spiritual practice gives them mental and emotional peace. Whether it's meditating, praying, reading a holy book, attending services, or participating in rituals, do whatever calms you. The more centered you become, the more inner strength you develop.

Share Your Story

We packed as much information as we could into this book, but so much more couldn't be squeezed into these pages. The stories of triumph and survival and the unique solutions not included here are YOURS. The best ideas are the ones you dream up yourself, the ones that are unique to you and your situation.

If you find solutions that aren't mentioned in the book, we hope you'll share them with us on Facebook at www.facebook.com/CyberSDefense. Your creativity and inventiveness may light someone else's path.

We'd also love to hear your success stories, the many different ways you've overcome. Use your real name if you can, but sharing anonymously or under a pseudonym is fine if you need to protect your identity. Do whatever you must to keep yourself safe, but do pass on your knowledge, your wisdom, your successes.

Celebrate your awesome power and potential by writing your own story. And then tell it to the world.

Appendix A

Checklists for Action

These quick checklists are general overviews, highlighting the most important steps at a glance. If you're overwhelmed and don't know where to begin, follow these steps first. More detailed steps can be found in chapters 11 and 12. Individual chapters also have additional information, but we gathered the basics in this appendix so you'll have them handy when needed.

Always Remember C-S-D-N: Cyber Self-Defense Now

Basic Steps:

> Call or Contact
> Secure
> Document
> Notify

Action Checklist for Dealing with Spoofers

Call or Contact

- Don't dismiss spoof calls as pranks; treat them seriously.
- Report calls to the authorities, especially if the spoofer issues threats.
- Contact your phone carrier and discuss the issue with its security department.

Secure

- Try not to react or give the caller any satisfaction.
- If you suspect it's the spoofer, don't answer the phone; allow calls to go to voice mail and save the messages.
- Change your phone number and make it unlisted.
- Never give out your unlisted phone number to anyone but close friends and family members.
- Don't talk about the incidents in public or to others; your spoofer may be listening for your reaction.
- If you identify your spoofer, it's better not to confront this person.

Document

- Save all texts and document dates and times of answered and recorded calls.
- Get written statements from family and friends indicating they didn't make the calls.
- Keep all phone records and voice mail messages.

Notify

- Contact a victim support group and/or a risk management consultant, especially those that deal with tech cases involving spoofing.
- Notify your local law enforcement personnel. Depending upon the severity of the situation, law enforcement may or may not react. Also, many law officers are not aware of the latest technology, so you may need an expert to explain it to them.

Action Checklist for Dealing with Cyberattackers

Call or Contact

- Call 911 or local law enforcement immediately if you receive any threats.

- Warn the cyberattacker that any further contact will result in the filing of a police report.

- Contact friends, family members, coworkers, classmates, and social media contacts to alert them that you have a cyberattacker; advise them to notify the authorities if they receive any messages. Also make sure they know not to give out any information about you, your plans, or your whereabouts.

Secure

- Change all social media accounts, passwords, and any links that allow the cyberattacker access to you or information about you.

- Secure all credit card, loan, and personal information.

- Block the cyberattacker from your phones, computer, and social media.

- Block any unknown phone numbers and text messages. Do not accept any new friend requests from people you do not know.

- Change passwords and create secret questions that will be impossible for someone else to answer. Be sure to save this information so that you are not locked out of your own accounts.

- Never give out logins and passwords to anyone.

- If you suspect a virus or other technology, such as spyware, a keylogger, or a GPS tracking device, contact a computer tech to analyze your phone, iPad, PC, laptop, and all other hardware.

Document

- Gather physical evidence. Print out screen shots of photos, emails, texts, and so on, and keep them in order by date.

- Create an events timeline with Date, Time, Incident Description, Matching Document, and Witnesses (if any) to correspond to the physical evidence (see appendix B).

- If gathering the evidence is too painful and you can't bear to look at it, ask a friend or family member to do it for you.

Notify
- Contact administrators at social media sites to have abusive messages erased.
- If social media sites have a "Report Bullying" button, use that to report all messages.
- Contact the harasser's Internet service provider. Often an ISP can stop the conduct by direct contact with the stalker or by closing the account.
- Take your timeline and all evidence to law enforcement. Continue to document and report all incidents. Take the evidence in person, keeping a backup copy of all records.
- Ask friends and family, if they are willing, to post positive messages to counteract cyberattacks.
- Seek counseling for emotional distress.

Action Checklist for Dealing with Abusers/Stalkers

Call or Contact

- If the stalker becomes violent or threatens your physical safety, dial 911 or local law enforcement.
- If violence occurs, allow police to take a full report, including the details of the incident and photographs of injuries.

Secure

- If your stalker is using the Internet to track you, follow all the steps listed for cyberattackers.
- If you are not in immediate danger, take time to plan and consult with a risk management expert to learn the best ways to protect yourself.
- Have easy access to a reserve set of money, credit cards, medication, important papers, keys, and other valuables in case you need to leave quickly. Have a safe place in mind that you can go in an emergency.
- If you share a home or space with the abuser, try to move to a space of your own.
- Change all the locks on the new space and install security devices.
- Take self-defense classes and learn to protect yourself.
- Stay alert when in public and vary your routine to prevent the stalker from tracking you.
- Take different routes to school or work. Go to places you normally don't frequent. Make some new friends.
- Travel with others, avoid dark and secluded places, and use well-lighted areas for banking, buying gas, and so on.
- If you choose to carry a firearm, get proper training and licenses.
- Regularly have your devices and car checked. Perpetrators may install tracking devices.

Document

- Gather physical evidence. Print out screen shots of photos, emails, texts, and so on, and keep them in order by date.

- Create an events timeline with Date, Time, Incident Description, Matching Document, and Witnesses (if any) to correspond to the physical evidence.
- Take photographs of property damage, physical abuse, or any other harm.

Notify

- Develop a safety plan. Inform friends, neighbors, and coworkers about the situation. Show them a photo of the stalker.
- Contact a private investigator and/or a risk management consultant.
- Contact a civil court to get a restraining order.
- Reach out to victim advocates, public officials, or other support organizations. Be sure to get emotional support as well.

Action Checklist for Dealing with Identity Theft

Call or Contact
- Contact one of the three major credit bureaus, and follow the action steps listed in the "Identity Theft Worksheet" in appendix B.

Secure
- Set up a credit freeze.
- Request that companies put a fraud alert on your accounts (see appendix B).
- Add a consumer statement to all credit bureau records instructing that no changes be made to your accounts without the creditors calling you first.
- Try opening a new line of credit to see if the credit bureaus are sending your message. If the creditor opens the account without calling you, contact the credit bureaus again.
- Monitor credit reports every six months to be sure that no old or inaccurate information is included.

Document
- Collect proof of your identity.
- Create an events timeline with Date, Time, Incident Description, Matching Document, and Witnesses (if any) to correspond with events (see appendix B).

Notify
- Notify law enforcement of the identity theft.
- Monitor all three credit bureaus and keep them updated as to your status.
- If these companies continue to give out incorrect information after they've been notified of the situation, contact an attorney or get in touch with NACA (see appendix D).

Appendix B

Documents and Logs

Every worksheet and piece of information a victim needs along with easy-to-follow step-by-step instructions is contained within this link on the SIA site: http://survivorsinaction.org/resources/victims-self-help-tools. In addition, key worksheets have been reproduced in this appendix.

Survivor's Guide

This guide is intended to help you as you navigate through the process of finding assistance. A victim's journey is full of unique challenges and difficulties, and in some cases victims are overly-referred, ignored or simply denied service. Without access to critical services, the victim feels forced to stay in the abusive relationship and is often unable to escape the cycle of violence and disenfranchised by the very system put in place to protect him or her.

Getting Help From Resources

1. If you are in immediate danger, please call 911.

2. For help finding a domestic violence advocate, call the National Domestic Violence Hotline at **(800) 799-SAFE.** **(TTY (800) 787-3224)**

3. Create a *Needs List.* A Needs List will include your needs as a victim. An example of a Needs List would be:

   - Pro Bono Attorney
   - Shelter
   - Transportation

   Keep your list simple, short and easy to understand.

4. Have an updated **Resource List** on hand. A Resource List should include the following:

   - Domestic Violence Shelters in your City
   - Your State Domestic Violence Coalition
   - Crime Victim Compensation in your State
   - Your Local Assembly Person/Senator
   - The District Attorney in your City
   - Contact Information for Legal Aid/Legal Assistance Resources

When reaching out for help through *email*, use the **Survivors In Action Template** for defining your needs. Here is an example:

Dear _____,

I am a victim of domestic violence in need of immediate help and assistance. I am suffering from chronic pain and in need of surgery. My children continue to get beaten by my abuser, I cannot pay child support because I do not have a job or the ability to work due to my injury-related disability. I am suffering and need help.

I need the following, or I face possible jail time because I cannot get to court:

1. A Pro Bono Domestic Violence Attorney
2. Crime Victim's Compensation to cover medical expenses and surgeries
3. Child Protection Services to step in and remove my children from the abuser's home

I have already contacted the following resources and have not received assistance:

1._____
2._____
3._____

Please respond ASAP. I fear for my safety and for the safety and well-being of my children.

The key is to avoid being caught in a cycle of referrals, and because you have clearly identified your needs and listed the resources that haven't worked for you, it will save time and avoid confusion. Always keep a paper trail and ensure that you are using an email account that you consider to be safe and that your abuser cannot access.

Self-Sufficiency Guide

This guide is intended to be included, but is <u>not meant to replace</u> your domestic violence safety plan. If you do not have a safety plan, please contact your local domestic violence service provider for assistance. If you are in immediate danger, please call 911.

1. Important Documents to Take With You:

- Order of Protection
- Social Security Card
- Medical Records
- Address Book
- Insurance Documents
- Pet Records
- Marriage/Divorce Papers
- Photo Identification
- Credit/Debit Cards
- Birth Certificate
- Copy of Your Lease
- Vehicle Registration
- Password List
- Vaccination Records
- Bank Statements
- Tax Records/W-2's
- Police Records/Photos
- School Records
- Checkbook
- Loan Information

2. If possible, **a safety deposit box at a bank is an ideal place to keep these records**. If you cannot get a safety deposit box, another option would be to leave them with a relative that you can trust. Your

important documents are essential and will be necessary if you plan to apply for benefits or take legal action.

A safety deposit box with a key lock can be purchased from a retailer like Walmart for around twenty dollars.

3. Take a **Financial Inventory.** Knowing where you stand financially is an important aspect to escaping abuse and reaching economic independence.

4. If possible, **begin setting aside money in a safe place**, if you can do so without jeopardizing your safety—even if it is just a few dollars.

5. **Obtain a copy of your Credit Report from** all three credit bureaus. This can be done (one a year) for free at www.annualcreditreport.com.

6. **If you suspect that you have been or are about to be a victim of identity theft**, you can place a Fraud Alert on your Credit File. If you suspect that your abuser has or will attempt to use your credit for financial gain, a Fraud Alert will prevent them from opening more accounts in your name. An initial Fraud Alert stays on your File for at least 90 days, but can be extended for up to 7 years. www.ftc.gov has more information about identity theft and fraud alerts. You also have the option to place a credit freeze on your credit file. Credit freeze laws vary from state to state. A credit freeze prevents potential creditors and other third parties from accessing your credit report at all, unless you lift the freeze or already have a relationship with the company.

7. **Do some research and find out what services and benefits are available to you.** This includes government benefits such as housing vouchers or temporary assistance for needy families. www.benefits.gov has an online tool to help you determine which benefits you may be eligible to receive. You may also be eligible for unemployment benefits if you had to leave work because you are a victim of domestic violence or stalking. Check with your state's unemployment commission for more information. Remember to perform this search from a computer that you feel safe using.

8. **If you do not have a cell phone** or will have to leave your phone behind, look into an income-eligible free cell phone program such as the program available through www.safelinkwireless.com.

9. **Use a Safe E-Mail Address** for all electronic communication. Ensure that you are utilizing an email account that you consider to be safe and that your abuser cannot access.

10. **Change ALL User Names and Passwords**, and we recommend avoiding any social networking sites. If you continue to use social networking, then remember that the Internet is a public resource and evaluate your privacy settings. Limit the amount of personal information that you post, and do not post information that would make you vulnerable, such as your address or your schedule/routine.

11. **Keep up-to-date documentation.** This is the most pro-active step that a victim can take. If a case goes to trial, victims will need to recall specific events and information for court proceedings. Document all incidents and injuries; it is important to keep track of facts, times, and dates of each incident.

Each situation is unique and this is not a comprehensive list. If you have a concern that has not been addressed, please contact your local domestic violence service provider for assistance.

Domestic Violence and Stalking Incident Log

Date and Time:	Description of Incident:
Location of Incident:	Witness Name and Phone Number:
Police Report Number:	Police Officer's Name and Badge Number:

Date and Time:	Description of Incident:
Location of Incident:	Witness Name and Phone Number:
Police Report Number:	Police Officer's Name and Badge Number:

Date and Time:	Description of Incident:
Location of Incident:	Witness Name and Phone Number:
Police Report Number:	Police Officer's Name and Badge Number:

Date and Time:	Description of Incident:
Location of Incident:	Witness Name and Phone Number:
Police Report Number:	Police Officer's Name and Badge Number:

A stalking log is necessary to document all stalking-related behavior and threats. This information can be used when applying for a protection order and can be introduced into evidence during court proceedings. Keep this log in a safe place that your stalker cannot access.

Getting an Order of Protection

Victims need to gather their data, evidence, important dates, and details together when filing for an order of protection. An Order of Protection tells the abuser to stop harming or threatening you. Domestic abuse can involve physical harm, injury, assault, rape, terrorist threats, or making a person fearful of harm or injury or assault. Examples include hitting, kicking, pushing, punching, slapping, pulling hair, choking, holding you down, threatening to harm or kill you or the children, forced sexual contact (even if you are married), or any sexual abuse/contact with a child.

Other Names for an Order of Protection:

- Stay away order

- Order of no contact

- Injunction for protection

- Harassment order

- Restraining order

- Stalking protection order

- Orders not to abuse, harass, contact, etc., that are part of bail, probation, or parole conditions

- Emergency, temporary, or ex parte order

Full Faith and Credit provision of the Violence Against Women Act says that a valid protection order must be enforced throughout the country. This means that if you get a valid protection order, it is good in the community where you received it, and all other jurisdictions or places you go in the United States. This includes protection orders issued in all 50 states, Indian Tribal Lands, District of Columbia, U.S. Virgin Islands, Puerto Rico, American Samoa, the Northern Mariana Islands and Guam.

How to File a Petition

Victims of Domestic Violence must go to their County Court and ask to file a Family Offense Petition with the County Clerk. You can get an Order of Protection from a civil (Family Court/Supreme Court) or criminal court. **An Order of Protection will not expire if a victim receives the order as part of a divorce settlement in Supreme Court.** If you are a victim going through a divorce, be sure to request an Order through your attorney as part of the divorce settlement.

Follow these steps to file a petition:

• Gather any evidence related to the crime. This includes threats in the form of writing, emails, text, or any phone conversations or instances of domestic abuse. Gather dates and times and be as specific as possible, including as many details as you can remember.

• Once you have gathered your evidence, write down a timeline of events with all the details gathered. See the example below:

{Example: Jan. 1, 2010-injury to face and body, verbal death threats made. /April 5, 2010-verbal abuse, threatening text message received at 10pm./ June 10, 2010-visit to the ER due to injury to the abdomen by abuser.}

• Clearly and thoughtfully follow your timeline of events and compose a detailed description of the crimes that took place in the form of a story. If there were many threats made, include all instances of abuse and threats into one petition and remember to be as specific as possible.

• Bring the timeline and the composition to the County Clerk and make sure the Clerk records your data into the petition, so that the petition is as clear and as accurate as possible.

• Be sure to call your local shelter in advance and ask for a Domestic Violence Advocate to accompany you to court on your court date. Plan to meet with your advocate before court so that you can obtain free legal representation for your court date.

Crime Victims' Compensation

Each state has an organization designated to providing services for crime victims. For more information, and a map to access state specific organizations, please visit http://www.ovc.gov/map.html.

Stay neat, very organized, and always make copies of anything you submit for your own personal files. This process can be long and time consuming, but if you need compensation for a crime, it is well worth the wait and paperwork.

Victim's Rights

Every state has a set of basic rights and protections for victims of crime called a "victim's bill of rights." In many cases, a victim's entitlement to a right depends on the seriousness of the crime. In some states, basic rights are afforded only to victims of felonies, while in other states victims of any violent crime, felony or misdemeanor, are entitled to such rights. In a number of states, rights have also been extended to include victims of juvenile offenders.

In addition to the crime victim, victim's rights may often be exercised by a family member of a homicide victim, or the parent, guardian, or relative of a minor, disabled, or incompetent victim. In some states, a victim's legal representative or another person designated by the victim may exercise rights on the victim's behalf.

- The right to notification of the proceedings in the criminal process
- The right to attend and/or participate in criminal justice proceedings
- The right to notification of other legal remedies
- The right to protection from intimidation and harassment
- The right to notice of the release or escape of the offender
- The right to privacy, including confidentiality of records
- The right to speedy trial provisions
- The right to discuss the case with the Prosecutor
- The right to prompt return of the victim's personal property seized as evidence from the offender
- Victim Compensation and Restitution

Many states give the victims or their families the right to be notified of important criminal proceedings and the outcome of the proceedings. Usually, the victim's rights include the right to attend the trial, sentencing, and parole hearing of the offender. Victims also typically have the right to make an oral or written statement at sentencing or at a parole hearing. Every state has a victim compensation program to provide financial assistance to victims, and in some cases family members or other eligible persons Usually a victim must have suffered actual physical harm or other tangible loss, and the financial loss caused by such harm or loss must exceed a minimum dollar amount.

In addition to compensation, victims often have the right to restitution, payment by the convicted offender for the harm caused by the crime. The court generally orders restitution at the time of sentencing. A lawsuit in civil court is usually required to recover punitive damages.

To find out more about victim's rights where you live, contact your state attorney general, victim assistance organization, your local prosecutor, or your local law enforcement agency.

Privacy Protection for Victims of Abuse/Stalking

- **Do not rely on Caller ID to accurately identify callers.** "Caller ID Spoofing" is a common practice used by high-tech cyberstalkers. It programs the Caller ID to reveal any name and number of their choice. Stalkers often use telephone numbers known by the victim in order to trick and deceive an unsuspecting victim into answering the phone. **Screen your phone calls.** Allow the answering machine to pick up first, and then answer. By allowing the answering machine to pick up, you may be able to use a phone message they leave as evidence. You are in control of your safety and security.

- **Password-protect all accounts, including utilities.** Besides adding a password to your accounts, request to have the agency/entity contact you if there are any changes made to your accounts including requests for account closures, electronic funds transfers, or account cancellations. It is common for abusers/stalkers to cancel credit cards, close accounts, transfer funds, and shut off the utilities of their victims.

- **Notify family, friends, employers, and co-workers not to divulge personal information about you to any third party.** Stalkers/Abusers may contact third parties under false pretenses to obtain information pertaining to the victim's activities and whereabouts. They may also pretend to be a member of law enforcement to obtain information. Ensure that those close to you are cautious and on alert, so that they will not fall prey to these methods.

FAQs

Why won't the victim just leave the relationship?

This can be difficult to understand. The victim may not feel emotionally strong enough to leave, they may feel isolated and alone, or perhaps the abuse is not constant so they view the abuser as wanting to change his/her behavior. Sometimes the victim grew up witnessing violence so they may feel that some form of abuse is "normal" in a relationship. The victim may be financially dependent on the abuser and fear homelessness if they leave. If the victim has children, they may have been threatened with the loss of the children, or perhaps the abuser has threatened to hurt or kill the victim or their family and friends. If this is the case, the victim might feel they are sacrificing themselves in order to save/protect those that they love from violence. When a victim leaves an abusive relationship, they are at the greatest risk of violence or even homicide. If a past attempt to leave has failed, the victim will most likely be fearful of trying to leave again. The best way to help a friend or family member who is a victim of abuse is to be caring and supportive. Make sure they know that you are there to listen. In the meantime, be proactive and learn about the resources that are available in the victim's community.

I'm a victim of stalking, what should I do?

Experts suggest that victims send the stalker/harasser a written warning, informing them that the contact is unwanted and ask the perpetrator to cease and desist further communication of any kind. Then, no matter what their response is, under no circumstances should the victim continue to engage the stalker in any form of communication. Victims should save copies of all communication with the stalker in both electronic and hard copy format. It is imperative to document the evidence, along with specific dates and times. If the harassment continues, the victim should file a report with local law enforcement or contact the local prosecutor's office to see what charges can be pursued. The victim should not agree to meet the perpetrator under any circumstances.

State by State Address Confidentiality Programs

Arizona	Voter Registration Only Secretary of State Elections Division 1700 West Washington Street, 7th Floor Phoenix, AZ 85007-2808 (602)364-4700 http://www.azsos.gov/Info/acp/
Arkansas	Driver's License Only Revenue Division - DL Services Department of Finance and Administration PO Box 1272 Little Rock, AR 72203-1272 (501)682-7052
California	Safe at Home Program PO Box 846 Sacramento, CA 95812-0846 (877)322-5227 http://www.casafeathome.org
Colorado	Address Confidentiality Program 1001 East 62nd Avenue Denver, CO 80216-1140 (303)869-4911 http://www.acp.colorado.gov/
Connecticut	Address Confidentiality Program PO Box 150470 Hartford, CT 06115-0470 (860)509-6006 http://www.ct.gov/sots/cwp/view.asp? a=3177&q=391912

Florida	Address Confidentiality Program The Capital PL-01 Tallahassee, FL 32399-1050 (800)226-6667
Idaho	Address Confidentiality Program PO Box 1737 Boise, ID 83701-1737 (200)334-2300 http://www.sos.idaho.gov/ACP/ACP.htm
Indiana	Address Confidentiality Program PO Box 6243 Indianapolis, IN 46206-6243 (800)321-1907 http://www.in.gov/attorneygeneral/2375.htm
Kansas	Safe at Home Program PO Box 798 Topeka, KS 66601-0798 (785)296-3806 http://www.kssos.org/safeathome/main.html
Louisiana	Address Confidentiality Program PO Box 94125 Baton Rouge, LA 70804-9125 (225)925-4792 http://wwwprd.doa.louisiana.gov/LaServices/ PublicPages/ServiceDetail.cfm? service_id=3368
Maine	Address Confidentiality Program 148 Statehouse Station Augusta, ME 04333-0148 (207)626-8400 http://www.maine.gov/sos/acp/
Maryland	Safe at Home Program PO Box 2995 Annapolis, MD 21404 (800)633-9657 ext. 3875 http://www.sos.state.md.us/ACP/ SafeAtHome.aspx

Massachusetts	Address Confidentiality Program PO Box 9120 Chelsea, MA 02150-9120 (866)723-3233 http://www.sec.state.ma.us/acp/acpidx.htm
Minnesota	Safe at Home Program PO Box 17370 St. Paul, MN 55117-0370 (866)723-3035
Missouri	Safe at Home Program PO Box 1409 Jefferson City, MO 65102-1409 (866)509-1409 http://www.MOsafeathome.com/
Montana	Address Confidentiality Program PO Box 201410 Helena, MT 59620-1410 (406)444-5803
Nebraska	Address Confidentiality Program PO Box 92921 Lincoln, NE 68509 (866)227-6327 http://www.sos.ne.gov/business/ acp_menu.html
Nevada	Confidential Address Program PO Box 2743 Carson City, NV 89702-2743 (775)684-5707
New Hampshire	Address Confidentiality Program 33 Capital Street Concord, NH 03301-6397 (603)271-1240
New Jersey	Address Confidentiality Program PO Box 207 Trenton, NJ 08625 (877)218-9133 http://www.njcbw.org/ gethelp_legalAdv_legaladdress.htm

Vermont	Safe at Home Program PO Box 1568 Montpelier, VT 05601-1568 (802)828-0586 http://www.sec.state.vt.us/otherprg/ safeathome/safeathome.html
Virginia	Address Confidentiality Program 900 East Main Street Richmond, VA 23219 (804)692-0592
Washington	Address Confidentiality Program PO Box 257 Olympia, WA 98507-0257 (360)753-2972 http://www.secstate.wa.gov/acp/
West Virginia	Address Confidentiality Program Building 1, Suite 157-K 1900 Kanawha Blvd East Charleston, WV 25305 (304)558-6000
Wisconsin	State Election Board PO Box 2973 Madison, WI 53701-2973 (608) 266-8005

This material is displayed in good faith and is for information purposes only. Clients should make their own assessments and use the external links at their own discretion. Many states do not yet participate in the Address Confidentiality Program. Contact your attorney general's office for more information.

Identity Theft Worksheet

If you are a victim (or suspect that you have been a victim of Identity Theft) it is important to take these steps as soon as possible:

1. **Place a Fraud Alert on your Credit Report.** This can be done by contacting:

TransUnion (www.TransUnion.com)	1-800-680-7289
Equifax (www.Equifax.com)	1-800-525-6285
Experian (www.Experian.com)	1-888-397-3742

You only need to contact one of the three reporting agencies - the one that you call is required to contact the other two, and they will also place an alert on your file. An initial Fraud Alert will stay on your credit file for at least 90 days but can be extended for up to seven years.

2. **Once you have placed a Fraud Alert on your Credit Report, you are entitled to one free credit report from each agency.** Remember to inform them to only use the last 4 digits of your Social on the report, so that they do not display your entire Social Security number.
3. **Review your Credit Reports carefully.** Look for inquiries with companies you haven't contacted, accounts that you did not open, addresses that you do not recognize, and debts or other information that you cannot explain.
4. **Close the accounts that you know (or believe) have been tampered with.** Call and speak with someone in the Fraud Department with each Creditor. Make sure that you follow it up in writing and include copies (not the original) of supporting documentation. It is very important to notify them in writing. Send the letters via *Certified Mail, Return Receipt Requested,* so that you have a record of when the company receives your information.
5. **File a dispute directly for new, unauthorized accounts by contacting the company using the contact information provided on your report.** Ask the representative if they accept the FTC's ID Theft Affidavit. (The ID Theft Affidavit can be found on the *'Resources'* page of our website). If they don't accept the ID Theft Affidavit, ask them to send you their Fraud Dispute Forms.
6. **File a Report with the Federal Trade Commission.** You can call the Identity Theft Hotline at 1-877-ID-THEFT or use the online complaint form: https://www.ftccomplaintassistant.gov/FTC_Wizard.aspx?Lang=en
7. **File a report with your local police department,** or in the community where the identity theft took place. It is best to do this in person, but if you cannot, ask if you can file a report over the Internet or phone. If they are reluctant to take your report, ask about a 'Miscellaneous Incident' Report or try the State Police. You can also check with your State Attorney General's Office to see if the law requires the police to take a report for Identity theft.

Continue to check your credit reports periodically, especially in the first year after you discover the identity theft, to ensure that there has been no additional fraudulent activity.

Credit Dispute Worksheet

It is important to review your credit report periodically to ensure the information is accurate, complete, and up-to-date. The Federal Fair Credit Reporting Act requires each of the major credit bureaus to provide you with a free copy of your report, at your request, once every 12 months.

1. **Get a Free Copy Of Your Credit Report**: (You are also entitled to a free report if a company takes adverse action against you, such as denying an application for credit or employment. If you are unemployed and plan to look for a job within 60 days, if you're on welfare, or if your report is inaccurate because of fraud.)

2. When requesting a Credit Report, ensure that you have specified that **only the last four digits of your Social Security number appear on the report.**

3. **Review your Credit Reports carefully.** Look for inquiries with companies that you haven't contacted, accounts that you did not open, addresses that you don't recognize, and any debts or information that you cannot explain.

4. Follow the **Credit Dispute Process**:

TransUnion:	http://www.transunion.com/corporate/personal/creditDisputes/creditDisputeProcess.page
Experian:	http://www.experian.com/disputes/main.html
Equifax:	http://www.equifax.com/answers/correct-credit-report-errors/en_cp

If you have statements, cancelled checks, or any other evidence to support your dispute, include copies of them (keep the originals for your records) with your statement. If you are mailing your dispute, send it certified mail, return receipt requested. This way you will have proof that you sent the dispute but also that the credit bureau has received it.

5. **The issuer of a credit account has 30 days from the time you dispute an item to respond to the dispute.** The reporting agency acts as the liaison between you and the credit issuer. Once the credit issuer responds to the credit agency, they will notify you of the findings. If the item is inaccurate, the agency will remove it from your credit report and issue you a new copy with up-to-date information.

Appendix C

Emotional Recovery Resources

EFT (Emotional Freedom Technique)

ABOUT EFT

For a description of EFT, what it is, and how it works, see the following sites:

www.thetappingsolution.com/#what-is-eft-tapping

www.bradyates.net/eft.html

www.youtube.com/watch?v=4ZDjAhuo_6Y

www.emofree.com/eft-tutorial/tapping-basics/how-to-do-eft.html (Good explanation of the basics down to the yellow box; the techniques that follow are more advanced.)

http://vimeo.com/14299752

www.youtube.com/watch?v=f6xm66XToEY

www.attractingabundance.com/eft/what-is-eft

www.attractingabundance.com/eft/wp-content/uploads/EFT-Directions .pdf

BASIC TAPPING POINTS

These sites identify the basic points that are used for tapping:

Pictures

http://eft.mercola.com/

www.dummies.com/how-to/content/emotional-freedom-technique-for-dummies-cheat-shee.html

Audio

www.bradyates.net/introtoeft.mp3

Videos

www.youtube.com/watch?v=GO4Sai4R-E0

www.youtube.com/watch?v=QzVd6Ww0as4

www.youtube.com/watch?v=1wG2FA4vfLQ

TAPPING SCRIPTS

If you need help with what to say as you tap, you can find many wonderful resources online. Here are some sites that have tapping scripts to help you deal with various problems.

EFT Wizard

www.youtube.com/user/eftwizard
Excellent series of tap-along videos by Brad Yates. Specific topics such as self-esteem, depression, guilt and shame, overcoming fear, and feeling safe again, among others.

Battletap

http://battletap.org/home.aspx
Originally developed for veterans, the resources and tapping scripts on this site also can be used for PTSD symptoms as well as other emotional and psychological distress.

http://battletap.org/SessionAssistant1.aspx
The Session Assistant lets you put in your emotion and a specific event, and then it creates a tapping video for you. This is most helpful if you familiarize yourself with the tapping points first, but it's also possible to follow along. You can use the site anonymously as a guest, but if you'd like to save the videos for future use, you'll need to create a user account.

The EFT Universe

www.youtube.com/user/TheEFTUniverse/videos
Offers a selection of videos on different topics. Select the ones that are relevant to your situation.

The Tapping Solution

www.thetappingsolution.com/eft-articles/nick-ortner
Select from the Categories list on the right for printed tapping scripts.

ADDITIONAL SELF-HELP RESOURCES

Journal Therapy

journaltherapy.com/journaltherapy/journal-cafe-3/journal-course

Radical Forgiveness

www.colintipping.com/strategies/radical-forgiveness-2/

Writing for Health

homepage.psy.utexas.edu/HomePage/Faculty/Pennebaker/Home2000/WritingandHealth.html

Appendix D

Resource List[4]

Hotlines

Covenant House NineLine (24/7 teen suicide hotline)
1-800-999-9999

National Center for Missing & Exploited Children CyberTipline
www.missingkids.com/cybertipline
1-800-843-5678
Online complaint form available to report sexual exploitation and to request the removal of underage sexual images posted online

National Domestic Violence Hotline (24/7)
1-800-799-SAFE (7233)
1-800-787-3224 (TTY)

National Hopeline Network (24/7)
1-800-SUICIDE (784-2433)
1-800-442-HOPE (4673)
Spanish-speaking suicide hotline: 1-800-SUICIDA (784-2432)
Teen-to-teen peer counseling hotline: 1-877-968-8454
Grad student hotline: 1-800-GRADHLP (472-3457)

---

4 Disclaimer: These are paid professional individuals, government-funded agencies and hotlines, and resources that are presently available in the United States; we've also included some agencies abroad. This is not a comprehensive list of every resource available, nor are these individuals, agencies, hotlines, or organizations endorsed by Alexis Moore or Survivors In Action. For the most up-to-date listing of resources, see the files at the Cyber Self-Defense Facebook page (www.facebook.com/CyberSDefense). Although SIA is actively working to reform victim resources and encouraging governmental oversight to ensure that all organizations effectively support victims, at present these resources are tools to be utilized with the awareness that victim support for cyberstalking, stalking, and abuse victims is limited and can be frustrating or even overwhelming for those in crisis. Think of this as a marathon rather than a sprint, and keep going. You will succeed.

National Suicide Prevention Lifeline (24/7)
1-800-273-TALK (8255)
www.suicidepreventionlifeline.org
To locate the crisis center closest to you: www.suicidepreventionlifeline
.org/getinvolved/locator

National Teen Dating Abuse Helpline (24/7)
1-866-331-9474
1-866-331-8453 (TTY)
You can also chat live online with a trained peer advocate:
www.loveisrespect.org/get-help/contact-us/chat-with-us

Rape, Abuse & Incest National Network (RAINN) (24/7)
To be connected to the rape crisis center nearest to you, call:
1-800-656-HOPE (4673)

Suicide.org
www.suicide.org
For a list of hotlines by state: www.suicide.org/suicide-hotlines.html

Outside the United States

Befrienders Worldwide
www.befrienders.org
jo@samaritans.org

International Association for Suicide Prevention (IASP)
www.iasp.info/resources/Crisis_Centres

Suicide.org
www.suicide.org/international-suicide-hotlines.html

Organizations

Corporate Alliance to End Partner Violence
www.caepv.org
2416 E. Washington St., Ste. E
Bloomington, IL 61704
Phone: 309-664-0667
Fax: 309-664-0747

End Violence Against Women International
www.evawintl.org
PO Box 33
Addy, WA 99101-0033
509-684-9800

National Center on Domestic and Sexual Violence
www.ncdsv.org4612 Shoal Cieek Blvd.
Austin, TX 78756
512-407-9020

National Coalition Against Domestic Violence
www.ncadv.org
1-800-799-SAFE (7233)
1-800-787-3224 (TTY)

National Family Justice Center Alliance
www.familyjusticecenter.org
707 Broadway, Ste. 700
San Diego, CA 92101
1-888-511-FJCA (3522)
619-980-8883

National Network to End Domestic Violence (NNEDV)
Safety Net Project
www.nnedv.org/projects/safetynet.html
1400 16th St. NW, Ste. 330
Washington, DC 20036
Phone: 202-543-5566
Fax: 202-543-5626
safetynet@nnedv.org

Office for Victims of Crime (OVC)
www.ovc.gov
202-307-5983

Privacy Rights Clearinghouse
www.privacyrights.org

Stalking Resource Center, National Center for Victims of Crime
www.victimsofcrime.org/our-programs/stalking-resource-center
2000 M St. NW, Ste. 480
Washington, DC 20036
Phone: 202-467-8726
Fax: 202-467-8701

Survivors In Action
www.survivorsinaction.org

Witness Justice
www.witnessjustice.org
106 W. Church St.
Frederick, MD 21701
301-846-9110

Working to Halt Online Abuse (WHOA)
www.haltabuse.org

Online Tools/Information

Electronic Privacy Information Center (EPIC)
www.epic.org

FightCyberstalking
www.fightcyberstalking.org/about-fcs/

US Government Organizations

Federal Bureau of Investigation, Internet Crime Complaint Center
www.ic3.gov/complaint

Federal Trade Commission (FTC)
Equal Employment Opportunity counselors (for harassment or discrimination)
www.ftc.gov/site-information/no-fear-act/complaint-process
202-418-1799

US Department of Labor's Civil Rights Center
www.dol.gov/oasam/programs/crc/
202-693-6500

US Social Security Administration (for ID change)
www.ssa.gov/pressoffice/domestic_fact.html

Additional US Resources by Topic

Bullying

StopBullying
www.stopbullying.gov

International Bullying Prevention Association
www.stopbullyingworld.org

National Bullying Prevention Center
www.pacer.org/bullying

STOMP Out Bullying™
www.stompoutbullying.org

Teens Against Bullying
www.pacerteensagainstbullying.org

Depression

Mental Health America
www.mentalhealthamerica.net/finding-therapy
1-800-273-TALK

Psych Central
www.psychcentral.com

Financial Fraud

Internet Crime Complaint Center (IC3)
www.ic3.gov/complaint/default.aspx

Equifax
www.equifax.com

Experian
www.experian.com

TransUnion
www.transunion.com

Identity Theft

Federal Trade Commission
www.consumer.ftc.gov/features/feature-0014-identity-theft
Document for reporting: www.ftccomplaintassistant.gov

The National Association of Attorneys General
www.naag.org/current-attorneys-general.php
List of current attorneys general for each state

Laws
Here are some laws that may be applicable to your case:

Truth in Caller ID Act
http://www.fcc.gov/guides/caller-id-and-spoofing
www.gpo.gov/fdsys/pkg/BILLS-111s30enr/pdf/BILLS-111s30enr.pdf
Prohibits falsifying caller identity or phone number

Revenge Porn
http://www.ncsl.org/research/telecommunications-and-information-technology/state-revenge-porn-legislation.aspx
The National Conference of State Legislatures maintains a list of states that have enacted laws against posting nude or sexually explicit photographs or videos of people online without their consent.

Cindy's Law
www.dcbabrief.org/vol241011art4.html
This legislation, which has been passed in some states, allows the use of GPS technology to track batterers who have violated their restraining orders.

Workplace Stalking Laws
www.dol.gov/oasam/programs/crc/2011-workplace-harassment.htm
These laws prohibit harassment in the workplace.

Legal Help

DV Leap (domestic violence)
www.dvleap.org
2000 G St. NW
Washington, DC 20052

Legal Momentum (Women's Legal Defense and Education Fund)
www.legalmomentum.org
5 Hanover Sq., Ste. 1502
New York, NY 10004
212-925-6635

National Association of Consumer Advocates (NACA)
www.naca.net
1730 Rhode Island Ave. NW, Ste. 710
Washington, DC 20036
Phone: 202-452-1989
Fax: 202-452-0099

National Crime Victim Bar Association
www.victimsofcrime.org/our-programs/
national-crime-victim-bar-association
202-467-8716 (attorney referral)

National Crime Victim Law Institute
www.ncvli.org
310 SW 4th Ave., Ste. 540
Portland, OR 97204
Phone: 503-768-6853
Fax: 866-301-8794

Restraining Orders

WomensLaw.org
http://www.womenslaw.org/laws_state_type
.php?statelaw_name=Restraining%20Orders&state_code=GE
Information on obtaining restraining orders in each state can be found using the pull-down menu.

Social Media
To report cyberabuse or have posts deleted, access the following pages:

Facebook
www.facebook.com/help/

Instagram
help.instagram.com

Twitter
support.twitter.com

Stalking and Domestic Violence
These additional resources may be helpful for those fleeing an abusive situation.

Angel Flight, Inc.
1515 East 71st St., Ste. 312
Tulsa, OK 74136
Phone: 918-749-8992
Fax: 918-745-0879
Email: angel@angelflight.com
Web: www.angelflight.com
Volunteer pilots offer free air transportation to those in need, including individuals escaping domestic violence.

Red Rover
http://www.redrover.org/redrover-relief-domestic-violence-resources
916-429-2457
Organization helps ensure pet safety for victims who are fleeing violent situations.

Resources Worldwide

1800 RESPECT
www.1800respect.org.au
1800 737 732
National sexual assault, family, and domestic violence counseling

Australian Federal Police
Report child/teen exploitation and abuse: https://forms.afp.gov.au/
online_forms/ocset_form
Submit info anonymously: 1800 333 000

Australian Government
Department of Communications
www.communications.gov.au/online_safety_and_security
Counseling, reporting, and educational resources

CyberActive Services
www.cyberactiveservices.com.au
Internet safety, social media investigation, and cybercrime prevention

Cybersmart
www.cybersmart.gov.au/report.aspx
1800 880 176
Report cyberbullying and exploitation; online counseling

Domestic Violence Victoria (DV Vic)
www.dvvic.org.au/index.php/about-us/our-mission.html
03 9921 0828

Kids Helpline
www.kidshelp.com.au
1800 551 800
Counseling for children and young people

Lifeline Australia
www.lifeline.org.au
13 11 14
Suicide hotline

Network for Surviving Stalking
nssadvice.org
National Stalking Helpline: 0808 802 0300
Victim Support: 0800 027 1234

White Ribbon
www.whiteribbon.org.au/finding-help
Local hotline links, domestic violence, teen resources, and legal aid

Women's Services Network (WESNET)
http://wesnet.org.au
Advocacy for domestic violence; resources for shelters, safe houses, and referral services

CANADA
Resources available in both English and French.

BullyingCanada
BullyingCanada.ca

Canadian Clearinghouse on Cyberstalking
A cooperative project between Victim Assistance Online (www
.vaonline.org) and the Canadian Resource Centre for Victims of Crime
(www.crcvc.ca)
info@cyberstalking.ca

National Office for Victims, Public Safety Canada
www.publicsafety.gc.ca/cnt/cntrng-crm/crrctns/ntnl-ffc-vctms-eng.aspx

PREVNet
www.prevnet.ca
613-533-2632
Bullying prevention

Victim Services Directory, Department of Justice Canada
www.justice.gc.ca/eng/pi/pcvi-cpcv/vsd-rsv/schp1-rchp1.asp

Victims of Violence
www.victimsofviolence.on.ca
1-888-606-0000

UNITED KINGDOM
If in immediate danger, call 999.

Child Exploitation and Online Protection Centre (CEOP)
www.ceop.police.uk
44 (0)870 000 3344
Online contact form available

National Stalking Helpline
www.stalkinghelpline.org
0808 802 0300

Network for Surviving Stalking
www.nss.org.uk
07501 752741
campaign@nss.org.uk
List of useful resources for stalking and cyberstalking: www.nss.org.uk/
useful-links/
Stalking quiz: www.nssadvice.squarespace.com/storage/police%20stalking
%20quiz.pdf

Papyrus Prevention of Young Suicide
www.papyrus-uk.org
HOPELineUK: 0800 068 41 41
Phone: 01925 572 444
Fax: 01925 240 502
pat@papyrus-uk.org

Protection Against Stalking
www.protectionagainststalking.org
pasofficehq@gmail.com

Samaritans (24/7)
www.samaritans.org
08457 90 90 90
jo@samaritans.org
Confidential support for emotional problems

Scottish Domestic Abuse Helpline (24/7)
http://77.68.56.8/sdah/
0800 027 1234

Victim Support
www.victimsupport.org.uk
0845 30 30 90

Index

About the Authors

Alexis Moore is a cybercrime expert. She frequently speaks on the subjects of cyberstalking, cyberbullying, and identity theft on radio and television programs such as CNN's *Headline News, Fox News,* ABC's *Good Morning America,* BBC *World News,* and Canada's *CBC News.* Her work has been the focus of more than one thousand magazine and news articles in publications such as the *New York Times, Ladies' Home Journal, Glamour,* and *Women's Day.* The founder and president of Survivors In Action, designer of the *Moore Secure* line of security software, and collaborator with state and federal legislators worldwide for cyberabuse legislation, Moore is considered a leading pundit on cybercrime.

Laurie J. Edwards is a freelance author, editor, and illustrator with an MA and post-grad training in creative and emotional recovery techniques. In addition to more than twenty-two hundred magazine and educational articles in print, some of her recent publications include the five-volume *UXL Encyclopedia of Native American Tribes, Pirates through the Ages, Rihanna,* and stories in four anthologies. She is also the author of a four-book young adult series set in the Wild West and several adult novels written under pseudonyms. Edwards speaks regularly at civic events, libraries, and conferences across the country.